JENNIFER O'NEILL

A NOVEL

CIRCLE *of* FRIENDS

Just off Main

A LATE SPRING FROST

PUBLISHING GROUP

Nashville, Tennessee

ISBN: 978-0-8054-4197-0

Published by B&H Publishing Group,
Nashville, Tennessee

Dewey Decimal Classification: F
Subject Heading: WOMEN—FICTION \
FRIENDSHIP—FICTION \ SPIRITUAL LIFE—FICTION

All Scripture quotations are from the HCSB, Holman
Christian Standard Bible™ © 1999, 2000, 2002, 2003 by
Holman Bible Publishers.

1 2 3 4 5 6 7 8   10 09 08 07

Praise God for his
love unleashed!!

Chapter 1

Morning Glories

The coming of a new day hadn't always been her favorite time. In fact, during Lauren Patterson's earlier years, she rarely had occasion to watch the glory of daybreak since she invariably snoozed her mornings away.

For most of her life, Lauren considered herself a night owl, sometimes spending entire twenty-four-hour periods awake on a creative tear. Perhaps she was driven to finish writing a song on the piano or paint her most recent portrait of a family member as she madly danced about to her favorite rhythms. Whatever her inspiration, she had a frantic need to express herself artistically, all the while ripping up the Manhattan pavement as a career "Headhunter." And in her spare time following her tumultuous divorce, she'd navigate the bevy of male suitors who trailed after her like a bunch of lovesick puppies. Yes, this woman had quite an interesting dance card to be filled.

⚜

As Lauren thought back on her life, she wondered what actually had prompted her to pack up everything she was familiar with and move to California to become a veterinarian some ten years ago. Her parents, Margaret and Sam, were stunned at her bold maneuver, never having recognized their daughter's passion for animals as anything but a phase she was going to outgrow. And that went double when it came to her obsession with horses.

"All little girls love horses," her father would point out. "Believe me, that will be short-lived as soon as you discover boys."

But that wasn't the case for Lauren; even though she did discover boys with a vengeance, she remained at the barn and kennels every spare moment she could carve out of her day. Still, when Lauren decided to radically change her life in her late thirties, Irene simply could not comprehend her little sister's move to a small California town to go back to school.

"What on earth are you thinking?" Irene grilled Lauren prior to her leaving. "This isn't the seventies, you know. The West Coast 'love the one you're with' and all that flower-child stuff is long past. You've already been there, so what's this exodus really about?"

"It's not about a guy, Rene. It's about the animals. I want to protect them . . . To save them, you know?"

"Wouldn't it be easier just to send the ASPCA a fat check?"

"No!" Lauren knew none of her family would understand her mission. Truth was, Lauren couldn't actually put her decision into words that made much sense, even to herself. The best she could say was that she had a stirring deep within her soul, and she was going to follow her dreams. And as it turned out, her yearnings were not folly; Lauren's move ended up to be one of the most positive decisions she'd ever made because it was there in California, of all places, that she had met the lover of her soul, Jesus Christ.

So at the not-so-tender age of forty, Lauren had finally come to her faith under the tutelage of her neighbor, Suz, a wonderful woman, ten years her senior and centuries beyond Lauren in her spiritual walk. What a gift to finally discover one's true footing and purpose in life with the support of a friend living a hundred yards away. A friend who had told Lauren she could bang on her door at any hour. Something Lauren had done frequently to ask Suz a flood of questions that filled her mind on a daily basis.

Replacing her creative all-nighters with a passion for the Word of God, Lauren voraciously went about getting steeped in her faith. Yes, when this woman did anything, she did it 150 percent. And so it was, a decade ago that Lauren's life began to radically transform. She went on to marry Brian, adopt their baby boy Tucker, graduate from veterinarian school, open an office, and buy herself a fancy show horse named Gracie as she settled into what seemed to be a bucolic life.

But as quickly as Lauren grew in her faith, her marriage helplessly fell apart, a crossroads that nearly threatened her walk with Jesus. But Lauren was soon to learn that that disappointment wouldn't be the first time she would come to a place of total and utter dependency on her Lord to sustain her while the details of her life spun out of control.

❧

Lauren loved reviewing God's choreography in her life. She marveled at the people God had designed to cross her path, as well as the favor she had found since she'd moved to Centennial a short six months ago. She couldn't help but smile at the thought of her bold departure from California to the small southern town just outside of Nashville, Tennessee, where she somehow had convinced her parents, Irene, and her niece Chelsea to join her. And although she missed Suz desperately, she felt lead to stay close to Brian so he could stay close to their son, Tucker. When Brian's work transferred him to Nashville, Lauren sold everything and followed suit. She had to admit, she did harbor some resentment for her ex-husband uprooting her life at first, but Lauren decided to make the best of the situation and focus on reuniting her family of origin. And although that desire was sure to be a challenge, Lauren felt she was up to the task. Nothing is impossible with God on your side, she often reminded herself.

One thing was for sure, Lauren had turned her life around, and she suddenly found herself bounding out of bed at predawn with enthusiasm for what the new day might hold for her. And this spring morning was no exception.

⁂

The horizon was barely showing light as Lauren made her way from the Grace Animal Shelter she'd recently opened as head veterinarian and cofounder. Knowing full well that her achievements were not a solo act, Lauren adored the fact that Mrs. Strickland, her benefactor, had supported her all the way, including allowing her to name the hospital after the horse she was financially forced to leave behind in California.

Beyond that, God had graciously opened so many more doors in Tennessee than he had on the West Coast. Yes, Lauren was still in shock at how fast her life was evolving, horse or no horse. She was also stunned that she had come to a place of peace and embraced her newfound sense of security. Oh my, what a gift!

⁂

Cruising along in her pickup truck, Lauren's eyes scanned the terrain of the quaint town of Centennial, so rich in history and architecture. The streetlights were still on, holding out for the end of darkness. These were the times Lauren felt she was the only one awake in the sleepy little village; a special quiet time for her before her hectic day would begin with predawn rounds at the shelter's hospital. She considered it a treat rather than a chore every morning to check on all the rescued animals well before the kennel help came to feed. Yes, this was her personal time to make sure all her furry, four-footed wards were progressing.

And oh, how it filled her heart with joy to be allowed to work in a career that had always been such a grand desire of hers since childhood. As she drove along, Lauren thanked God yet again for placing those desires in her heart and then allowing her to fulfill them. She had learned firsthand that God doesn't put passions in any of his children to frustrate them. She also had accepted that he designs each and every one of them with particular yearnings and talents to be used for his service beyond their wildest imaginations.

Yes, what God had in mind for Lauren's life was already laid out; it was now up to her to choose to walk in the path he had made clear for her.

As Lauren approached Norros Diner just off Main Street, she pulled over, her mind flooding with memories. She imagined she could see through the now darkened diner's windows that the establishment was filled to the rafters as usual with customers for all breakfast, lunch, and dinner servings. And at the center of the hubbub was her dear friend, Stephanie, single-handedly serving up the patrons the finest vittles found anywhere in the Nashville area.

An eclectic clientele was drawn to Norros, renowned as the "gathering and feasting" place to be. But for Lauren it had also become a special place of solace and profound exchange. This was where she gathered with her *circle of friends* for prayer at least once a week—depending on the challenges life put before them. But despite the ladies ongoing scenarios, this group of five showed up regularly to stand in agreement, praise, thanksgiving, and prayer for renewal, wisdom, and deeper fellowship.

As Lauren stared more intensely into the diner's shadowy window, she was transfixed as if she were viewing previews from a movie. She watched on as her friends gathered inside; she could see Eleanor's tears streaming down her glistening brown skin. All the women were laying hands on her in powerful prayer concerning the healing of Eleanor's recent bout with breast cancer. Thank God, despite medical reports, the power of faith triumphed over Eleanor's disease. Yes, Miss Eleanor simply refused to throw in the towel at age forty-seven; she had far too much living and loving to do.

It had only been within the last six months since Lauren had known Eleanor that she'd witnessed her new friend go from diagnosis to surgery, and then on to healing victory, not only over the dreaded disease but over her personal fears as well. All the *circle* had witnessed Eleanor engage her powerhouse of faith, and in the end, she and her husband resurfaced with an even deeper and more abiding relationship and love than they had shared over their thirty years of marriage. Oh, what a grand example Eleanor and Hamilton were of lives lived for the Lord.

Then Lauren imagined seeing Pam, her stunning long blonde hair framing the sweetheart of a thirty-year-old. It was hard to imagine one at such a young age so filled with vision, enthusiasm, and compassion. Pam was determined to renew the spiritual well-being of young ones and create a safe place for education and reconciliation in a town known for generations of division between blacks and whites. Despite the past, Pam had enough gumption to overcome what had previously been impossible; her template was called The Hope School. But hers was not a singular vision; Eleanor and Ham (as his friends called him) were all on the journey together to bring their vision to reality.

But despite Pam's lofty aspirations, she had recently been experiencing some personal struggles as evidenced by her need for her fair share of time in "the *circle*" to be prayed over for release of her ongoing battle with the demon of depression. Lauren, who was the newest member of this diverse group of friends, quickly learned that there was more to Pam than what immediately met the eye. And then there was the story of her brother's teen suicide years before. Yes, it seemed that not only Lauren had a past to deal with.

This was also true of Tonya, Pam's best friend. At twenty years old, this African-American tall drink of water with Cover Girl looks and Harvard intelligence was already a single mother of a four-year-old boy, Bobbie. Lauren quickly respected how her young new friend had successfully managed a high school pregnancy and single motherhood. You see, her little boy's dad, Shooter, had thus far sidestepped a marital commitment with Tonya. This was deep disappointment to the young woman. Still, Shooter had always stepped up to the plate as a dad. He never shirked his responsibilities as a father like most eighteen-year-olds would have due to teen self-centeredness. And then there was the complication of the heart for Shooter and Tonya; they had always loved each other since they were preteens. Lauren simply couldn't get her arms around why this couple wasn't married, but then she couldn't understand why she was divorced.

Lauren thought back on the first time she and her niece had walked into Norros:

A slight breeze rushed through the empty restaurant as the front door opened admitting Lauren and Chelsea who was carrying a half-eaten bag of popcorn under her arm. Stephanie and Eleanor watched the two take the first booth. "Wonder if they're new in town or just passin' through?" Eleanor queried, grateful for the change of focus. "I've never seen them before. Pretty girl though, huh?" Stephanie noted.

She wasn't the only one that noticed Chelsea's good looks. While the girl was scanning the menu, Trace came into the restaurant through the kitchen entrance. He locked eyes with Chelsea for a fleeting moment before moving on to talk to his mom. Chelsea blushed slightly, then looked out the window trying to act aloof.

Approaching Stephanie with a triple burger clutched in his hand, Trace greeted the women with a wide grin. "Hey, Miss Eleanor."

She smiled back at the boy, happy to see him looking so up. "Trace, that hamburger's bigger than you are."

"Yes ma'am, it's one of Bubba's specials." He stared at Eleanor's disfigured face, not quite sure whether to say, "I'm sorry," or, "What the heck . . . !?"

Eleanor saved him the trouble. ". . . Allergies."

"Wow . . ." After closer inspection of Eleanor, Trace finally turned his attention to his mom, "I gotta get some school stuff, so Bubba said I could work in the kitchen this afternoon to make some extra money."

Stephanie nodded, "I'll be thanking him for that. Just get everything you need to start the year off right."

Exiting, he waved his hamburger, splattering some of its juice on the floor. Trace bent to clean it up when his mom shooed him on. "I'll get it. I have to take care of those folks in front anyway."

"Thanks. Bye, Miss Eleanor. I hope you feel better." And with that he was off, but not without checking Chelsea out again before disappearing behind the kitchen doors.

Stephanie straightened her apron, regarding Eleanor who was finishing the last vestiges of the doughnut. "I'll be right back. I just gotta take their order. Do you have time to sit for a while?"

Eleanor nodded, holding her hands over her eyes as if she could simply wish away her bloating. "Lord, I don't have bags under my eyes; I have suitcases! Yes," she sighed in frustration, "I have some time. Ham's over at the school doin' inventory of the team's uniforms. He's comin' to get me in about a half hour." Stephanie gave her a thumbs-up.

As she approached Lauren and Chelsea, Stephanie offered a welcoming smile. "Hello, ladies. How's the day treating you?"

"What a nice thought. . . . Just fine, thank you." Lauren returned the smile; predictably, Chelsea didn't bother to respond.

Stephanie pulled out her order pad, "Well, good then. . . . What can I get ya?" Chelsea instantly rattled off, "Double cheeseburger and fries with a Diet Coke."

"That's sort of an oxymoron, isn't it?" Lauren teased her niece, "A Diet Coke and fries?" Stephanie laughed, but Chelsea didn't find the comment the least bit amusing, stuffing some more popcorn in her mouth for effect.

"I've got a son 'bout her age with a bottomless pit for a stomach, too." Stephanie chatted. "Don't you just hate that kids can eat anything they want and never gain an ounce?"

Lauren looked at Stephanie, taking an immediate liking to this woman, "Obviously, they haven't heard about mad cow disease. I have to admit, I'm scared to death to eat hamburger."

"Oh, I can promise you, ma'am, our meat is good," Stephanie quickly assured her. "That was my boy going through here a minute ago slamming down a triple 'Bubba Burger.' . . . But, if you prefer, our southern fried chicken sandwich is real tasty."

"Perfect. . . . And I'll have a real live Coca-Cola for good measure."

"Be up in a jiffy." Stephanie wheeled about and headed toward the kitchen.

Lauren noted her niece's distant gaze, realizing she'd made zero headway as far as rejuvenating their friendship thus far. Still, she was not about to give up. "How'd you like Braveheart? I thought it was an amazing movie."

Chelsea mumbled, "I liked Sling Blade better." After a moment of silence, Lauren tried again. "You drove really well. And don't you worry about the fender. . . . It was just a tap."

"Sorry." Chelsea offered unconvincingly. "Don't tell Mom, OK?"

"OK, why not? . . ." No response. "So, what's your favorite music these days?"

The girl crumpled her popcorn bag, then wiped away some butter from her mouth with the back of her hand. "Seal." Lauren looked at her, waiting for a bit more information. Finally Chelsea relented, filling in the gap, "Seal is the singer's name. The song's 'Kiss from a Rose.' It's number one."

"Oh, . . . will you play it for me sometime?"

"Sure." Chelsea grunted.

Undaunted, Lauren continued. "So, the other day I read that Janet Jackson got the biggest record deal ever . . . eighty million bucks. Isn't that amazing?"

"That's rad." Chelsea's interest perked slightly. "Eighty million . . . " She gazed off. "When I'm a country star, I'm going to make more than that."

"Gee, I knew you had a sweet voice." Wrong word, Lauren thought. Powerful. Maybe not powerful. Kids don't have powerful voices. "I just didn't know you had those kinds of aspirations."

Chelsea looked out the window again nonplussed, "Well, we haven't talked in a while, ya know."

"Yeah," Lauren responded, embarrassed. "Time flies when you're not having fun, huh? Hey, do you think milk comes out of a cow's nose when it laughs?"

Chelsea scrunched her face up, "That's gross."

Lauren became slightly defensive, "It was just a joke."

"Yeah, maybe for a five-year-old. Don't forget, I'm seventeen."

"Sorry. You're right, I'm kind of used to hanging out with Tucker. You'll just have to bring me up to speed with what interests you. I really do care."

After another moment of silence, Chelsea decided to grace her aunt with a response. "Yeah, well, I'm not interested much about being here in this stupid town. Mom knows I'm moving into Nashville to do my music the minute I'm eighteen."

Lauren tried not to look shocked. "What do you mean? You're going to finish high school first, right?"

"All I know is that I'm going to be doing my music." Chelsea's attention was drawn to the window once more in avoidance of Lauren's stare.

❧

Lauren finally pressed her foot down on the gas petal, pulling her truck away from the diner that early spring morning. But despite her physical getaway, her thoughts lingered, and she giggled to herself about the *circle of friends* photo exposé a few months before in response to Norro's misbehavior. Yes, there was a man behind the diner's name, "Norros." This gentleman, if one could call him that, started up the eatery as a cheap southern truck-stop version of fast food located on Main Street in Centennial. Truth was, he actually won the building in a poker game in 1990, and under his lackluster ownership the establishment barely made enough in revenue to pay its property taxes. But Norro knew that property was ultimately the operative word; the ground the diner sat on was a proverbial gold mine since Centennial was recently growing in leaps and bounds thanks to an influx of residents to man the new Nissan Company headquarters. Oh, the luck of the draw.

Still, it was not until Stephanie offered her waitressing expertise and finesse as well as "the cook team extraordinaire" three years ago to the diner's equation that the establishment exploded into the best kept secret on Nashville's fine culinary discovery list. With the help of Stephanie's influence, Norro had cashed in big time on an endeavor that wasn't rightfully his—not the land, not the diner's reputation, nor its ongoing business. Without a doubt, if there was any justice in the world, 1997 would be the year Norros Diner changed hands. At least that was Stephanie's plan.

Lauren hummed to herself as she continued on her way through the quaint town. And by the time she pulled into the cul-de-sac where her modest yet prim house stood atop a hill, she sighed with satisfaction. "Oh goodie, home." Lauren was determined to take her post on her back porch as she did every morning before the sun rose to pray the new day in with thanksgiving.

Chapter 2

Skid Marks

At what seemed to be her sister's darkest hour, Lauren stalwartly declared, "Rene, God is always in control, so Chelsea's miscarriage must be a blessing in disguise . . . even if we don't understand his plan right now."

For once Irene had to agree. Still, Lauren's sister was quick to point out, "I only accept the 'blessing' part of your statement, not the 'God is always in control' concept. As far as I'm concerned, if God actually exists, why does he let such horrible things happen to people?"

And although it was like containing a toddler in a teacup, Lauren uncharacteristically zipped her lip, knowing full well that the hospital was not the time or place for a debate about God's purposes. She also knew that the only thing Irene cared about at the moment was the fact that her seventeen-year-old daughter was in no way prepared to decide the fate of the baby she carried, especially once she found out that her deceased stepfather was responsible for her pregnancy. So, was it better the teenager had miscarried?

Leaving the hospital the night of Chelsea's loss wasn't the first time Irene had vehemently stated to her parents and Lauren that it was a good thing her "slime of a husband," Ford, had died of a heart attack; otherwise she'd have to have shot him dead for sexually abusing her little girl! And as horrifying a thought as Irene's threat was, truth be known, Lauren would have delivered the two-timing pedophile dressed in thousand-dollar suits her own brand of "death sentence by way of international bad press" if he'd still been walking this earth.

Lauren was thankful God had already taken care of the retribution of Ford Williams. Yes, on a rare occasion there seemed to be some justice in the world as evidenced last February 5 when the so-called "Big Three" banks in Switzerland announced the creation of a $71 million fund to aid Holocaust survivors and their families. And although Norro was shy of the heinous offenses of Ford Williams and Adolf Hitler, Lauren held fast to the belief that God surely would make a way for Stephanie to buy the diner; she so deserved a gift from God for all her faithful prayers and hard work.

Of course, Stephanie was always the first one to remind anyone who would listen as she'd served them their meals at the diner, "Good thing we can't earn God's love. . . . None of us would make the grade." Then she'd beam as she handed her clientele their bills. "Now, Jesus paid our way to heaven, but you'll be needing to pick up the check for your food while you wait!"

Then she'd wink as the customers would invariably give her a fat tip. Everyone just adored Stephanie.

Oh, what a time the last three months had been. Lauren often revisited the dramas and traumas that had taken their toll not only on her immediate family but on her friends as well.

As she sipped on the dregs of a still steaming cup of coffee, Lauren momentarily cuddled amid comforting pillows she'd surrounded herself with atop her floral couch. Sometimes it was hard for her to sit still since everything Lauren did seemed to move in double speed, a trait she'd never been apologetic about. In her mind, time was not to be wasted.

The generous enclosed porch had become her favorite spot for prayer and renewal in the six months since she and her family had moved to town. Lauren couldn't deny the ever-present calming beauty of her backyard, which was presently bursting forth with life, despite the late spring frost in the air. Her surroundings never failed to inspirationally frame the recent seasons of her life that were dramatically shaping her future. She smiled fleetingly in relief that the worst must be over for her loved ones—at least that was what she was claiming.

She recalled how she'd brought in the new year feeling more convinced than ever that she had made the right decision to move her entire family to the outskirts of Nashville in hopes of reconciliation and repair for all. And although the past winter months had delivered them more than their share of twists and turns of what seemed to be life's ongoing soap-operatic story lines, Lauren felt a peace that she could only attribute to her ever deepening faith.

Lauren glanced down at the Bible in her lap, scanning her *answered and yet to be answered* prayer lists sprawled across its opening pages. Clearly, she was a blessed woman despite the fact that her prayers for Irene, Chelsea, and her parents to come to know Christ had not yet been answered. Still, she had high hopes and no doubt in the promises of God that her prayers would be heard for her family; she so wanted to share with them the grace, peace, and forgiveness she'd found in her faith a decade earlier.

"God's timing," she reminded herself over and over. Lauren had always been such an "alpha" individual; she constantly had to reassure herself that she had sown the seed of God's Word in her loved ones. Actually, she had done so to the point of trying to pound it into their heads, which all clearly resented.

She chided herself, knowing, according to the Word of God, that it is up to the Holy Spirit to soften her family's individual hearts to truth, and all of her persistent persuasions were not required or requested. Bottom line, Lauren needed to "chill out"; God had managed quite well for eternity *without* her personal *press* card. Oh, how she prayed for patience. And yes, she was doing better at trusting the Lord of late, even if it rubbed her controlling personality the wrong way. Surely she would eventually get over herself, wouldn't she?

Despite all the positive momentum Lauren had seen displayed in her life, the last several months had been a heart-stopping roller-coaster ride. From the discovery of Chelsea's sexual abuse and pregnancy, to Irene's bogus arrest and never-ending-impending court trial, to learning for the first time that Irene had had an abortion in college. Wow!

As she did with all of her "missions," Lauren researched the aftermath of abortion with verve in an effort to help her sister cope with the reality of what she'd done in secrecy so many years before. And as she studied the documented facts of the crippling effects on those experiencing abortion, all the pieces of the puzzling quilt of guilt and shame Irene had suffered finally made more sense to Lauren in light of her sister's past. The root of Irene's pain and following destructive behaviors had finally been uncovered, yet they still remained festering emotionally like an open wound, robbing Irene on a daily basis in one fashion or another.

Again, Lauren thought about the day last winter Chelsea spent in the hospital, hoping against hope that her baby would survive. How she had watched Irene struggle to make the right decisions for her daughter, during which time the chasm between Lauren's faith in Christ and her sister's unbelief was never more evident. To Irene there seemed to be no reasonable answer available for Chelsea since her stepfather was the father of her baby, not her high school boyfriend, Trace. Irene waffled about telling her daughter that the baby she was carrying was the product of her sexual abuse, according to the ultrasound test. Surely Chelsea hadn't known she was six weeks pregnant when she had met Trace right after moving to Centennial from New York City. Following that logic, the young couple's "one time" act of love-making was not responsible for her pregnancy. Irene knew that that information alone would send her emotionally damaged daughter right over the edge. But Irene also knew that she couldn't, in any good conscious, allow Trace to believe he had been the father of the baby.

And then there was the fact that before the miscarriage, Chelsea, Trace, and Irene had all seen the baby's humanity on the ultrasound screen earlier that fateful day. They had all heard his little heartbeat. And the truth was, the very image and sound of that baby's life was what shocked Irene into recognizing what she had really done when she had aborted her own pregnancy thirty-two years before. She could no longer tell herself, as she had been told, that she had simply "eliminated an inconvenient blob of tissue or a cluster of cells."

As all the events unfolded that winter's day in what felt like a slow motion runaway train wreck, Lauren privately thanked God that at least there hadn't been enough time to address the option of abortion concerning Chelsea's impending mother-hood. Before it could even become an issue, Irene and Stephanie had been called in by the doctor to Chelsea's bedside.

As she was losing the baby, Chelsea refused to let Trace go, clutching him in horror throughout the entire ordeal. It seemed there was no chance of survival for the premature infant—a baby boy, as evidenced not only by the ultrasound's display of his leaps and bounds prior to succumbing to his mother's infection-induced contractions, but also from his still form delivered by Dr. Logan when he tenderly placed the fetus on receiving blankets in the incubator at the foot of the girl's bed. There was an intense yet brief flurry of a prenatal medical team standing by Chelsea's hospital door, but in response to the shake of Dr. Logan's head as he examined the tiny, lifeless frame he'd just delivered, the medical team silently dispersed.

Nary a detail went unnoticed by either Irene or Stephanie's ever watchful eyes; the picture of the premature yet fully formed body of the baby was indelibly imprinted in both women's memories prompting Irene to step closer to her daughter to shield the physical evidence of loss from Chelsea.

Enveloped by hysterical grief, the girl buried herself in Trace's arms that held her fast with reassurances he himself needed. The truth was, he was numb and scared too, and his mother knew it. As Stephanie covered the young couple like a hawk over her nest, the woman's arms spread wide open, showering prayers and words of loving encouragement. And so it went for a short while.

Lauren had reluctantly obeyed the hospital staff's request to stay out in the hall instead of inside Chelsea's room while the rest of the girl's family and friends continued to pace the exterior waiting room. Knowing her own short fuse for waiting, Lauren was just about to disobey orders when a gurney was pushed into the hallway by a stout nurse; Irene was sprawled across its sheets.

"She fainted. She's fine," said the woman in a professional tone. "I'll be right back, darlin'."

Obviously Irene had crumbled under the enormous pressures of the day. The nurse returned with smelling salts, and Irene awoke to find herself awkwardly dangling half off the gurney. While the nurse took her pulse, Irene slowly focused on Lauren and then on Stephanie, who had since joined the women in the hall.

Suddenly Lauren gasped for air, realizing she'd been holding her own breath from all the tension. Her dramatic inhale alarmed the rather blasé nurse who immediately dropped Irene's wrist like a dead mackerel on the gurney's metal side to attend to Lauren.

"No. . . . Sorry, sorry. I'm fine. I just forgot to breathe." Lauren offered the nurse a sheepish grin as she spluttered, turning her attention back to her sister. "You fainted, Rene, but you're OK. Now just relax and get your bearings." Lauren flashed her sister a thumbs-up as the nurse disappeared down the hall.

Within moments Irene stubbornly tried to sit up, but Lauren slammed her back on the pillow. Irene growled. "Stop it, Lauren! The baby . . ."

Lauren cut her off, ". . . Rene, Dr. Logan promised Chelsea's going to be alright. And you're not going to help her a lick by cracking your noggin open." Lauren gently kissed her sister on the forehead.

But despite Lauren's reassurances, Irene desperately grabbed her sister's arm, "I have to talk to you. I have to talk to you now!" Then she glanced wildly at Stephanie who took the hint, deciding to withdraw back into the Chelsea's room. But before she exited, she leaned over to Irene for a quick hug. "I'll just wait with the kids."

Irene nodded weakly, "Thank you."

As soon as Stephanie was out of earshot, Irene sat up, warning Lauren with her eyes not to dare thwart her physical efforts of recovery. Obedient, Lauren immediately started rubbing her back, but Irene pushed her away. "I don't know what to do! The baby died. . . . It was a baby, and the *baby* was *Ford's baby*, not Trace's!"

Lauren would have given anything not to overreact to the insane news she'd just heard, but she couldn't contain the shock on her face. "What do you mean, *Ford's baby*?"

"Remember in the hall just before Chelsea miscarried? The doctor wanted to talk to me alone?"

Lauren's eyes widened like saucers, "What?"

Irene buried her head in her hands for a beat. "Don't yell at me!"

Lauren started to hug her but thought better of touching Irene at that particular moment, "Sorry, sorry. . . . Go on, please."

With that, Irene took a deep breath and began slowly, "The doctor told me that everything was going to be alright, . . . that the baby had a good chance of survival since it was *four and a half months along* and that he was aggressively treating Chelsea's infection!"

The two sisters just stared at each other, recognizing that no one could deny the math of the situation. Obviously, Chelsea hadn't even moved to Centennial when the baby was conceived. Nonetheless, it took several minutes for Lauren to respond with any kind of clarity as she reviewed the news she'd just heard. "Does Chelsea know? She couldn't have, . . . could she?" But before Lauren could come to any conclusion, Irene pressed on.

"*Obviously* she thinks Trace was the father." Irene's speech pattern radically increased as she continued. "*Trace* thinks he was the father. . . . *Stephanie* thinks she was a grandmother, and I don't know what to do now that the baby's gone because I know it would be easier for Chelsea to believe that Trace was the father, but that's . . ."

Lauren finished the sentence for her, ". . . not right."

"Oh, this is horrible!" Irene was up and off the gurney in a leap, dragging her sister over to a more sheltered corner of the hospital hall. "I have to consider Chelsea's condition! She's so vulnerable, especially now. I'm afraid telling her about Ford might completely destroy her."

Irene started to sway as if she were about to faint again. Lauren forced her down into a nearby chair, then pressed her head between her legs for a moment. When Irene came up for air, she looked at her sister like a pleading child, totally at a loss for words.

"You have to tell them, Rene. Maybe you can wait to tell Chelsea for a little bit until she gets stronger, but you've got to tell Stephanie, and you've got to tell Trace!" Lauren's eyes darted about as she attempted to gather her thoughts. "And then when Chelsea is feeling better . . . No, that's not right either because then . . . Oh this really is a mess. I think you need to tell everybody and get Chelsea a giant sedative so she'll sleep for a year and a half. . . . But she has to stay in the hospital so they can watch her." Lauren started to spin in circles. "We'll all stay with her! As long as it takes until she's OK. . . . We won't let anything happen to her, Rene. Promise. . . . But I think she needs to know the truth."

Now Lauren slowed her pacing and took an uncomfortable pause before continuing. "And in a weird way, knowing Ford's involvement may even help Chelsea with the loss of the baby."

And that's when Lauren said, "Rene, God is always in control, so Chelsea's miscarriage must be a blessing in disguise . . . even if we don't understand his plan right now."

Chapter 3

Minor Details

The sisters decided that Lauren would be the one to tell Stephanie about the baby's father being Ford since she knew Stephanie better from their prayer circle. But when Lauren called her out of Chelsea's room to the far end of the hall, all Lauren wanted to do was run. No one deserved any more bad news, especially Stephanie.

"How are the kids doing?" Lauren looked deep into her friend's eyes.

"They're hurting, crying and hugging a lot." Stephanie glanced down the hall through the dividing window to Eleanor, who locked eyes with her momentarily, then continued to pray with Tonya, Pam, Margaret, and Sam. Stephanie saw Sam glance up, clearly uncomfortable with the hand-holding, prayer-warrior gathering. Nonetheless, she sensed from a distance that Sam was actually finding comfort in the support.

She then turned her attention back to Lauren, "I've never seen Trace so broken up. . . . But actually I'm really more concerned about Chelsea. She seems inconsolable. It's a lot for these kids to take in." She paused for a moment while her emotions got the best of her. "It's a lot for any of us. There wasn't even time to digest that they'd been intimate, let alone . . ." Stephanie stumbled over the word *intimate* before continuing, ". . . let alone deal with Chelsea's being pregnant." Suddenly Stephanie turned her face to the wall, not out of embarrassment of showing her emotions to Lauren, but rather she was simply worn out from the intensity of the day.

Finally Stephanie continued in a small voice while Lauren laid hands on her friend's exhausted shoulders. "Ever since Trace was a wee one, I've covered him in prayer and dedicated him to the Lord. . . . I know God only lends us our children for their earthly care. And I do trust God as I stand in the gap for Trace. Especially since his daddy died, I've known in my heart that my boy is a child of God. I believe that he will choose a relationship with Jesus and grow into a godly man. I believe that as surely as I am standing here. I see it in his spirit and know it by his heart. But he's been so confused since his father was killed, so angry at God. . . . I've tried hard to put the right values in my boy. I know they're there, Lauren."

Stephanie began to sob and turned back to Lauren for physical support; they hugged for several minutes in silence before Stephanie continued.

"I'm confused about my emotions. I know God doesn't make mistakes. The baby was his conception. I had actually

already come to agreement that the baby would be a blessing, . . .
a gift somehow, even though all the timing seemed wrong. I just
kept saying to myself over and over, 'God doesn't make mistakes.
This baby is here, and he is here for a reason. So be it.' And then,
before any of us could practically catch our breath, he's gone."
Her eyes filled with pain. "I don't understand. I guess I'm not
supposed to. . . ."

"Steph, you're the best mom I know. You work yourself to
the bone. You're there for your boy first before yourself. Trace is
a wonderful young man. Look how he stepped up when Chelsea
told him she was pregnant. Yes, the kids made a mistake, but
I could think of a million different ways that he could have taken
the news. He took it like a man. He took the responsibility.
He's treating Chelsea with tenderness and affection well beyond
his seventeen years. That doesn't happen out of thin air, Steph.
It happened because you sowed those seeds in him, and God
will harvest them. In fact, you saw some of their fruit right there
. . . the evidence. Trace is going to be fine. And you're right,
I'm more concerned about Chelsea because she's been so damaged
by the abuse from her stepfather. At least when Ford died, Chelsea
finally told us what had happened to her. . . . Oh and Stephanie,
. . . I don't even know how to say this, but there's more . . . "

Stephanie pulled away, shaking her head slightly at the
concept that there could be *more*. "What, . . . what is it?" She
stammered. "Is it Chelsea? . . ."

Lauren grabbed Stephanie's shoulders in assurance.
"Oh, . . . sorry, sorry. I didn't mean to scare you. It's about
the baby. The father of the baby."

"Trace? What's wrong with Trace?"

"Stephanie, Trace is not the father. He couldn't have been. I know everyone thought he was, but that's why Irene has been so overwhelmed."

Stephanie stared at Lauren, totally caught off guard. "What are you saying?"

"Just before the miscarriage happened, the doctor told Irene that the baby, according to the ultrasound-sona . . . whatever that machine is called. The doctor said that the baby was four and a half months along. The doctor was encouraged by that because he told Irene that the baby had a real chance of survival since he was that far along."

Stephanie continued to shake her head. "What? Y'all hadn't even moved here four and a half months ago."

"I know. . . ." Lauren looked at the floor as if she were somehow responsible.

Stephanie's next words came slowly, as did her realization of the truth. "Are you saying that the baby was her stepfather's, that man, Ford's . . . who molested her?"

"Irene and I talked about this. It wasn't something we could just sweep under the carpet. We couldn't let these kids keep on thinking they had lost a baby . . . or that you'd lost a grandchild. Yes, a baby has been lost, and it was Chelsea's baby. And that's so sad, . . . but Irene and I both knew we had to tell you the truth. We're going to tell Chelsea, and I'm just praying that somehow . . . I don't know. I don't know how you can make a loss like that any better, but I'm not sure she would've wanted to have Ford's child. Oh my God, the baby is the innocent one here, but so is Chelsea . . . and Trace. And I just want to take that sick man Ford and . . . "

Now it was Stephanie who consoled Lauren. "Listen to me. . . . You've done the right thing. Now we just need to pull it together for the kids."

"When are you going to tell Chelsea?"

Lauren withdrew, drained. "I don't know. I think soon would be best. I think that's best." Stephanie nodded in agreement. "We can't keep this from Chelsea even though she's emotionally distraught right now. Maybe the truth will set her free in some strange way."

Lauren lowered her voice to a whisper. "Steph, you know it says in the Word of God that Jesus has all of our children in his arms. That means the baby is already in heaven. . . . And we're the ones who are left behind to grieve." Stephanie's eyes welled with tears again.

"I'm so sorry about all this, Steph."

"I know. It's not your fault. It's no one's fault. It just hurts so much."

Relief was the wrong word to describe Trace's reaction when his mother called him into the hall and told him the truth about Chelsea's baby. Confusion was more descriptive of the boy's state. He had only considered the fact of being a father for less than a day, and yet the idea had settled into his heart rather quickly since he had true and deep feelings for Chelsea. And although he didn't know how he was going to handle school, his basketball career and starting college in the fall as a young father, those details seemed to blur next to the emotions he felt when he held his girl in his arms. And when he had seen the ultrasound of the baby, the little being he believed to be his son, everything changed—his heart, his plans, his life.

Stephanie had her own struggles about the situation. Yes, she'd be lying if she said she wasn't thrilled as she watched the baby move about in Chelsea's womb. He even sucked his thumb for moment, like he was showing off for his family. Becoming a grandmother at that juncture in her life was certainly not the timing Stephanie had in mind, but in the few hours she had thought her son was about to be a daddy, she had already settled into her role, determined as always to be there for Trace. Yes, she was sure God would see them through this surprise package. In fact, Stephanie quickly opted to view the situation as a glass half full, not half empty. For her the pregnancy could be an opportunity for these teenagers to recognize the grace of God through the miracle of life; and as young parents, they most assuredly would be drawn to their own father in heaven.

But her positive thinking was short-lived. And so, as Stephanie informed Trace that he was not the father of the baby, both mother and son experienced a deep and profound sadness. Their disappointment was not only for themselves but for the loss of the baby, no matter whose he was, and surely for the pain that was certain to claim Chelsea at such striking news.

"I want to be with her, Mom . . . when she's told. I really love Chels, you know. It's not her fault all this happened." Trace's gaze was steady and determined.

Stephanie couldn't remember being more proud of her son than at that very moment. "That's good Trace, but we have to ask Chelsea's mother if you can go inside and . . . " Before Stephanie finished her sentence, Irene and Lauren approached from down the hall.

"Is it OK if I go in with you?" Trace stepped toward Irene in anticipation, but the woman just shook her head; her expression was devoid of emotion.

"What's wrong? Is Chels OK? Did you tell her yet?" Trace started down the hall when Stephanie grabbed his arm. "Son, Mrs. Williams said no." Trace froze as if shot by a tranquilizer gun.

"Trace . . . " Lauren waited for him to slowly turn his gaze toward her. "Irene's already told her about the father of the baby. Chelsea's sedated right now. She seems to be totally nonresponsive. The only thing she said was to have everybody leave her alone, and then she refused to talk anymore."

Trace was shattered, "She couldn't mean me."

"I'm sorry, she said 'everyone.'" Lauren reiterated. "I'm afraid the doctor insists that none of us go in to see her at this time. Most importantly, she needs to rest. In fact, Dr. Logan wants us all to go home. He's heavily sedated Chelsea so she'll be able to sleep through the night. She must rest. That's all he said, and we all need to go home now."

"I'll wait until she wakes up." Then all the events of the day suddenly hit Trace like a Mack truck; he started crying uncontrollably.

"Please, son," Stephanie held her boy. "We have to go home. Chelsea's not going to be up or seeing anyone all night. We'll come back in the morning. You need some rest, too." All the women nodded in agreement as Trace slumped against the wall in defeat.

Despite everyone's instinct to hover in the hall for any indication that Chelsea might need them, they finally decided to take the doctor's advice and go home. But not before each personally peeked in her room to see for themselves that Chelsea was in fact sleeping soundly.

And it was not until all well-wishers had left the hospital that the devastated girl opened her eyes and stared blankly at the wall before her; no sedative could override her grief or anger.

Chapter 4

Hindsight

Lauren slowly extracted herself from her mound of pillows and moved into the kitchen to get herself another cup of coffee. She knew what was next in her daily review; it had been happening this way since the details of her family's lives had caught everyone so off guard. A total recount of dialogue and actions played out in her mind; and try as she may, she could never seem to skip a single chapter.

She patted William, her ever-loyal black shepherd-mix dog, on the head when suddenly she flashed on the decision to call her dog "William." At the time Lauren thought the connection to her sister's married name was amusing, but given who Ford Williams turned out to be, he didn't deserve to be her dog's namesake.

Lauren felt a flush of anger rise in her, but she was brought back to reality when she almost tripped over Bingo, the kitty, who impatiently waited for her mistress to finish her time on the porch so both she and William could be fed their breakfast. Not that the feline was concerned about the dog's growling stomach—she only cared about the tidbits he would carelessly drop for her hasty clean sweep.

The sun was just peaking over the treetops while the rest of the household remained still. Standing by the sink at the end of her wood and tiled kitchen, Lauren poured another cup of coffee and bathed in the stream of light that hit her window for a moment of glory. She plopped a double dollop of heavy whipping cream into her cup, a habit she refused to give up even though lately she'd noticed its slight lingering effects collecting on her hips. Yes, Lauren was at the age of body-shape changes, which seemed to occur like clockwork in five-year increments.

She told herself that it was normal to be an extra five pounds heavier than she was in her thirties; just a pittance of poundage compared to some of her heftier friends, she consoled herself. Hers was not an unkind thought; Lauren didn't have a catty bone in her body. It was more of a self-preserving observation because the truth was, she resented the fact that by the time she would be sixty, at the rate she was going she'd be wearing an additional ten pounds! "And that wouldn't be OK," she cautioned herself. Especially since Irene was two years her senior and was still pencil thin. Of course, her sister had always insisted on maintaining her New York high-society look that she had established for years as the shipping magnet, Ford Williams's, wife.

Clearly Irene was blessed with a stunning figure, and she took care of it in her former big-city days with dance classes, private work-out sessions, and a nip and tuck here and there. But lately Irene had just flat out forgotten to eat due to the stress she was experiencing, and her former lithe build was now looking a bit haggard. And that made her even more stressed.

Lauren tried to encourage her sister with her well-worn concept that she really didn't mind her own wrinkles as long as they pointed up from smiling. Or, for that matter, her few extra pounds that had popped up here or there as long as they were fit, not flabby pounds. Frankly, Lauren didn't even worry that much about her encroaching flab since she and Brian had been divorced—Oh my, was it going on over a year now? Nope, she wasn't going to go down that memory lane this morning.

She had made it all the way back to the porch before her thoughts flashed once again on the events following Chelsea's miscarriage. Although everyone was well aware of how fragile Chelsea had been emotionally, no one would have ever imagined what was about to happen next in the string of events.

The day following the miscarriage, Chelsea spiraled into a deep and profound depression, regressing emotionally to when she was twelve years old. Together, her family and medical team decided that after a few days of sedation and observation to make sure the teen had recovered physically from her fluke vaginal infection that had caused her miscarriage, she was to be transferred to the psychiatric ward of the hospital and put on suicide watch. The doctors told Irene that even though her daughter was talking and physically appeared to be fine, she was not.

Chelsea absolutely refused to recognize or discuss any of the events that followed the beginning of the sexual abuse she'd suffered years before. All memories of Ford and her miscarriage were obviously too overwhelming for the girl to handle emotionally, so to protect herself she mentally returned to a time in her life before the extensive traumas had robbed her of her innocence, a time before all her psychological and physical pain had begun. And for the days following her withdrawal, no family persuasion, medication, or attempt from the psychiatric team was able to reach the girl. Chelsea seemed stuck in a time warp, and she refused to abandon her place of refuge.

Eventually Chelsea was transferred to a private institution for the mentally disturbed where her new league of doctors suggested shock therapy as an avenue to jolt the girl back to reality. The medical team explained the shock procedure to Irene and Lauren at length, noting all the great success they had experienced with that sort of treatment. Then they asked Irene for permission to use it on Chelsea; Irene refused, at least for a time.

It seemed ironic to the family at large that Chelsea was getting the best and most costly medical care via insurance available courtesy of Chelsea's offender since her mother had still been married to Ford when he had died. And although Irene continued negotiating her legal strategies for her rights to the inheritance of Ford's estate, she remained virtually penniless while living with Lauren and their parents. In fact, all the family's financial responsibilities had fallen on Lauren's shoulders, bankrolling everyone's needs since they had moved to Centennial. This included Irene's airfares and hotels as she shuttled back and forth to New York City and the hospital where Chelsea remained.

Lauren was happy to take on the monetary load, knowing how blessed she had been to land her recent job as head veterinarian, manager of Nashville's private Grace Animal Shelter. Thanks to Mrs. Strickland, she was not only fulfilling her aspirations as a DVM, but she was able to give her family the support they individually and collectively needed at that time.

Still, the last months had sponsored events so challenging, it was close to impossible to imagine a purpose to it all, much less a happy ending. Lauren reminded herself once again, by definition, that happy endings mean tough beginnings. Oh, how she wished she could comfort her sister and the others with the words she clung to, but the promises Lauren held in her heart from God remained silent for the rest of her family.

And as much as she wanted to protect Chelsea, Lauren could only imagine how she would react if Tucker, her five-year-old bundle of joy, were to be put in harm's way. But when she and Brian had dedicated their adopted baby boy to the Lord, they knew that Tucker was then under God's watch until he could make his own choice in faith. Lauren recognized there would inevitably be times she'd feel helpless when it came to parenting; after all, she had watched her dear friend Suz struggle with fear of the unknown concerning one of her six children who had gone astray during their teen years. But Suz was quick to point out to Lauren how the enemy delights in stealing everyone's peace and joy, and Lauren marveled as her seasoned sister in Christ called upon the promises of God that Lauren now repeated for Chelsea and her family. Moreover, she was able to stand in agreement with her *circle of friends,* declaring, claiming, and praising God for his assurances that he would never forsake them. And whenever Lauren would "let go and let God," her peace would return.

⚜

After much debate and the fact that Chelsea was not improving, Irene finally gave permission for her daughter to have shock therapy treatments, which, after only two courses, seemed to do the trick in terms of prompting the girl back to real time. That was the good news. The bad news came when Chelsea returned to her present state; her depression, anger, and emotional withdrawal had exacerbated the situation. She refused to see anyone who tried to visit. She refused to eat and had to be put on IVs for sustenance. And according to the doctors, she said she hated her mother and did not want anything to do with Trace, sure that he must hate her, too. Beyond all that, she wouldn't talk about her feelings.

Imprisoned in the hospital over the weeks leading up to her eighteenth birthday, Chelsea was determined not to cooperate with her captors in any way. Stoically, she battled her demons alone as she managed to elude her core issues, coping rather by the aid of antidepressants. Chelsea knew she soon would be of age; and if she could just contain any violent or self-destructive behavior while she was being observed in the hospital, she would finally be free of all outside authorities including her mother, family, counselors, and doctors.

Yes, Chelsea was on a mission to leave the hospital the minute she could sign herself out to follow her dreams of becoming a country singing star of a magnitude yet to be discovered. And to that end she poured all of her energies and focus into her plans, leaving her past in the dust, dead; but she was to find out soon enough, not entirely buried.

As a woman, widow, and especially as a mother, Irene continued to experience overwhelming feelings of helplessness. Unable to positively affect her daughter's ongoing destructive decisions, Irene was stung from the venom and rejection Chelsea relentlessly displayed toward her. And, she was spiraling out of control trying to deal with the reality of her abortion. Most times during the last months that the subject was broached, it was "not up for discussion" despite Lauren's efforts to bring Irene's feelings to light.

And then there was another thing Irene couldn't control, her publicly scrutinized legal situation in the small southern town that continued to elude the local courtroom despite the appeals of her two lawyers. Her charges of disorderly conduct and assaulting an officer from months ago reappeared in the newspaper headlines on every occasion her day in court was yet again postponed. Plus, there were those exhausting trips to Manhattan to mind-wrestle her grown stepchildren in the case of the pending Ford Williams's estate. It was safe to say that Irene was at the end of her rope.

Still, through it all, Lauren recognized that the very personality traits that outwardly sustained Irene during such suffocating adversity were also what seemed to hold her at bay concerning her "pending decision for Christ," as Lauren called it.

Irene had confessed on more than one occasion that she felt if she "let go and let God," as her sister was always encouraging her to do, she would simply lose whatever grip she had left on her life. She was convinced she'd fall into an abyss she called "the helpless victim of people and circumstances" and simply curl up and die. Therefore, Irene was not about to turn over anything to some invisible force, especially not her heart, life, and soul.

"Lauren, don't you get it? If I don't take care of things, who will?" Irene argued during one of their late-night talks.

"God will, Rene. Promise."

"Why do you keep saying that? Dad never protected us. . . . My husbands certainly didn't. Both abandoned me, both cheated on me, and Ford abused Chelsea! If your God loves us so much, how could he let so many horrors go on in the world?"

"Rene, God doesn't make bad things happen. That's sin."

"I thought you said, 'God is always in control. . . .'"

"He is, but he's . . . "

". . . Stop it. It's stupid. I've told you, I'm happy for whatever you've found, but it's not for me."

And that's where their conversations about faith usually ended, leaving Lauren right back in her place of waiting on God.

Chapter 5

Ticket to Ride

N o ma'am, I've decided." The bronzed-skinned, hazel-eyed
beauty held fast as Eleanor considered her friend across the
fifties-styled kitchen table while enjoying their afternoon tea.

"But you've waited so long, Tonya. Why don't you just give
it through graduation and see if he comes around. You can always
start modeling in the summer."

"I don't care if the man comes around and meets himself
on the way back. Hey, listen . . ." The twenty-year-old suddenly
bounced up and down in her seat like a child. ". . . I wrote a lyric
for a country song!"

"Girl, what are you talkin' about? You don't sing. You don't
write songs."

Tonya flashed a mysterious smile. "I know, but this keeps rolling around in my mind. . . . 'I'll wish you well as soon as I recover from you, the male-child-heartless-lover.'"

Eleanor couldn't help but laugh. "Maybe you should put that on the front of your portfolio." Standing, she made her way back to the sink to give herself a moment to think. She didn't want her young friend to make wrong decisions at such a vital time in her life. But Eleanor also didn't want to preach to her, knowing full well that Tonya had been more than patient with Shooter. As she slowly washed her cup in the sink, her mind sought wisdom. She had so hoped that Tonya and Shooter's love would evolve to where she was with her husband, a place everlasting and solid. But that was not what seemed to be playing out, at least for the time being.

And oh, how Hamilton had tried to have Shooter come around to right decisions. Ham and Eleanor would sit and talk about the young parents till the wee hours of the morning as well as during lunch breaks at Greystone High School. Ham and Eleanor always appreciated the fact that her being school nurse and him being basketball coach afforded them extra time together during the day, and they surely needed it for all their mentoring appointments.

They were also concerned about Trace, who was recovering from all that had happened with Chelsea. And although both Shooter and Trace had been working hard to keep their basketball games up, both boys' personal lives were in flux.

Hamilton consistently commended Shooter for how forthright he had been since becoming a father at the tender age of fourteen. Clearly the maturity of his actions belied his years. But despite that fact, he hadn't followed through with Tonya in marriage. And although there was no question that both Shooter and Tonya were loving parents to Bobbie, Ham could never quite get it through to Shooter that he needed to make things right with the mother of his child. Shooter was more than stiff-necked about the issue, arguing that he loved his girl, but he wasn't going to jeopardize his future in sports. He had always promised to take care of his son and Tonya, but he was going to do it his way, in his timing. And now that he had been picked up by the Chicago Bulls to play on their team, he was on his way, and nothing was going to stop him, despite Tonya's concern about his moving to a big city. In fact, her concerns really messed with his mind; did she think he couldn't handle a big town? Was he that stupid or something?

Ham confided in Eleanor that he thought insecurity was the real issue with Shooter. Tonya was so beautiful and so bright; she had been ahead of the athlete emotionally, spiritually, and mentally. Of course, being a year older, she graduated high school before Shooter and immediately started local college. Yes, she had been offered several scholarships to big-name schools but opted to stay in Centennial for Bobbie's sake. And yes, Tonya always had believed that she and Shooter would get married, so she had always put their relationship first over her potential career. That's why it hurt her so deeply when Shooter insisted on becoming a star before becoming a husband. She finally chalked his stubbornness up to his needing to be in control like he was on the basketball court. But the truth was, Shooter needed to feel like the head of the household, and so far he had always felt like he lived in Tonya's shadow. In his mind, being a success would change that.

The hole in his thinking was that he was about to lose Tonya before he even stepped foot in the big leagues.

It had been interesting for Hamilton to watch Trace and Shooter on the basketball court over the last few months as they formed a partnership of give-and-take teamwork. Yes, these young men had gone from being archenemies on and off the court to becoming best friends. And what an odd couple they were— a six-foot-eight-inch black boy from "The Bucket of Blood" projects and a backwoods blond from Alabama.

Shooter and Trace started hanging out after classes, having a lot more to talk about than just their shots and how they would strategize their game. The competitive tension between the two had lifted once both had been chosen by the scouts at the end of last year. Trace was off to college in Lexington in the fall on a scholarship; Shooter was heading straight for the pros, something that virtually never happened. Yes, both these young men were excited about their futures, but they were also torn up about their love lives. Trace was trying to recover from his relationship with Chelsea and her rejection of him since the incident in the hospital. He couldn't even get her to talk to him. And as much as that hurt, he was finally getting tired of her attitude, especially since she'd left the hospital and taken off to Nashville proper to build her singing career with not even a word to him.

As for Shooter, he never thought that he'd hear Tonya say she was actually going to leave Centennial to go to New York City and model. And although he recognized that that was as big time for her as the Chicago Bulls was for him, he always thought his girl would wait for him to make it big first. Truth be known, he was getting extremely uncomfortable with Tonya's recent show of independence. And the thought of not being able to see Bobbie every day was beyond his imagination. Unfortunately, he was not bothered enough to ask Tonya for her hand in marriage.

Still at the sink, Eleanor tried to take Tonya's assurances to heart, but she had to admit that she was uneasy in her spirit about the girl's decision to leave.

"Miss Eleanor, the agency has everything figured out for me. I'll be fine." Tonya reiterated. "They bring girls over from Europe all the time at fifteen and sixteen years old, and they do great. They've got an apartment picked out for me, a preschool for Bobbie. I already have a booking in two weeks, and I haven't even finished getting my test shots together. I'm going to school at night on the computer. . . . It rocks! I'm excited. So be excited for me, . . . please!"

Eleanor finally turned from the sink; her cup had been washed clean ten times over. "I am, girl. You know me, I'm just a mother hen. You'll be fine, and I'll be visitin' a lot."

"Yes, ma'am. You better. I'm going to have a pull-out couch in the living room so you and Ham can have a weekend on the town anytime you want. I can stay in Bobbie's room, and it will be just like I never left." Tonya was back to bouncing up and down in her chair in excitement.

Now Eleanor sat back down at the table while Tonya guzzled down another cup of tea. "I've got to go get Bobbie." She glanced at her watch when Eleanor grabbed Tonya's hand.

"You'd better quit takin' all that caffeine. You're clear about to jump out of your skin, and your hand's a shakin'."

"I'm just happy, Miss Eleanor. Once I finally made the decision to go to New York, I felt two tons lighter. . . . But listen, I gotta confess. . . ." Tonya's expression suddenly turned somber. "When you told me to get my head on straight about Brian and Lauren being my friends and all . . . And that I shouldn't even put my toe in that doorway . . ."

". . . What doorway might that be, girl?" Eleanor gave her a knowing look.

Tonya blushed, "You're gonna make me say it, aren't you?"

"Does a chicken have lips?"

"OK, fine. The 'doorway' was considering Brian in any way at all as a man thing until I figured out what was going on with Shooter and me. But actually, my feelings for Brian helped me make my decision about New York. OK, so I didn't pursue it . . . him. You were right; I shouldn't have. Now he's moved closer to Centennial, he's being an incredible father to Tuck, and he's supporting Lauren with her new shelter thing and all the time she has to spend at work. They're practically raising Tucker together again instead of Brian being just a weekend father."

"And he's going to church, even though it's a different one from ours." Eleanor pointed out, minus any "I told you so" attitude.

"I know. . . . I just wanted to thank you for not letting me step into their space."

"More like into a slippery slope, not 'space.'"

Tonya exhaled deeply. "True, true. Listen, I've been praying that they can get back together for Tucker's sake as well as their own. Anyway, I'm just saying that I really think that it's going to be good that I get away for a while. And I don't want you or Ham to worry; I've got the Word of God etched on my heart. I'm not going to mess up, no matter what comes at me."

"Don't be too cocky now. Life's tough in the big city."

"I'm not cocky; I'm determined. And you know what I'm like when I stand for something. Gosh, I've waited on Shooter for almost five years now. I think I've done my part. I say 'his loss'! This wild crazy girl calmed down after I had Bobbie, and I'm not ever going to put myself in that position again. I'll be waiting on my man. If it's Shooter, he's going to have to jump through a few personal hoops to get me back, but that door of my heart is not entirely closed."

"Amen."

"Yes, Miss Eleanor. You'll see."

As both women stood, Eleanor gave Tonya a big hug. "I'm so proud of you, girl. I know we've talked about this 'big city thing' ad nauseam. You're goin' to be out in the world, and the world doesn't think the way we do. But I'm just gonna be prayin' that you're going to take all that beauty of yours from the inside out and show the world what Jesus looks like in the flesh . . . You!" Eleanor took Tonya by the shoulders. "Father God, I ask you to cover this girl with an impenetrable hedge of protection around her and her son and give her wisdom beyond her years.

I rebuke you Satan in the name of Jesus! You go back to the pit of hell and take all your little demons with you that would adversely affect this glorious child of God. And Satan, you've already lost the battle, so you keep your evil hands off Tonya and Bobbie . . . and Shooter. Guide them, Almighty God. . . . And I ask this all in Jesus' name above all names!"

Tonya nodded in agreement, her eyes suddenly pools of tears, "Amen, in Jesus' name." Then she squealed like a little girl. "Oh, I'm so scared and excited at the same time. I can't believe I'm actually leaving tomorrow! But not before I see the girls for our Thursday afternoon. I'll have everything packed up, and I'll be by before I take off with Bobbie."

Eleanor wagged her finger, "You better, or I'll slit your tires."

"Listen to you sass!" Tonya took in her friend's curved figure. "Ever since you've been 'remodeled,' you've been pretty . . ."

Eleanor cut in, ". . . spunky?"

"Yeah, I guess you could use that word. But the one I was thinking about also begins with an *S* . . . Sexy!"

Eleanor winked. "Well, if I can beat cancer, you can beat off the men who are goin' to be falling all over your feet once you hit the city." With that thought Eleanor looked worried again.

Tonya put her fingers to her lips. "Sshh . . . I'll be fine. Hey, I have my man. He's about three feet two inches and still sucks his thumb. His name is Bobbie, and . . . oops . . . I wasn't supposed to tell anyone about his thumb-thing. The boy wants to be so grown-up all of a sudden."

"His secret's safe with me." Eleanor escorted Tonya to the front door with hugs of assurances along the way.

"All of our thoughts are safe with you, Miss Eleanor. Thanks for being such a good friend." And before both ladies started to cry, Eleanor hustled Tonya out the front door with an emotional fanfare.

⚜

As Tonya made her way down the street from Eleanor and Ham's small brick house smack-dab in the middle of the projects, she drank in the neighborhood as if it would be the last time she'd ever see that part of town. Yes, she was definitely 'moving on up to the east side,' and she couldn't wait.

Unlocking her car, she thought to herself that it was OK she had waited so long to make her decision. Eleanor was probably right; she wouldn't have been ready before. She also knew she was lying when she said with such assurance that she would be fine. She was a little scared about going to New York City by herself. Clearly her twenty years in a small town had not afforded her the kind of experiences necessary to traverse that kind of world, let alone the fast pace of runway and photography modeling.

And of course, she had heard on the news and read in the newspapers some of the horror stories of living the high stakes of metropolitan lifestyle. In fact, if Chelsea's experience had been a realistic glimpse into Tonya's future, she would unpack her bags before she even left for New York. You see, Tonya had witnessed the eighteen-year-old's life spin even more out of control as soon as Chelsea had hit Nashville on her own.

It surprised Tonya that she and Chelsea had become friends after Chelsea fled the hospital a few months ago. Since Tonya was more sophisticated than her other friends, Chelsea had come to her for advice, albeit cautiously, making Tonya swear that whatever they talked about stayed between them. Unfortunately, the time they shared was brief. Tonya felt Chelsea was in some deep trouble but had no idea how to help the floundering teen. Tonya also knew that the only thing that made her different from any other wide-eyed beauty in a big bad world was her foundation in Christ, and Chelsea clearly didn't have that rock-solid unconditional love to lean on. Nor did she have a *circle of friends* to pray with—but little did Chelsea know, that despite her lack of faith, she still had a *circle of friends* that prayed for her.

When Tonya had advised Chelsea to go back to live at her aunt Lauren's and start her singing career out of the safety of a home base, she stopped calling. And although Chelsea wasn't talking to her mother, she was smart enough to check in every so often with Lauren so nobody put out an APB on her. Chelsea's conversations with her aunt had been brief, expressing only the girl's increasing need to be independent. To her, family meant emotional ties that she clearly rejected. Chelsea did share with Lauren that she was working as a waitress, had her own place, and was making the rounds and taking vocal lessons, all in the period of a few months.

Yes, the wayward teen's fate remained a frightening question mark for everyone who loved her. Still, Irene and Lauren decided that they couldn't push the point of communication further for fear Chelsea would completely disappear from their radar screen.

Lauren gently encouraged her niece to please check in, and so far she had. Just maybe Chelsea was finding out that it was not always cool to be so independent.

✿

Tonya double-parked and quickly approached the office at the back of her church from the parking lot behind Centennial's courthouse. Although in a hurry, she did take a brief moment to breathe in the crisp spring air, wondering if Centennial's famous spring blossoms would reveal themselves despite the lingering frost.

Just before she reached the office door, it flung open, and her son bounded out followed by Pam, her best friend of years and years. When Bobbie jumped into his mother's arms, he almost knocked her over by his sheer impact; Tonya was used to her four-year-old's brawn, having always called him "a bag of rocks" to Pam.

"Mama, Miss Pam had a cake for me for going away! I got some in my backpack for you."

Tonya looked up at Pam with affection. "Thanks, Sweetie."

"Oh, don't thank me, girlfriend. I just thought it'd be fun for you to have Bobbie all hopped up on sugar for his last evening in town."

"Gee, thanks. . . ." Tonya regarded her boy, who looked as if he had been plugged into a wall socket as he ran over to the swings in the yard next door. Tonya yelled after him, "Bobbie, just a few minutes, kiddo. . . . We have to get home and finish packing!"

"OK, Mom!" As he threw his backpack on the ground, Tonya and Pam realized the cake was now squashed dead.

"Darn, I really was looking forward to stuffing my face."

"Aw, . . . poor baby!" Pam gave her a sincere hug. Yes, these two were also quite a pair; Tonya loomed over Pam's petite body by a good foot and a half.

Wiggling out of their embrace, Pam indicated that she needed to get back inside. "I've still got a couple of kids in there who haven't been picked up yet, and, I'm sure one of them is eating the rest of the cake single-handedly."

"OK, but I'll see you later, right?" Tonya shooed Pam into the doorway. "I've got to put you to work, remember? Hey, what am I going to do about unpacking once I get to New York? . . . You've got to come with me so you can help arrange my new life!"

"Oh no, Miss Pied-Piper, it's your life and your adventure. But I'm sending my favorite pillow along with you so I won't have to drag it on the airplane."

On that note Pam disappeared into the door with a swish of her golden locks, barely dodging a piece of chocolate cake, which not so mysteriously flew through the air.

As Tonya gathered her son up at the swing set, she was happy that Bobbie seemed so excited about their move. She had definitely lost sleep over whether her boy would miss his friends, but thankfully he seemed to be up for the adventure. But Bobbie would ask, "When's Daddy coming to New York?" Tonya would founder as she explained to her son that his dad had to finish school here, and he'd be visiting soon. Still Bobbie seemed to accept her answer. Since the boy had always known his dad to be there for him, in Bobbie's little mind, he couldn't imagine it being any other way.

Chapter 6

Changing Hands

The takeover had been a brilliant move of righteous indignation on the part of the *circle of friends*. It wasn't exactly blackmail, the women told themselves as they hovered around the back booth of the diner over the last several months plotting their strategies. After all, Norro never appreciated Stephanie's Herculean talents of running and serving his establishment, nor did he recognize the value of the finely tuned cook team who, as easily as flipping pancakes, presented the renowned southern dishes.

Then, of course, there was Norro's personality, or lack of it. No doubt, the man was less than a stellar individual with questionable character. He was known for his cheap politics and sleazy business dealings. To put it bluntly, as Stephanie had often said, "He is merely a grease spot on the kitchen floor, a slime that sneaks around and spies on people for his own ends."

So, when the girls gave the sixty-something, pot-bellied low-life of the month a taste of his own medicine, they felt no remorse. After all, they had found out Norro was responsible for, and benefited financially from, taking some of the photos that kept appearing in the newspapers concerning Irene's court appearance and charges. And once the ladies collectively confronted Norro with evidence of his unacceptable behavior, he folded like a stack of bad cards.

Lauren's photos snapped at the Easy Motel, home of Centennial's hot political poker games, had done the trick. They were all they needed to support the gals' plans to stop Norro from anymore spying, as well as squelch any ideas of his returning to public service. Having been the sheriff of Centennial years before, the "grease spill" was planning to pretend to right his crooked ways and run again for town mayor, a concept that would have sent chills up any of the citizens' backs if they knew the truth of Norro's utter lack of integrity.

And to that end, Stephanie, Eleanor, Tonya, Pam, and Lauren felt they could kill two of Norro's bad plans with one good picture of his plotting while playing poker with the towns' riffraff.

The diner's business had been booming, thanks entirely to Stephanie's efforts, so the *circle of friends* decided that it was time for the venue to change hands. And they had their eight-by-ten glossy trump card heading their negotiations. After confronting Norro with the damning photo, they convinced him that it would be wise to pursue his political aspirations in another part of Tennessee. And with that, things started to take shape. At first Norro was not going to back down or be "blackmailed," but Stephanie was able to convince him that he should probably have a meeting with the others frequenting his poker room to get confirmation from his cronies that his refusal to play the lady's game was a poor decision for all concerned.

It was a bold step for the gals to challenge the good ole boys in a Southern town, even in 1997. But miracle upon miracles, Norro folded, recognizing that he and his buddies had all been caught with their proverbial pants down. The men concluded that Norro had a zip of a chance at winning the mayoral election due to his ongoing shenanigans. So, after much ado, he decided to get out of town after he accepted Stephanie's hefty offer for the diner—one he couldn't easily ignore.

What the girls had considered at first to be a harebrained idea quickly turned into reality. And that reality was now, not just about making the deal, but rather how to pay for the deal. Obviously, Stephanie did not have the credit or even the down payment to buy the diner. And it didn't matter that the idea was something she had dreamed of since she had first stepped foot in Centennial three years before. "Wishes don't buy mortgages" was a concept she knew all too well. Point being, no matter how many shifts Stephanie worked, her waitress pay would never create a nickel's worth of a savings account.

It wasn't long after Norro had accepted Stephanie's proposal that the reality of the financial resources needed to close the deal hit the ladies. Eleanor called a special meeting of her *circle of friends,* offering up a partnership between her husband, herself, and Stephanie to buy Norros. After all, what are friends for?

Oh yes, it was a sweet time. The support Stephanie felt from the girls as well as Hamilton's financial genuflecting was actually going to bring her dreams to fruition. More importantly, the purchase of the diner was Stephanie's confirmation to her son that God does work in mysterious but never failing ways. She pointed out to Trace that God always likes to show up at the very last minute, just to make sure we know we are not responsible for his masterful miracles.

And there was also another positive note after so much recent pain; Ham had gotten closer to Trace over the last few months. The boy was thankful that his mother could finally be in the position of ownership as she had worked so long and hard for what Trace called a "twig of a paycheck." And through all the changes in this young man's life, he was finally allowing Hamilton to step slowly into the shoes of surrogate father in addition to basketball coach. And, no doubt, Hamilton Walton Robert James III was up for the job.

On that late spring afternoon Stephanie waited in the bank for Ham and Eleanor to arrive so they all could fill out the loan applications for the diner. Her knees were literally knocking in excitement as she tried to contain her joy over the recent changes in her life. Yes, the diner meant the world to her, but more importantly, she had been watching her son spiritually move toward his faith, and that was better than a double-dipped chocolate fudge brownie covered with Haagen-Dazs ice cream smothered in hot chocolate sauce. In fact, that's exactly what she had in mind to make for Ham and her *circle of friends* in celebration as soon as the ink on the paperwork was dry. Oh my, God was so good.

Stephanie observed the hustle and bustle in the bank foyer with curiosity. This was not an establishment she'd spent a great deal of time in short of cashing her weekly checks. No, high finance was not in this Alabama girl's vocabulary. In fact, she felt out of place in her white waitress's uniform among the suited entourage of bank employees.

Glancing at her watch for the sixty-millionth time since she'd arrived, she whispered to herself, "Stop it. . . . They're not even supposed to be here yet." Still, Stephanie's eyes moved intermittently to the front door as she waited for her friends to arrive.

Eleanor glanced at her watch while waiting under the welcome sign at Greystone High for 11am to arrive. When she was finally joined by her husband, he greeted her with his ever-present look of love and hug for the wife he so adored. "Sorry, I just had to put the finishing touches on the board."

Eleanor kissed him on the ear as she looked up to see Ham's tidbit of wisdom for the day scrawled across the school sign.

> "YOU CAN GIVE AS MUCH AS YOU MAY—BUT
> NOT MORE THAN YOU HAVE; SO 'FILLER' UP BY
> LOOKING UP."—HAM

Satisfied with his workmanship, she cooed, "It's so delightful to be married to a man who can mix a romantic touch with intellectual prowess." Hamilton puffed up like a pelican at the compliment.

As the couple headed for their car, hand in hand like high school kids going steady, the afternoon sun splashed shadows across the parking lot. They carefully dodged some students who wove in and out of various parking spaces as school let out for the afternoon.

Ham put his arm around his wife, then winked at her. "I know you're just trying to get on my good side with all your sweet talk."

She giggled, "I'm already on your good side. . . . You're buyin' me the diner today, remember?"

"*We're* buying the diner, darling. And you and Stephanie better not outvote me on all the decisions just because I'm the only male investor."

"Mr. Ham, you'll be makin' all those decisions for us. We'll be relyin' on it. After all, you are the headship of this family, and you handle it quite well, I might add."

Again he looked pleased with himself as he opened the car door for his "bride" as he liked to call Eleanor. "Uh-huh, . . . and you make it so easy to love you."

She paused for a moment before getting in the car to hold his face in her hands with such tenderness. "What I know is that this morning before we got out of bed and I was lying there with you, all I kept thinking was how safe I felt in your arms."

Eleanor's last statement of amore actually caused Hamilton to blush, "Woman, you're going to have to write these down. My head is about to explode." He gallantly closed the car door and jogged around the front of the vehicle to the driver's side. And all the while, Eleanor's eyes were glued on her man.

No, she had never been sorry for marrying this gentleman; not that all their days had been perfect, by no means! Still, they had grown together intimately as each had grown more intimate with their Lord. And under God's umbrella and direction, their marriage kept getting better and better.

Not only that, their purposes individually and collectively for their lives kept broadening. Eleanor and Ham had mentored in their private time so many students over the years, and they continued to do so, staying close to the most needy kids by not moving out of the projects. What made their decision to stay particularly sweet was that they well could afford to have moved up and out years ago. And despite the fact that their son had located his law practice in Washington D.C., they remained where they felt they were most needed.

Hamilton had reminded Eleanor as recently as last night that one of the reasons he always wanted to have a secure savings program was so they'd have a nest egg to invest. Hamilton's motto was, "When God blesses us with money, it's only to flow through us to others. The fun part is to see who God wants to bankroll."

But despite his well-honed overview of blessings, both Eleanor and Ham had not sidestepped frustration in respect to their plans with Pam to open the Hope School. All three were beyond curious as to why the source of funds for the project hadn't been revealed thus far. Since the financial necessities to build and support the school were well beyond Ham and Eleanor's bank account, it was clear that alternative doors of revenue needed to open.

Pam had finally sat down with Mrs. Strickland last winter for a meeting about the school as soon as the shelter project had opened its doors, but to no avail. Although Mrs. Strickland couldn't have been nicer, she declined to invest due to her family's donor schedule.

"Perhaps next year we can revisit the subject, Pamela." Mrs. Strickland chimed with a supportive smile. "Your school sounds just lovely. What could be more important than giving the opportunity for all children, despite their financial or ethnic backgrounds, to become tomorrow's leaders? Splendid. . . . And I give you my word that I'll bring it to our board for year-end consideration."

Hers was not the answer Pam was looking for. Even though there was potential of funds in Mrs. Strickland's promise, the thought of waiting another year to get the school started totally frustrated the young woman. And only when she and her *circle of friends* called out to God for direction and patience did Pam's optimistic attitude finally return. That's when Ham, Eleanor, and Pam stood in agreement once again that God would loose the needed finances at just the right time through the right individuals or group because surely Hope School was a spiritually solid concept of reconciliation with Christ at the helm. And that had to be pleasing to God.

But as Eleanor pointed out, "Today we're all about the business of buyin' a diner."

❦

Stephanie was at the bank's revolving entrance door by the time Ham and Eleanor finally arrived. And she was about to jump out of her skin with excitement as the three hugged in the corridor.

"Come on, come on, come on! Ms. Bratchet's waiting for us."

Hamilton checked his watch, "Steph, calm down. We're *exactly* on time."

Stephanie took a breath. "I know, I've just been here for a year and half waiting for y'all. I feel like a kid in a candy store, and the tooth fairy is about to arrive!"

The three headed toward one of the private offices where Ms. Bratchet stood waiting for her next clients. Suddenly Stephanie stopped and grabbed both Eleanor and Ham by their arms. "Are you sure you want to do this? I mean, just because I got carried away with myself and made an offer I couldn't afford doesn't mean that you two have to come up with the goods."

"Steph, you are going to make us so much money in that diner, even as part owners." Hamilton reassured her. "Eleanor and I believe that we'll make enough money to open the Hope School from this venture. So, believe me, you're the one that's doing us the favor. We're just putting up money and prayer. . . . You're the one putting in all the love, sweat, and *no* tears."

Hamilton put his arms around both women and ushered them toward the office. "Let's take our first vote, what do you think? Should we change the name of the diner?"

Stephanie looked stunned, "No! Everybody knows about Norros. . . . It's famous for its food, and me of course." She giggled. "Seriously, most folks don't even know there's a real *Norro*, especially the out-of-towners."

Ham wasn't convinced, "Well, we'll see how it all unfolds. I'm just not sure I want any lingering attachments to that man."

And as Ms. Bratchet led the three into her cubicle, a bona fide dream was about to come true. What fun!

Chapter 7

Big Business

There was a light knock on the office door. Buried in paper-work at her formidable desk, Lauren didn't bother to look up from the piles of bills before answering, "Come in."

William, the dog, was already at the door in quick response to the knock, so as it flung open, the heavy oak barrier smacked the canine hard on the nose. William yelped, retreating to his cushion in the corner of the room.

"Sorry, William." apologized Clive, the heavy-set African-American seventeen-year-old kennel assistant.

Lauren looked up over her reading glasses at her dog. "William, if you keep that up, you're going to wind up looking like a boxer instead of a shepherd." Then she regarded the boy in her doorway, "I've asked you to please open the door slowly. In fact, why don't you put a note on the hall side of the door so everyone will remember that William is a nosy-body, and when you bang on the door, he's going to be up trying to protect me." Lauren scoffed at the thought. "Although I don't know what the dog would do if somebody actually came in and tried to hurt me. . . . He'd probably lick them to death."

Then Lauren noticed her cat, "What are you doing with Bingo?" The fat feline was stuffed under Clive's kennel jacket looking disgruntled at being manhandled.

"Sorry, Miss Lauren, but Bingo was down in the dog corridor driving them hounds crazy."

Lauren's eyes narrowed. "She is soooo bad. What a tease! I don't know how she got out of the office again. Do you think she's figured out how to open and close the door by herself?"

Lauren maintained a serious expression while Clive actually considered her question, "Don't know, ma'am. She's kind'a short to reach the knob. Maybe William helps her."

Lauren giggled at the thought. "Actually, I think she lays in wait until I have to go through the door, and then *zoom*. It seems to make her day to strut up and down in front of the kennels while the dogs go nuts because they can't get at her. I didn't know she had such an evil streak. . . . Maybe she's bored. But she hates to stay home. You should see her face when she gets really, really mad." Lauren regarded the cat who was now curled up on her spot atop the couch.

"Why don't you put a big bell on her or something so you know where she is."

"Clive, what a great idea! A big cowbell she'll trip over so she's not so fast. . . . Just kidding." Now, Lauren seriously considered his suggestion. "Do we have any collars from the strays with bells on?"

"Yeah, I think maybe in the back. From a little dog. I'll go check it out."

"Thanks." And with that mission on his mind, the kid was gone in a flash.

❧

Lauren enjoyed a sip of her coffee, as she took a moment to peruse her office. It appeared as if she had lived in it for years; almost every inch of space was now occupied in stark contrast to the opening day of the shelter a mere three months earlier.

Oh, she so enjoyed how her life seemed to be turning out. She thought back on how insightful Mrs. Strickland had been in giving Lauren her own space by way of her office that was big enough for Tucker to come after school and bring friends. The area even had its own little kitchenette and bathroom, much like a miniature house. And given the hours Lauren had been spending at work, she'd practically moved in.

Tucker absolutely adored coming to his mom's work to play, and it warmed Lauren's heart that everyone who ran the shelter also adored her five-year-old, including all the animals he played with for hours on end. Yes, Tucker had become quite the little helper, and with his dad being available to take the boy to dinner or even overnight if Lauren had an overflow on her surgery schedule, her life seemed almost too good to be true.

Lauren often pinched herself. Everything had worked out so well, with only one exception—time. There just didn't seem to be enough hours in the day to complete all she wanted to accomplish. But when she'd catch herself in a hurried moment, she'd remind herself of Mrs. Strickland's words of wisdom, "Everyone has the same amount of hours each day. If you're running out of them, you're running too hard." The seventy-year-old lady would then wave her cane in the air for emphasis.

But despite Mrs. Strickland's warnings, Lauren was once again *out of time.* As she regarded the clock on the wall surrounded by thank-you notes, pictures of animals, and drawings from Tucker, she applauded herself for making the entire side of her office wall one big bulletin board of written celebration. She allowed herself a moment of enjoyment, then pulled herself out of her seat; she was about to be late, and there was no keeping Irene waiting at the airport.

❧

Lauren had been tempted to let her dad pick up Irene, but oh how she loved the short ride from the airport to Centennial when the phones weren't ringing and she could spend some catch-up time with her sister alone. Poor Irene seemed to be a bundle of escalating nerves, and Lauren was convinced that the least she could do was try to lift her sister's spirits at every turn possible. Airport runs were part of that plan.

Slamming through the front door of her house shadowed by William, Lauren cradled Bingo in her arms; the kitty's look of consternation had reached new heights. Bingo had already given up on flipping her head back and forth in physical denial of the pink collar with small snow bells attached tightly around her neck.

As Lauren kicked the door shut behind her and started to delicately place the cat on the floor, Bingo propelled herself from her mistress's arms like a rocket ship. Yes, with her tail twice its normal size, clearly the cat was in a total kitty snit-fit. Bingo batted furiously at her collar, all the while the annoying bells the cat had only heard at Christmastime clattered about her neck announcing her every move.

At the cat's visual frustration, Lauren noted that she'd give Bingo the evening to settle down, but if her kitty still hated her motion detector by bedtime, Lauren would remove it.

Heading to her parents' apartment, Lauren banged on their door and entered, barely waiting for a "come in" from Margaret and Sam. The couple was nestled on the end of their couch together under a big overhead light madly working on a crossword puzzle before the start of their regular evening news program.

Margaret, as always, was twirling Sam's hair at the back of his neck around her forefinger. No doubt, Lauren's mother was a whiz at crossword puzzles, and it had always been a debate between Irene and Lauren as to whether Margaret simply let Sam get a few words just to keep him happy.

Upon entering the room, Lauren thought how cute her parents could be sometimes but then pulled her attention back to the reason she was there. "Just wanted to say, 'Hi.' I'm running out to get Irene. You'll hear the explosions if I'm late, so pray there's no traffic." Before Margaret and Sam could respond, she was out the door yelling over her shoulder, "Tuck's eating with Brian! I'm going to pick him up for church tonight, and we'll be home around 8:30! Love you!" And with that, she was gone.

Sam pulled his glasses off and looked at his wife, "Can you ever remember a time when she *wasn't* late?"

Margaret thought for a moment, "Not really. She was even late for both her weddings. There was also the fact that she could never resolve the snoring issue with either husband, as I have with you." Margaret gave Sam a knowing look.

"What does snoring have to do with being late?"

"Appreciation. I'm never late, and I handle the hard times."

Sam bluntly responded, "You don't handle anything. You pinch my earlobes off every time I snore. I don't know if that's 'resolving' or not. I do know that my earlobes are at least a quarter of an inch longer than they ought to be from years of woman-handling."

Margaret affectionately rubbed the side of her husband's face, then pulled on one of his ears. "No, no darling. Ears grow and noses grow as we get older. You can't blame your nose extension on me."

"I blame my nose on my parents, but I blame my earlobes on you."

"Well, whatever you say, dear." She pointed down at the crossword puzzle. "Seven across is albatross . . . a-l-b-a-t-r-o-s-s . . . as in around your neck."

Frustrated, Sam stared at his wife; he never could figure out how she came up with such tough words.

"As Maya Angelou said once," Margaret continued, pleased with herself, "'I've learned that people will forget what you said, people will forget what you did, but people will never forget how you make them feel.'"

"You're starting to sound like Lauren."

"No, Sam. That's not from the Bible. It's just from an interview I saw on TV of Maya's thoughts on growing older. When I told Lauren about another one of her quotes, she had to add on to it."

"And what was that?"

"Alright, the quote was, 'I've learned that life sometimes gives you a second chance.' And of course, Lauren added, 'But God *always* gives you a second chance. There's a difference.'"

"Actually, Lauren's add-on sounds a little bit more appealing."

"Here's one I was going to write to you on your next birthday card. 'I've learned that even when I have pains, I don't have to be one.'"

Sam finally cracked a smile. "Those are pretty good, Margaret."

"No, plagiarism here. That's also from Maya. And here's one . . ."

". . . Enough."

But Margaret was not about to be silenced. " Here's one I told Irene the other day although I'm not sure she got my point. 'I've learned that regardless of whether you like your parents, you'll miss them when they're gone from your life.'"

"Is that a statement or a promise?"

"It wasn't about us, Sam. It was about Chelsea. I was just trying to cheer Irene up. Surely, Chelsea will outgrow her rebellious stage at some point."

"Only if she survives it. I don't blame Irene for feeling so vulnerable." And then, in a surprising moment, Sam looked as if he was about to cry. Yes, this hardhead had gotten a bit more tender in his later years, especially since he too was feeling vulnerable; his and Margaret's reliance on Lauren's generous heart was out of their comfort zone. Sam had tried to tell himself that their current financial situation was not his fault. But the truth was, they had not planned his retirement well; and at the end of the day, despite what both would concur over their cocktail hour, there was no real excuse for their predicament other than poor planning and overspending.

Sam often wondered since he had retired and both he and Margaret lived off their Social Security checks alone, what would he do if they didn't have a free place to stay? But then he would immediately push that agonizing thought out of his mind. He was good at that.

No, it hadn't been often that this seventy-nine-year-old man expressed contrite gratitude. But lately both he and Margaret were sure to make Lauren understand how much they appreciated her graciousness. And whenever they expressed those sentiments, Lauren would respond, "Mom and Dad, it's a blessing to have you two so close to us. Tuck will get to know his grandparents. . . . It's all good!"

But despite her assurances, somewhere deep in Sam and Margaret's hearts they knew, given the pattern of both sides of their families' behavior over generations, Lauren's present style was unique; everything from her vocabulary and attitudes to her outlook had turned around. Yes, the Pattersons simply couldn't deny that something life altering had happened to their daughter ten years ago, and Lauren insisted that change had everything to do with accepting Jesus Christ in her life.

It seemed a universal conclusion within the rest of this family of nonbelievers that all had to take Lauren at her word since her actions were actually speaking louder than her words. And simply put, whatever it was that was going on with their youngest daughter, it was really beginning to soften Margaret and Sam's hearts. Yes, certain boundaries had been drawn in the sand within the rather volatile family for the sake of their survival together in close quarters, but Lauren simply loved them all through their idiosyncrasies (including her own). And that kind of unconditional love seemed to be working.

Now none of this was to say that Lauren was a piece of cake to live with. She still had times of profound dismay, stubbornness, sadness, and anger. But the difference was, when she felt out of control, she would come into her parents' apartment like a child and confess all her negative feelings, thoughts, and deeds. Then she'd humbly repent before them, which invariably made Margaret and Sam uncomfortable. Nonetheless, the process always put Lauren back on track.

Still, Lauren's new style of handling life was in direct opposition to Sam and Margaret's lifelong method of dealing with a bad night, harsh words, hurt, anger, or scathing remarks that so often flew back and forth within the Patterson household. Their style was to sweep all the hurtfulness under the carpet the next day and act as if nothing had ever happened. Unfortunately, the painful patterns would simply raise their ugly heads over and over since the root of the issues was never recognized, understood, grieved, forgiven, or healed. Oh, the last few months had been so revealing.

Margaret asked her husband, "Do you remember the time Lauren went through E.S.T.?"

"E.S.T.? As in estimate?"

"No, no. Don't you remember years ago when she went through that *truth-thing*? . . . She took some course that she couldn't even afford to take, and they kept her in a room for hours and hours and wouldn't ever let her go to the bathroom?"

Sam looked blank.

"Come on, don't you remember she told us that in E.S.T., whatever the heck that stood for, the leaders tore you down like the Marines do and told everyone that they were 'worthless, nothings . . . liars' or whatever made them recognize the evil in them. Something like that, to what end, we could never figure out. Don't you remember?"

Sam finally nodded, "Ah, yes. That was a really ridiculous time for her, with many more to follow, I might add."

"Oh, I know," Margaret agreed. "Lauren was convinced that nonsense was what it took to become an honest person, and that everyone needed to confront everyone else they knew and review every event of their pasts, . . . and then tell them honestly everything they thought. Which we thought was just destructive."

"And self-centered, I'd say."

"Thank goodness she's since apologized, and we've all actually laughed about it. . . ."

Margaret and Sam sat in silence for a long moment.

". . . But don't you think this being a Christian thing seems to have stuck with her? It's certainly brought about good things, I think. Don't you, Sam?"

But Margaret's husband had had enough by then. "I'm going to turn on the news."

And that was his notice to his wife to stop talking, a command she'd never taken seriously. Plain and simple, if she wanted to keep talking, she did. No, Margaret was not a woman to be bullied, but this evening *she* decided there was not much more to say at that particular moment.

Chapter 8

U-turn

Unable to land in Nashville, the plane was in a holding pattern due to thunderstorms. As she glanced out the window, she caught her image that shown in the glass. "If life is a stage," she pondered, "I want better lighting."

Without lingering on her reflection, she turned off the overhead reading light that had illuminated the writings from Lauren now spread about her lap. Irene gingerly flipped over the pages her sister had sent her during the last several years so that the woman sitting next to her in first class wouldn't be able to take a gander. Recently Irene had zero tolerance for nosy people; between all the press and various strained situations in her life, she felt like the proverbial open book. Yes, Irene had become overly protective about her sense of self-preservation concerning anything of a personal nature. And who could blame her?

Apologizing for the delay, the pilot announced they had been cleared for landing and should be on the ground in approximately twenty minutes. And as the cabin lights illuminated, the flight attendant quickly made her way up and down the aisle picking up last-minute glasses from the passengers, while Irene glanced once more out the window to catch her reflection, now happier with her backlit image. She thought of how thankful she was she'd been able to close at least one of her negotiating points during the ongoing period of dispute over Ford's will; substantial numbers of his unused frequent-flyer miles had been put into Irene's account. At least she was allowed to continue to fly in the status of which she had become accustomed over their twelve-year marriage.

For Irene the thought of sitting back with the masses in coach class was horrifying, not due to snobbery mind you; it was more born of the fact that she felt she couldn't take one more intrusion of her space. Life simply had become too stressful not to be able to have some cocktails and a bite of decent food as she traveled the hours between Nashville and New York, especially since she had been making the regular commute for almost half a year now. In fact, she traveled so often that Irene had come to know just about every flight attendant and most employees at the ticket counters as if they were personal friends. Ah, she thought, the little details that made life's pressures bearable.

Having embraced the solace she had found in the comfort of first class, Irene glanced once more over the letters Lauren had sent, her sister's written efforts to communicate details of her life and passions while maintaining a long-distance relationship with Irene.

She had questioned herself when Irene grabbed the portfolio of Lauren's writings as she packed for her most recent trip to New York. She wondered why she had even kept her sister's correspondence all this time since she didn't much agree with her sentiments. Nonetheless, there was no denying that Lauren had radically changed for the good, her renewal expressly witnessed by her family since they had all moved in together. So, despite herself, Irene thought perhaps she should review some of her sister's "steps of progress" in Lauren's own words. After all, whatever it was that she had discovered, it had moved Lauren into a place far more appealing than Irene's world.

Thinking back, Irene noted that her sister had always written excerpts, if you will, of her beliefs from the time she was a kid. Then Lauren would insist on sending her thoughts on to family members and friends like a monthly Christmas letter from a ten-year-old sage. Lauren had even sent one of her poems to the local newspaper, sure that she would be published. And she was.

Irene felt herself tense at the memory; after all, *she* was the writer in the family. *She* was the artist, even if she was only self-published. Hey, Lauren was the tomboy! Thankfully, after a moment, Irene settled down again, deciding that she should be complimented that her little sister had followed in her footsteps of expression. Actually, if Lauren had gleaned any kind of talent as a writer, it was because Irene had guided her style and vocabulary with loving care. "So there," Irene whispered.

In fact, Lauren had become an extremely effective writer. Irene recalled her sister's article in the local newspaper when they all had first moved to Centennial. Lauren had exposed the town's use of chutes for animal control for what it really was, inhumane and totally barbaric. It was beyond comprehension to Lauren that the residents of Centennial would actually drop any unwanted animals or critters down a drive-up chute to be contained in a one-room cell until animal control would pick up the poor beasts, dead or alive. The doomed ranged from cats, dogs, raccoons, birds, squirrels . . . whatever. Lauren's article was so stirring that in a matter of months she had closed down all the chutes in the area (by popular demand) and was now running the Grace Animal Shelter. Talk about making a grand entrance and a profound difference.

But instead of reveling in triumph for her sister's achievements, Irene's thoughts turned on her, and she suddenly felt personally frustrated and worthless, invisible under her little sister's shadow since she had moved to Tennessee. No, Irene couldn't deny that Lauren was making a better bid on life than she seemed to be. Clearly her baby sister was more successful as a mother; Tucker was growing up swimmingly well whereas Chelsea was not a reigning example of health, happiness, and prosperity. The truth was, Irene didn't have a close relationship with her daughter like Lauren had with her son. And upon that realization the word *relationship* stuck in her craw. "Close relationship with Chelsea," she thought. "*No* relationship was more like it."

Irene's eyes darted across one of Lauren's letters entitled "The Drought."

May 1990
Dear Rene,

I've been going through a lot of changes (as usual),
so I thought I'd keep you posted. I've written the

following about relationships. It reminds me of the fact that when a tree is experiencing a drought, its roots go deeper underground seeking living waters. My conclusion is: although I'm going through some difficult times, they're causing me to draw nearer to God and deeper in my faith because he is the living water.

Irene reviewed Lauren's written words for a minute, trying to grasp her full meaning before continuing . . .

Life is all about relationships, don't you think, Rene? I do. And I just want you to know how much I miss you. Here are some more of my thoughts—not that I think I've got some special wisdom. . . . Please! But I'm searching, I'm wondering; how do I put growing in my personal relationship with Jesus Christ, moment-to-moment communication with the Holy Spirit and God, at the top of my list? What about my spouse, my child, parents, and sibling? It occurred to me that the most important relationship that I do not have a choice in is my immediate family. How many bad experiences growing up still rob my todays? How many of my good experiences do I recycle? And how well have I done in choosing partners in life, starting with the most intimate in life, marriage? Where do my friends and business associates fit into my mix, and what is my church family really supposed to mean in my daily life? What are my choices really based on . . . need, fear of being alone, codependency, social pressure, insecurity? How do I heal and grow in the commitments I've already made, and how do I make solid reciprocal commitments in the future?

Lauren signed a little "xo" with a smiley face on the page and then continued.

What do you think, Rene? I'm about to get married for the second time. Do I know what I'm doing? I hope so. Anyway, I know this much, . . . I miss you and Chelsea and Mom and Dad, and I wish you'd come visit. It's a little hard for me to get away with the clinic and all, but let's make it happen. I believe we can if we really want to.

Tons of Love,
Lauren

Irene ran her fingers over the letter, taking her attention to the next one peeking out from underneath the pile. Its title caught her attention once again: "On Submission." Irene reeled; that was a word that really got her hackles up. Still, she decided to read on.

Dear Rene,

How art thou? Hey, what do you think? Can we negotiate the truth? . . . Can we be a little bit pregnant? I had a revelation over New Year's. . . . I'm just trying to get all this "submission" stuff right—how it works with Brian as a husband and how it works with God. I wrote this letter to Brian as a New Year's resolution of sorts. Love to know your thoughts.

"What happens when I stomp out of the house, late as usual, frazzled and belligerent about not needing directions? I get lost. Not only that; sometimes I never make it to my destination at all.

"Submission is a touchy subject, isn't it? It seems immediately defensive to our sense of self. Isn't it so much more attractive to follow our own path; after all, we've been taught to mythologize and rely on ourselves since we were children. And if any higher power needs to be included in our agenda for spiritual growth, let's choose the ones that teach that at the end of our 'enlightenment tunnel' we'll evolve into absolute 'oneness' with God; therefore, we become God. Pretty cool? The only problem is, it's not the truth. I am not God; I'm his child, and he's the boss.

"I love to negotiate with God. I've wanted to do things my own way my whole life, and I brought new meaning to the word impatient. *Fact is, it only brought me unhappiness. God loves us enough to mold and shape us even if we don't like the discipline, and he'll leave us out there as long as we insist on our own way, not his. But then he'll bring all things to good if we love him, will rest in him, and let him drive. In the end the only one that's going to change is me. I'm the work in progress, not God."*

Well, what do you think, Rene? I keep asking you like a kid, don't I? I wonder what that's all about? (Smile) Anyway, I closed by telling Brian I was sorry I was such a hardhead, and then that made me think

*about Dad being such a hardhead. And I thought, that's
something I don't want to inherit. Of course, I can't
say for sure that my views on submission have been the
Band-Aid Brian and I need, but I think it's a start.
Again, love to hear what you think.*

*Tons of xoxo,
Lauren*

With two happy faces, Irene noted.

Irene pondered the letter for a moment when the pilot broke
in again, "All passengers, please make sure that your seat belts are
buckled, your seat backs are in their upright position, and your
tray tables are firmly stowed. We are about to land in Nashville.
Thank you for your patience, and have a good evening."

Irene stood in the nippy early evening air at baggage pickup. She
couldn't believe that Lauren wasn't there since her flight's arrival
was fifteen minutes late. But just as she told herself to take a deep
breath and calm down, Lauren's truck headlights smacked her in
the eyes. Wincing, Irene stepped back, surprised that her sister
had brought the monster vehicle.

Lauren jumped out of the truck like a gazelle and ran
around to help Irene put her bags in the backseat. "Sorry, sorry!
I was here. . . . I was waiting, but they only let you sit in the parking slots for ten minutes. Then they make you go around and,
wouldn't you know, just the minute that you get here, they make
you go around again! I could actually see you coming down the

escalator and bam! The guy said 'Go!' . . . How very un-Southern hospitality of him, don't you think?"

Rene gave her a quick hug, "It's OK, I was only standing there a minute."

"I know, I told you I saw you coming down. I recognized your legs. Gorgeous, as always!"

Rene pulled the door open, "Let's talk inside; it's cold."

"OK." Lauren dashed around the truck and hopped into the driver's seat ready to go while Irene was still struggling to get on board.

"Your vehicle is definitely not designed for high heels!"

Lauren guffawed, "*I'm* not designed for high heels. . . . I don't think anyone's designed for high heels, really. I believe men should be required to wear high heels for one day, and then they'd know that their fantasies were actually Chinese torture."

Lauren pulled her truck out into the traffic lane, barely allowing Irene to close the door. "Sorry, sorry I didn't pick you up in your car, but I have to go get Tuck so there's no time to switch up autos."

Irene regarded her sister. "You'll at least slow down so I can get my bags out."

"Course, Rene. I'm not going to shove you out of a moving vehicle. . . . You can jump when I slow to five miles per hour." Lauren winked at her sister.

"You're nuts."

"Oh goody, I thought I'd lost my touch. So how was New York?"

Irene looked disgruntled as. "It's still there."

"Did you make any headway?"

"Headway in this matter is simply getting everybody in the same room together, and by the time they all pour their coffee, have their chitchat sessions, and line us up on opposite sides of the conference room table, it's time to go. It kind of reminds me of the court system in Centennial."

"Sounds infuriating."

"It is." Irene tried to adopt a more pleasant attitude. "So how are you and Tuck and Mom and Dad?"

"Tuck's great. Like I said, I have to pick him up for church tonight. Brian's been pretty incredible lately, and Mom and Dad are cool, but Bingo is definitely miffed. I made her wear a collar with bells on it so I could track her movements. Kind of like *Mission Impossible*. . . . She's totally insulted."

Irene couldn't help but laugh, "Well, wouldn't you be?"

Lauren took her sister's observation to heart, suddenly experiencing deep remorse for what she now recognized as induced humiliation to her cat. "Good point. I'm going to have to make amends as soon as I get home."

"I didn't mean to imply you had to go to the confession booth over it."

"That's Catholic. I'm nondenominational. The difference is . . ."

"Please, I didn't mean to open the envelope to one of your religious discussions."

"Rene, I'm not religious. Religion is man-made. I believe in the Bible and that . . ."

"Uncle!"

"OK, sorry, sorry."

Lauren glanced at her watch, noting that she was running late. As Irene glanced out of the window, it just so happened that they were traveling the exact run of road where the whole legal incident six months prior had happened, and Irene fell into a full-fledged flashback. Although she could hear Lauren chit-chatting in the background, Irene couldn't seem to pull her focus away from the rerun in her mind. It seemed the whole scenario repeated itself every time she and Lauren made their way from the airport to home.

Yes, it was right there on that stretch of the road that Lauren had pulled over to calm her sister down, but Irene was simply over the top with despair. Irene's flashback started with the appearance of the police car:

It wasn't that Officer Chet Monty didn't believe the sisters' story of having pulled over to talk, and it wasn't that he recognized them from that morning's newspaper because they were both so incredibly disheveled; he simply deduced that they were drunk after having witnessed their previous antics outside the school. Unfortunately, his conclusion was confirmed by the smell of alcohol on Irene. She told the officer that she had ordered some cocktails on the plane. "I wasn't driving; I was trying to relax. The pilot was driving!" The more she talked, the more upset she became having started the conversation already on the verge of hysterics. She just wouldn't shut up, "I am an adult, and I'm perfectly capable of having drinks. My drinks are none of your business! My sister was driving."

That's when the situation escalated, and he escorted her to the side of the road, "Get your hands off me!" The policeman asked her to walk a straight line while shining the light in her eyes. Lauren was horrified as Irene became more and more belligerent due to her extreme emotional angst. She clearly didn't know what not to say and took this "southern pie," as she called him, excuse for a policeman on like a barracuda. The more Lauren objected, the more intense the fray became between Irene and the officer.

Lauren ran back to the car to get her license and registration, then politely told the policeman that she just wanted to take her sister home; but by that time this officer had an attitude bigger than his pot belly. His macho southern disdain for out-of-towners clicked in, and his control mode took over as he ordered Irene to take a Breathalyzer test. "So as to clear up any misunderstanding that you were driving intoxicated ma'am," he said sarcastically.

Now Lauren lost her cool. "Officer, I was driving. I picked my sister up at the airport. We have to get home. Just release her to me, and we'll be on our way." She waved her license and registration in front of his face. "I'll 'Breathalyze' anything you want! Here's my license; here's my registration. Why are you doing this?"

When Irene smacked the Breathalyzer out of the officer's hands, he escorted her to his police car and slammed her into the backseat. "You're goin' down!" he spat at her. Lauren just stood there horrified, looking at her sister behind an iron-mesh divider. Then, trying to block him, she begged the policeman to stop this insanity. But by then, he was into his full defiant mode and wasn't about to let Irene go. As he walked around to the driver's side, he ordered Lauren, "Ma'am, step back, or you'll be goin' with her. You can find her down at the precinct police station just off Main.

I'm going to have to clarify a few details with your sister before she can be released in accordance to her behavior. She just struck an officer."

Lauren started to go ballistic.

"Ma'am, I'm warning you. Now, step out of my way!"

And with that, all Lauren could see were the red lights and sirens screeching as Irene was carted off into the night.

Lauren finally stopped her incessant babbling, now aware that her sister had been drawn into the past once again. Lauren had tried to figure out a different route home, but there was no going around that particular stretch of highway. It seemed Irene was a helpless bystander when her mind decided to review the past, awake or asleep.

Interestingly Irene's nightmares had decreased somewhat according to the sisters' chats over morning coffee. Lauren was hoping that Irene's mind was settling somewhat, but in reality her concern was more about Irene's self-medicating just to get a sliver of rest at night. No doubt, the woman was heading toward a breaking point.

Lauren gently nudged her sister on the shoulder. "Are you in the police car yet?"

Irene exhaled in frustration. "Don't be cute." She yanked out a pack of cigarettes, lighting up without even a hint of concern as to whether Lauren would object. Anyway, Lauren always let the issue of smoking slide when her sister was so upset. She did, however, open her truck window, practically blowing the cigarette out of Irene's fingers; sparks flew off the cigarette embers.

Irene held fast to her bad habit, now opening her window so the smoke at least disappeared from the passenger side of the truck. And then, with the precision of the dance routine, she pulled out her mints and a little green Christmas tree-shaped air freshener that she slapped over Lauren's rearview mirror.

"Have you heard anything from Chelsea?" She asked without looking at Lauren, tensing at what she knew would most likely be the answer.

"No, Rene. Not for a while."

Irene inhaled deeply on her cigarette.

"The only thing that makes me feel better is that Brandon sees her on occasion at the clubs. He's keeping an eye on her from a distance when he covers the entertainment section of the newspaper."

Irene threw her cigarette out the window and glared at Lauren. "It makes you feel better that Chelsea's hanging out at song clubs? And . . . Brandon is doing what? Why didn't you tell me?"

"Rene, I'm just trying to keep track of her as best I can. He's not a private eye; he's a newspaper guy. I haven't heard from her, but he said he saw Chelsea over the weekend at a café. He said she was there and looked fine and that was all."

Irene put her hand on her forehead and closed her eyes. "I'm sorry. I know you're just trying to help, but if I had two *nickels to rub together*, I would hire a private investigator!"

Lauren broke in, "And do what? She's of legal age. You can't stop her from living her life. The best thing you can do is just wait till she comes around and keep your arms wide open for her. She'll come back, Rene. We're all praying so hard for her. I know that she'll be OK."

"I appreciate all your prayers, but I don't have those assurances."

"I'll assure for you, Rene." Irene closed her window as Lauren followed suit.

"So you and Brandon are ah . . . Are you just friends? You seem to spend a lot of time with him."

"He's the editor of the newspaper, as you know, and thankfully he covers a lot of the activities we have at the shelter. So he's on my A-list."

"Business or pleasure? I thought he was going to be in your little black book. At least that was what you told me a while ago."

"Yeah, well." Lauren turned her windshield wipers up to high as the truck moved through a torrential rain spot. "Ah, Noah's ark." She focused intently on the road. "Did you *fashion* your seat belt?"

Like an obedient child, Irene pulled her seat belt around her. "It's *fasten* your seat belt."

"I know. But the only way I remember putting it on every time is to make it part of getting dressed. That's what I tell Tucker. Anyway, we were talking about Brandon, not how my mind works."

"I gave up on your mind management a long time ago." Irene drove home her point. "For instance, how you categorize your phone book. It makes absolutely no sense."

"Of course it does." Lauren adopted a defensive tone. "I have all my cat owners under *C*, all my dog owners under *D*, anyone who's involved with horses under *H*, and all my Christian friends under *JC*. I think it makes perfect sense."

"It's a good thing that you don't do your filing. You wouldn't be able to find anything at the shelter."

"Brian is totally organized, and he finally admitted my system works. Although he clarified that it worked for me and no one else. . . . But then again, it only has to work for me. It's *my* phone book, and I'm not a secretary."

"How true."

"Don't act like I'm the only eccentric in this truck."

"What?" Irene objected.

"Do you know that your outfit for your next Centennial court date has got about an inch of dust on it?"

"I'm not moving it," Irene dug her high heels into the floor, "until the ordeal is over."

"But you always change your clothes every time you go to court."

"I know, Lauren. And when I do, I just lay a new set right back on the chair." Suddenly Irene looked concerned. "And you think that's eccentric?" She flashed to the last time she'd gone to court, noting with irritation that it had been over *three months ago.*

Irene's pristine outfit was carefully laid out on the chaise lounge. Every button was fastened, and all accessories were in place as if she were actually wearing the suit—minus her body. She stood over her empty clothes, considering what a fantastic book cover they would make. Irene actually thought of pulling out her camera and taking a snapshot of her outfit, pearls and all, then art-directing it onto the front page of the imaginary autobiography of Irene Patterson Williams appropriately titled, The Disappearing Woman.

"*Uh, no, . . .*" Irene considered. "*. . . I'm beginning to think like my sister.*"

Once again, Lauren nudged Irene. "Come back little Sheba."

Irene refocused, shrugging. "I'm not sure I want to. Revisiting the past is taking up all my present, and since I hate my now as much as my then, I'm stuck in a time warp. I just wish that I could move forward!" She took a tension-relieving breath. "And speaking about moving forward, what exactly are you up to with Brian? You always avoid that conversation. He seems like a perfectly good guy; but then again, I don't know him at all, other than what you've told me."

Suddenly Lauren swerved, barely successful in avoiding a car that had run a red light. "Gosh, a snowflake, a raindrop, and they all go nuts! Can you imagine any of them in New York City?"

"No," Irene said flatly, "And stop changing the subject."

"I wasn't changing the subject! We were almost in a car accident."

"OK, fine. So what's going on with Brian?"

"Nothing really. He's just being nice lately."

"So isn't that *nice?*" Irene looked at her sister with a discerning eye. "I know I've been out of the loop lately, but I wasn't born yesterday. Brian's moved virtually down the block. He sees Tucker and you all the time."

"No, Rene, he sees Tucker all the time. Then I pick up Tucker, and sometimes we chat. . . . But I don't know, he seems different. I've talked to Mrs. Strickland about him *very briefly.* You know how conservative she is. But since Brian's been attending her church, she does bump into him. . . . She's never seen him with anybody else. He's acting so . . . well, just different."

"And you've never gotten over him. I see the way you look at him when he drops Tucker off and he's walking to his car."

Lauren blushed slightly, "What do you mean? How? What? I'm just looking at him."

Irene was amused at what a silly liar Lauren had become. "That's my point. If you didn't care about him, you wouldn't have your eyes glued on his every move. You'd just close the door, and that would be it."

"I . . . I . . . I find the man attractive. I always did. But I'm not going to forget the issues we had."

"And what exactly were those issues."

"Well, for starters, we fought all the time. After we adopted Tucker, Brian just didn't seem to be that interested in me. I don't know, maybe I was insecure."

"Well, you shouldn't be." Irene paused for emphasis. "What *you* don't see now is that he watches you the same way you watch him."

"Who are you, the hall monitor?"

"I'm just looking out for your best interests. God is not the only one who sits in that seat."

Lauren's eyes widened. "Are you being rude about God?"

"Never, so shush and answer me. Tell me if you want to resurrect this thing with this guy, and I'll be all for it. . . . And don't tell me that you don't care when it's obvious that you do. Mom and Dad have noticed it too."

"You've been talking about me to Mom and Dad?"

"Who else am I going to talk with about you? You? You have your friends, you have Brian, you have church. . . . You work nine thousand hours a week, and you have Tucker. And I've got baggage claim tickets and lawyers."

"Well, Rene, you know you're always invited to come to anything I have and do."

"I know, Sweetie. I just have no interest in all that stuff. And we can't even go out to lunch in this town or to the cleaners without being ogled. . . . And we . . ."

". . . Hey! Where's my girl who always says, 'Who cares?'"

Irene was grateful that they had just turned up the cul-de-sac to Lauren's house; their conversation was escalating to subjects she didn't care for. "Well, uh," Irene started to gather her things. "I don't know, maybe 'the girl who doesn't care about what people think' will pop up again at the annual Bloomingdale's designer sale. I guess I'm *on hold*, Lauren. And that's the best I can do . . . barely hold on."

As they pulled up the driveway, Irene started to open her truck door.

"Whoa! I haven't stopped yet." Lauren screeched. "I'll help you in with your bags."

Irene looked at her sister, deflated. "Well, thanks. I appreciate that."

As Lauren dashed around the truck, she gave her sister another quick hug. "Oh, and Rene, . . . thanks for asking about Brian and all, with everything else on your mind. I'm just trying to figure out what the best thing to do would be. It'd be pretty amazing if we could make it right for Tucker and all. So I'm just trying to focus on that and see if that's what God has in mind."

"Did you ask God the first time you married your ex?"

Lauren gave her a wary look, "Come on, Rene. Don't be mean. Yes, I did ask him, but maybe my ears weren't on straight."

"All I know is that I'd seriously think about what would make it different this time around. Not just *wishing* it so. Remember, you're the 'two out of three ain't bad' heavyweight contender. Might I remind you that with everybody you've ever been involved with, you always said, 'Well, I'll fix that part later.' And that part was usually the scenario that took you down."

"I know, I know."

"Don't forget, you're the one who would call me up in hysterics when Brian was in one of his rages. Then you'd tell me how you had looked at him that very morning and thought, *Who are you and how did you get in my bed?* And I had to remind you that *you invited him there!* Listen, I'm not trying to be nosy; I'm just trying to be your big sister . . . although I realize that I don't qualify in the advice department. No one has picked worse men than I." Irene's eyes suddenly started to tear. "And I'm really proud of you for being such an amazing sister and a good mom to Tuck, and how well you treat Mom and Dad. . . ." And then she choked up, unable to continue.

It wasn't that Irene didn't want to commend her sister further; it was just that in recognizing the areas Lauren had grown, it painted such a dismal picture of where Irene felt she was at fifty-two years old. And with that thought came a full-fledged, whammo hot flash, turning Irene's beautiful pale skin tomato red within nanoseconds as perspiration flooded her forehead.

"Ooh, I hate this," Irene seethed. "I'm totally losing it!"

Panicking at her sister's despair, Lauren clapped her hands together to divert Irene's attention.

"Stop that! I'm not a dog you're calling to attention."

"Oh, Rene. I didn't mean it that way. Wow, you're really scaring me."

"Well, you just wait, little sister. If you're going to get back with Brian, you'd better hurry up because you'll never forge a renewed relationship during menopause. You won't even know who you are for at least three years."

"Three years. No, it can't be that bad. You make it sound like I'll turn into a pit bull with lip gloss!"

Irene gave her sister a knowing look. "Let me put it this way. . . . On my flight today the pilot announced they had reached cruising altitude and would be turning down the cabin lights for the passenger's comfort . . . *and to enhance the appearance of the flight attendants*! Menopause equals *out of control* in everything from wrinkles to sweat glands. And you know that none of us Patterson women handle *out of control* well. . . . Remember that time when we were kids and Mom finally ventured out to get a tan?" Irene relaxed slightly as she thought back. "Oh, that was so insane."

"What am I missing here? What does Mom's mishap have to do with menopause?"

"It's the control issue, or lack of it. Just stay with me. . . ."

"Rene, I have to go. . . ."

"Not until I finish."

Lauren leaned against the truck, aware there was no immediate escape for her until her sister had made her point.

"Remember when Mom slathered herself up with suntan oil because she had never tanned, let alone been in a bathing suit in public in her life? And we were swimming in the pool?"

"Yes! . . . And she went way up the hill and sat down on a chaise lounge virtually out of sight from the masses." Both girls started to giggle.

"And then mother slowly leaned back on the lounge after she had carefully taken down each strap of her bathing suit so she wouldn't get tan lines. Oh, she was so modest. She tried so hard to stay out of everyone's way."

"Ooh!" Lauren gasped, "And when she leaned back, the chair collapsed, and she went rolling down the hill. She looked like a greased taco madly holding onto the front of her strapless bathing suit so she wouldn't fall out of it!"

Now both were roaring with laughter, tears streaming down their faces. "She just kept rolling and rolling down the hill," Irene spluttered, "gathering up all the freshly cut grass that stuck to her oiled white body. Ah! Talk about feeling out of control!" But by then neither sister could talk anymore.

Lauren finally grabbed Irene's bags, and they stumbled up the entrance stairs in utter hysterics.

Waiting impatiently at a stoplight in the middle of town, Lauren picked up her cell phone to dial Brian.

He answered on the first ring. "Hey there."

"Hey," Lauren was always caught off guard simply by the sound of this man's voice. "Irene's flight was a little late, so

I'm there in about five or so. I stopped at your house to get Tuck and got your note that you guys went out to eat."

"Are you hungry?" His words floated over the phone.

". . . Oh, sure, thanks, Brian. Wrap me up two slices of cheese pizza, and I'll eat it on the way to church." She was taken by his kind offer to feed her, smiling into the phone as if he could see her pleasure. "You're sure you don't want to come with us? Oh, I forgot, you have that men's study group. . . . Right, OK. Well, I'll be right there. . . . Hope I didn't make you late. OK, . . . see ya."

Lauren was so entranced with her conversation that the line of traffic behind her had to honk to urge her on through the now green light. "OK, OK! Hold your noses. . . ." She punched in another phone number, then forged ahead.

Suz picked up on the last ring before the answering machine responded. "Oh goodie! You're there!" Lauren squealed.

Manning her position at her sewing table where she spent most of her time, Suz was expertly working on a pair of curtains. This was her life of late, that is, other than caring for her invalid husband. The sixty-year-old woman with piercing blue eyes and a year-round California tan had clearly aged over the last several months since her husband's illness had turned from bad to worse. Yes, a wariness shown through in Suz's expression although she never lost her aura of softness. And the sparkle in her eyes had not dulled as this godly woman had come to terms with the fact that, although her husband was barely there in body, she could feel his strong spirit even after his last two massive strokes. Yes, it seemed hers was to be a life of servitude, and she had made peace with that.

During Lauren's short but meaningful phone call to California on her way to pick up Tucker, Suz shared with her friend how she really felt concerning Fred's incapacities. "It may have sounded corny to the world when I vowed I was going to spend the rest of my life with Fred. And of course, our commitment to each other didn't come with a coloring book full of pictures of what that was going to look like."

Lauren probed gently since Suz hadn't been inclined to divulge her deeper thoughts recently. "How does it look to you now, Suz?"

"Well, I surely didn't see myself at age sixty-something dealing with a shell of a husband, but I've survived my invisible fear and insecurity demons many moons ago, so now I just have to hunker down and get on with my reality reprogramming. What else can I do or say? Some trials are harder to take than others. . . . Hey, I was always so intent on calling the shots; now my new job is to take the hit and smile. The strokes weren't Fred's fault, God knows. . . . He always ate well, exercised, loved the Lord. It's my honor to watch over him."

Oh, how Lauren loved this woman of strength. What an inspiration their friendship had been to her. "Suz, remember when we used to talk about the oil that was poured on Jesus when he went to visit Lazarus, Martha, and Mary? That incredible woman, Mary, anointed his feet with her hair, perfume, and tears. She used the value of a year's worth of labor to honor her Lord, lavishing him with what was probably her dowry for marriage. And the oil, oh, I remember you told me that just one or two drops alone would fill a room with its aroma for days. Gosh, I can only imagine what a whole bottle of that intense oil would smell like. It would permeate everything. . . . While Jesus was flogged and tortured to the point that he was unrecognizable, the entire process, including his crucifixion and burial, was covered with the presence of that woman's oil. I have to remind myself that the presence of Jesus remains steadfast through even our worst times, and the Holy Spirit never leaves us no matter what. Like the oil, God's love will surround us with the essence of love."

Suz held her phone to her chest for a moment, gathering her emotions before she responded to Lauren's sweet sentiment. "I've forgotten how lyrical you can be when you're not being silly." Suz sighed. "That was a good reminder to keep this trolley on track because frankly, left to my own pity parties, I want to get the first red-eye to Nashville and camp out at your already overbooked home."

Lauren melted. "Anytime, with 'bells on.'"

"Just knowing I'm welcome helps. But I'm OK, really. I have a peace about all this, thank God. And my kids have been super."

"They better be, or I'll punch them."

"Touch my children and you're minced meat."

"Ooh, you're such a lioness about your kids."

"And you're not? Speaking of . . . how's my little man, Tuck?"

"He hasn't outgrown his Batman cape yet. He's doing super."

"You give that boy one of my special hugs."

"I always do. Express airmail from his godmother."

Suddenly Lauren's focus was split between trying to find the location of the restaurant and talking with her friend. "Suz, I'm a dog. I called you, and I've only got a minute and a half to chat. Sorry, sorry! Anyway, I think I'm about where I'm going."

Suz laughed. "Oh, that would be the day. As you put in one of your letters of luminous thoughts, 'If I knew where I was going, I'd know which way to turn.'"

"Oh, give me a break! That was ages ago."

"It doesn't mean it wasn't good. So now you're growing and knowing where you're going!"

"Hey, 'poet and you know it,' look who's rhyming. . . . Suz, are you really OK?"

"I am, promise."

Lauren spotted her destination. "That's my girl. . . . Well, I've miraculously arrived. Gotta go!"

Suz whispered in the phone, "Be careful, squeeze the boy and thanks for calling. . . . I love you."

"I love you more. . . . Bye-O." And with kisses blown through their phones, the two friends reluctantly hung up.

⚜

Lauren zigzagged her massive truck through the jammed parking lot like a pro, pulling over to the local pizza parlor at the far end of town. As she did, she spied through the swipes of the windshield wipers her Tucker, looking like a miniature fireman with his orange raincoat, hat and boots, standing next to his handsome dad.

"Oh my," Lauren thought, "what a picture." She had to admit she felt like she was being drawn in again by Brian, the very man who had caused her to build a wall of protection around her heart just to survive. And OK, she recognized that it had taken two to tango; both had sliced and diced each other up in their own inimitable ways over their rather short marriage. Still she needed to remind herself to *go slowly.*

But then there he was with Tuck; she couldn't seem to control her heart from beating faster as she pulled her truck up to the curb. Yes, she loved Brian's best behavior, but she would not accept his bad behavior ever again. Or hers for that matter.

Chapter 9

Exit Ramp

Pam dodged the flying pillow that missed her head by mere inches. In quick retaliation, she flung a chair cushion across the room, hitting Tonya square in the stomach. Then it was Bobbie's turn; squealing, he popped up from behind the couch nailing Pam on the side of the face with his favorite teddy bear. She dropped like a rock, feigning death from the teddy's blow.

After a motionless moment Pam pleaded, "Truce, truce!" Gathering herself into a sitting position, she looked around for Bobbie, but before she could steady herself, the four-year-old tackled her with an upper body hit like a pro.

Tonya was quick to swoop her two-ton tyke off her friend; his weight was swiftly becoming equal to Pam's. "Bobbie, you're not supposed to tackle girls, remember?"

"But we're playing, Mom."

"I know, buddy, but we have to stop now. . . . And no more sugar for you or pillow throwing. We have to get packed, or we'll be up all night, and you don't know cranky till you see your mama with no sleep."

Rubbing her back, Pam concurred. "Here, here." She pulled herself into the cushion-less chair.

The girls took a brief gander around the room, which basically looked like a bomb had gone off; boxes were strewn everywhere and half-filled mounds of clothes and pots and pans were stacked in various heaps.

Pam chuckled. "It's a good thing your uncle is driving all this stuff to New York for you."

Tonya shrugged, still holding Bobbie in a vice grip. "Right. I can't see fitting two bedroom's worth of junk in my Volkswagen, can you?"

"Not my point. . . . I'm just glad he's going to be following you in case anything happens on the road."

"Let go, Mom!" Bobbie wiggled out of Tonya's arms and ran to his bedroom. "I'm gonna get the rest of my toys. I have to take two, . . . no three with me, . . . in the car, . . . OK?"

Tonya sighed as her little boy disappeared through the doorway. "OK, *two* . . . big ones, if you want!"

She turned to Pam, "Nothing's going to happen on the road. We've got troops from above. I've asked for an angel's escort to cover our trip for a month now."

Pam continued folding clothes and putting them in a box that rested on the coffee table, while Tonya headed for the kitchen. "Do you want a soda?"

"I've told you a zillion times, carbonation is not good for your bones."

Tonya returned with a Coca-Cola. "You don't have any bones. You're like the Pillsbury Doughboy. You barely exist."

"That's not very nice."

Tonya giggled, "Who am I going to tease like this when I move? I mean, I can't play verbal volleyball with Bobbie. He'll grow up with low self-esteem and hate me. You, on the other hand . . ."

". . . I what?" Pam threw a blob of sweaters at Tonya.

"Now don't start again."

"Well, I what? You think I don't have insecurities sometimes?"

"If you do, I don't see how. You had ten guys calling you from the *slopes* after just two days of skiing."

"Tonya, it's not about who *calls*; it's about *who* calls. I wouldn't even know what to talk about with most of those guys. They just thought I was something because I beat them down the slopes half the time."

Tonya stood back in amazement at her friend. "Girl, I'm not sure how you do that since you never practice. . . . Give it up or stop bragging."

"It's a gift. It comes naturally to me. It's like your looks." Pam gave her a sassy once-over. "You didn't earn them, but there they are. Soon you'll be jet-setting around the world making a million bucks a year, and you won't even remember my name, snow bunny or no snow bunny."

Even though Pam was playing with Tonya, she was only half kidding about her concerns. Oh, how she was going to miss her friend, the one she'd been able to open up to more than anyone other than Eleanor. Pam had found it kind of interesting to be the "middle sister in Christ" of these two wonderful black women. Yes, the trio had been like three peas in a pod until Stephanie arrived in town, and now there was Lauren, bringing the *circle of friends* to five strong. Although their group was growing rather slowly, each knew their foundation was solid. No, there would be no amount of miles that could keep their hearts and prayers divided.

Beyond that, the ladies knew there was nothing any of them could ever do, at their worst moment or lowest ebb, that would damage their fellowship; no criticism flowed in their veins for each other—just accountability and unconditional love.

What a comforting thought, one Pam had held close through her many times of pain and loss. She thought back on the occasion when she and Tonya were meeting with Eleanor in her kitchen about five years earlier. Pam had just bared her soul about her ever-present ache for her brother who had committed suicide on his high school graduation day some years before. Pam confessed to her friends her sense of utter failure as a sister; her eyes were filled with frustration and questioning. "How did we all miss it? I should have been able to see how out there my brother really was . . . how upset he was."

Eleanor got up from the table that sunny summer morning and grabbed a box of Kleenex; as she put it down in front of Pam, she placed her hand on the back of her friend's shoulders. "Darlin', you were a child. Don't forget, your parents were ultimately responsible for your brother. But the truth is, they weren't responsible for his suicide. They did the best they could."

Pam began to object, but Eleanor continued in a soothing tone. "Listen little one, Ham and I know what I just said is right because we've worked with kids since we were kids, and there's an epidemic of teen suicide going on. Your brother had deep-rooted issues, to say the least. Remember, that's why he was sent away to that military school."

Now Tonya grabbed a trash can; Pam was going through Kleenex like Cracker Jacks. "But they were supposed to help him at school!" Pam wailed. "They were supposed to be professionals at that place. Mom and Dad just passed him along, and they didn't save him! How could they mess up so badly? Why do you think I want to counsel and help kids? Because I messed up so badly."

"Hey, girl," Tonya stepped in with authority beyond her years, "you always told me that suicide is one of the most selfish acts at its core. Yeah, it's a cry for help, but you said it's also a punishment from who's doing it to the people they blame. You let me read his letters, Pam. Your brother was brutally mean to you. He blamed everything in his life on everybody else. So your parents messed up . . . divorce and all that. But a lot of kids go through that and don't kill themselves. Hey, you're always helping everybody else. How about you?" By then, Tonya was on her feet next to Eleanor, laying her hands on Pam's back, whose shoulders were now wrenching from her uncontrollable sobbing.

"I have this depression. I've fought it all my life. I probably have the same thing my brother had, which scares me so much! I'm this overachiever, and if I'm not helping someone else, I seem to fall apart. . . . So maybe it's all just about keeping busy for me."

Eleanor calmed her once more. "Depression is real, Pam. It doesn't mean that you don't have strong faith. As long as we're in this world, we're goin' to be hit upside the head with every human frailty, whether or not we're believers. Look what Ham went through after Vietnam."

"I wasn't in a war. I have no excuses."

"Oh, but you are in a war, sweet pea, if you're in this world. Spiritual warfare. Still, as believers we have God's promises and his armor to protect us. But that doesn't mean we don't need to talk about things sometimes. And if we do, that doesn't mean we're failing, or that our belief is weak, or that we don't trust God. What it does mean is that we're takin' on too much by our own might. Talkin' it out just means you're recognizin' you have an issue. And Tonya's right; the next step is you've gotta let us pray over it. Let's nip this thing in the bud. God didn't design us to go it alone. And he doesn't expect us to be perfect. God expects us to rely solely on him, and he expects us to be in fellowship while we're doing it. That's why he puts us all together. And if I sound like I'm preachin', it's cause I am. If you're not sick, you don't need a doctor. If the human race didn't need a Savior, Jesus wouldn't have come. We all mess up. You've just got to give yourself more of a break. Perfectionism is not pleasing to God 'cause if you could be perfect on your own, you wouldn't need him."

Eleanor lightly patted Pam on the back when Tonya suddenly sat down again and grabbed herself a handful of tissue. And within moments she was emotionally shattered. "I need to tell y'all somethin'." Her intensity of emotions rendered her speechless for a moment.

"I messed up." She started again slowly as if trying to pry a rock out of cement. "I . . . Shooter and . . . we . . . I messed up. I'm pregnant." And with her statement came silence; now all three were at a loss for words.

❧

Pam pulled back from her memory as Bobbie sped across the living room, throwing his arms around her legs in a show of affection. It was as if the boy suddenly realized that he was leaving everyone and everything he'd known his entire little life.

Tonya had been concerned that this might be her son's reaction to the move, but the boy hadn't shown an inkling of reserve until this moment. But there he was, clinging to Pam, tears streaming down his face. "Please, come with us! You can sleep in my room. I'll share Teddy with you."

Although it was a struggle, Pam picked up her godson and held him tight. "Hey, Bobbie boy, I'm going to be there before you blink. And we're going to have the best time. . . . We'll go to the Central Park Zoo and Radio City Music Hall and anywhere else that's fun! OK?"

And as children are capable of doing on occasion, the boy calmed immediately. "Is it a big zoo?"

"Yeah, it's a *very* big zoo." Pam's eyes widened for emphasis. "They have all the animals we've talked about in the books I got you. *And* they have carriages in New York City that are drawn by horses so we can ride around in the park, even when it's cold. The horse has a blanket on his back, and we have blankets. It's so fun and so cozy! And gosh, they have that big giant tree with all the lights I showed you on TV last Christmas."

Tonya reeled from seeing Bobbie so emotionally distraught, even for a few moments. No, she had never wanted to uproot her son; and as convincing as she had been to others when she'd say everything was going to be alright, she was still concerned as to whether she had made the right decision in moving to NYC.

At this point all she knew was that her child needed to feel safe and encouraged. She flashed her biggest smile at her son. "And Bobbie, they have ice skating! Not on a pond, but it's right under where the big tree is, and it's there all the time, so we can go over whenever we want! Oh, and there's F.A.O. Schwartz, which is the biggest toy store ever!"

And with his mom's words in his heart, the boy was satisfied that all was well in his world again. When Pam put him down, he simply said, "OK. I'm gonna keep packing." And off he went again, happy as a clam.

Tonya looked at Pam, both moved by the little one's concerns. "Wow," Tonya simply stated.

"Yeah, wow. . . ."

And as they pondered the future, a knock at the door drew their attention from their chores. Before even opening the door, Tonya tensed, knowing after seven years together that the knock was Shooter's. She looked like a trapped animal glancing at Pam for some sort of direction and support. "Should I answer?" she hissed in a whisper.

Pam's mind raced. "I don't know. Maybe he wants to see Bobbie. . . . You should let him in."

"But we've been over everything, and it's just torture. Besides, he saw Bobbie after school today." And then another bang resounded in the apartment.

"Alright, I'm coming!" Tonya gathered her composure and headed for the door while Pam dismissed herself, "I'll wait with Bobbie in his room."

And as she disappeared, Tonya opened the door without reserve; whatever trepidation she was feeling, one could not read it on her face. Shooter just stared at her, unaccustomed to the resolve that was set in her expression. He started to crack one of his charming smiles, but that idea was fleeting. Instead, what surfaced in him was the anger and hurt he'd been harboring since he'd heard of Tonya's leaving.

It was nothing that he planned to say; actually, Shooter had considered picking up some flowers to let Tonya know that he still cared. He wanted her to know that, although he was confused, he still loved her. See, Ham and Shooter had shared hours and hours of conversation after school about the situation. Ham assured the boy that there was nothing unmanly about letting the woman he loved know how much he cared for her. Still, Shooter stubbornly remained bound to his decision not to marry Tonya just then. And with that unswayable fact, Ham advised Shooter at least to try to keep the door open with the mother of his child.

So there he was, ready to try to achieve that goal, but within an instant this barely eighteen-year-old's lack of maturity failed him. "I came to see my son." He said flatly.

"We did our good-byes earlier. It's just going to make it hard for Bobbie and . . ."

Shooter stepped through the door without invitation, his huge frame filling the front of the room. "I'm never sayin' good-bye to my son."

Tonya was taken aback by his aggressiveness. "I didn't mean it that way. I'm not saying that to Bobbie. 'So long' are the words I use. I tell him that we're going to see Daddy soon. But that's all up to you, Shooter. I hope you don't make me a liar about that."

Tonya closed the door to the hall. "It's like it's always been all up to you, and I can't. . . . Never mind. We've been through this."

And then there they came, a burst of tears. She hated herself for giving in emotionally, but she simply could not help herself. Turning away quickly, Tonya tried not to let Shooter see her pain. She searched her mind for some stability in her thinking. She hadn't allowed herself to review Shooter's hurtful words since she'd made the decision to leave, and yet there they were ringing in her head again.

⁕

"The NBA wants me, girl! I'm going directly to the NBA from high school, and that practically never happens. The Bulls are one of the best teams in the world, and they want me! You should be screaming happy over this."

"I'm happy, I am. . . . I just, I don't know. . . . I'm just surprised."

She fumbled for words while Shooter stared at her in disbelief. "Tonya, it's what I've worked for all my life, and it's here faster than I thought. There's nothing bad about this."

"I know, but what about your education?"

"Man, you sound like the father I never had." The young man tried to control himself, taking a breath to settle. "Now I'm gonna go by to tell Ma the good news, and then we're all gonna go out and celebrate. Are you comin' or not?"

Tonya glanced at four cars behind him packed with his high school friends and cheerleaders with their pom-poms tied to the car antennas. Cigarette smoke billowed from the windows, and exhaust from the cars' pipes created a surrealistic background behind Shooter's head.

"That's good. Go talk to your mom, but then let's go to Norros to celebrate. Bobbie can come with us there, and he can be part of the excitement."

"I ain't going to Norros to sit and have no cheeseburger with all those uptight . . ."

". . . Don't. Come on, Ham and Eleanor are going to be there."

"I'm goin' over to Billy's."

Again Tonya looked around Shooter at the cars, noting that Billy and Robert Jack were waving Shooter over. "Hey man, let's hit it. It's freezing, man," they yelled.

Then Billy stepped out of the car and opened the back door for his teammate. "I gotta get things cranked up at the crib. Come on!" Everyone was hooting and hollering as if they had already been on a bender. Clearly, Tonya was worried about how the night would unfold.

Shooter waved his friends off for the moment and addressed his girl again. "Look, like I said, I'm goin' to get my Ma and go to Billy's. If you don't want to come, I'll drop you and Bobbie off at Norros. . . . Whatever you want."

Tonya couldn't believe what she was hearing. She felt like she was looking at somebody she didn't even know. "Shooter, what's going on? We've talked for years about getting a college education. I know how important basketball is to you, but what if something happens? What if you get hurt? You've got nothing to lean on. Our future . . ."

Shooter pulled away. "I don't want to hear this stuff right now. You talk to me like I'm a kid, and I'm not. Last year I got recruited by Columbia, and you didn't want to go to New York City. So I said OK, I'll wait, . . . take a chance and get something nearer to here to make you comfortable and all."

Now Tonya's voice escalated. "It wasn't about me; it was about raising Bobbie in New York City. A lot of great colleges are in towns that would be better places for us to get started in our marriage."

"I'm takin' the best place for me to play ball . . . period! If you want me to cover the family, then get out of my way. Especially seeing that one of the best in the world just picked me up! I'm going, and I want you to come with me. Get this sweet deal signed, and we'll get married, OK?"

Tonya took his hand again. "I just need you to tell me you'll think about it. You could get lost there. Chicago's so big, so fast. People get hooked up . . . killed even. Tupac Shakur just got shot and died. It's dangerous!"

By now Shooter was seething. "Tonya, that guy was a rapper. He got shot in Vegas, not Chicago. I play ball, and I'm gonna stay clean!"

Fed up, he started to walk but stopped a few feet away, then turned slowly to face her. His voice was low and even; he looked like he had aged years within moments. "Girl, you got to believe in me or forget it. I'm going in the fall as soon as I graduate to play for the Bulls, and if you ain't by my side . . ." He just shook his head.

"No! You're going to get your mama so you can go with your friends and go drinking. I'm not interested in that kind of celebrating. You can't go out and buy beer legally, so you're going to be sitting in Billy's house doing stuff you're not supposed to do, and your mama's going to be right there doing it with you. And that's what I'm afraid of . . . that you're going to end up like her."

It was the first time since Tonya met Shooter that he'd ever stared at her with pure hatred. "Don't you never talk about my ma like that! At least I have a mama standing by me. You got no one but your stupid little sewing circle. Go on with yourself, grow old with them in this stinkin' town. I'm gone."

She could tell by his expression he had a lot more to say, but he walked away instead, and for that she was thankful because she already had been served up more than she could digest.

Tonya stood frozen in disbelief. What just happened? How could he drive off without her and Bobbie? She started to choke back her emotions, at first wanting to scream after him to stop, but she didn't. Was it her pride? Or was it her pain? It didn't matter. All that mattered was that the love of her life had walked away, and she knew if she was really honest with herself, this was the moment she had feared for some time now.

Tonya turned to Shooter in what felt like slow motion as she recovered from the hurtful memories she'd just revisited. And as she faced him, her tears were gone, and so was her hardened look of resolve. What remained was a woman with a broken heart that filled the room with sadness well beyond the massive physical presence of Shooter.

Tonya's dismay enveloped her; she had no fight left. It wasn't about some snippy battle; it was about the fact that there was nothing more she could do. Either Shooter loved her enough to step up beyond his fears, or he didn't. Yes, the time had been approaching; she now knew with assurance that she must move on.

Although Shooter had been in the habit of missing her meanings for many years, the way Tonya presently looked at him was not a mystery to him. There was no strategy left. There were no more words to say, at least for the time being. So Shooter simply opened the door and left but not without glancing over his shoulder with a look of deep regret and longing. The young tiger had just lost the battle for his mate, and Shooter didn't even know who his opponent was. And for the sake of this young couple, hopefully it wouldn't be too long before Shooter figured out that the enemy was none other than himself.

Chapter 10

Mood Swings

A musical adventure has the ability to propel one to soaring heights or dash them with crushing despair. But to either end, music reigns in its impact to lift or languish its listening audience. Lauren's Wednesday night church meeting promised to deliver such music along with the good Word, especially when Pastor Mark spoke and Eleanor sang. Often as not, Miss Eleanor would share the stage with Stephanie; their duets had been heralded by professionals and captivated audiences alike as breathtaking, and that's saying something, considering the talent in the Nashville area.

Trace was never more proud of his mother than when he heard her sing, even though it was usually in the early morning hours while she praised her Lord in song. It had been some time since this young man had heard his mom "on mike" and accompanied since he hadn't, for the most part, been attending church—not since his dad had died. But following the incident with Chelsea and his big break in his athletic career, Trace had been drawn somehow into the safe haven of church support and healing his mom labeled "fellowship."

Needless to say, Stephanie was thrilled her boy was attending services with her, sure that he was finally beginning to answer God's call on his life, albeit one baby step at a time. Yes, there was still a side of Trace that rested on his personal plans and timing, not unusual for a young man his age. And no, he wasn't about to let go of all control. Oh, how Stephanie knew that feeling so well. But she also knew that after time her son would begin to trust God more and more as she had and ultimately surrender to the love of God.

Trace was not so different in his spiritual stepping-stones from Shooter, but in other ways these young men were poles apart. Control remained a giant issue for both boys; but, Trace had to admit, the more he got to know Shooter, he recognized that his friend was actually under more personal pressure than he. After all, Shooter had grown up with no dad at all. Not only that, but his mom didn't seem to be the same kind of mom Stephanie was—not by a long shot. It was obvious that Shooter had been doing it on his own for a long time. And becoming a dad at fourteen was something Trace couldn't even imagine pulling off.

Ham engaged the guys to talk about their feelings in respect to Tonya and Chelsea. The conclusion was pretty clear: there's not much one can do when one person out of the couple does not want to move forward. That was the case with Chelsea when it came to Trace and with Shooter when it came to marrying Tonya.

Interestingly, the distant place where Shooter would withdraw in order to protect himself emotionally was integral in unleashing some of Trace's own angers and disappointments concerning his father's passing. In trying to get Shooter to open up, Trace had discovered some of his own difficulties in handling the hurtful feelings he'd suppressed for so many years.

In the end Trace could commiserate with Shooter's pain, and the fact that Shooter actually had a harder row to hoe revealed to Trace areas of grace in his own life.

Beyond his relationship with his friend, there was the surprise gift of Ham in Trace's life. He had come to realize the deep-running wisdom his elder possessed, far beyond the fact that Ham was a heck of a basketball coach. Not only that, but he now finally bought into the fact that Ham really cared about him and his future. Yes, Trace was beginning to see that he had to stop pushing people away who were truly on his side.

In his private moments, Trace couldn't deny that he had been feeling a sense of well-being and belonging that he hadn't enjoyed since his dad had been killed. And although his success in obtaining a scholarship was big enough to turn somebody's life around, Trace often thought about how close he'd come to blowing it all. And with that review, he finally had to conclude that what his mom had always said was true; God was looking out for him in a way no person could, not his dad or mom or Ham or anyone else.

The congregation surrounding Trace that Wednesday night was enthralled with the sounds, sights, and soarings of praise and worship to their Lord. Looking about, Trace took it all in as he listened to his mother and Eleanor sing "The Sweetest Gift . . . (A mother's smile)" in the most exquisite harmony; it was as if the two women were created for just that moment of God's glory and the edification of the congregation.

Trace had always been torn between his natural musical abilities and his athletic prowess. Of course, top that off with his caring heart and outstanding good looks, and it was no wonder the boy had always been special.

But since Chelsea had come into his life, the heart part of him had shut down. Not to her, mind you, but to other girls. And although Chelsea wouldn't return his calls, and he kept telling himself he didn't care anymore, she remained landlady of the place in him that had never been touched before. And he guessed at times that the special place he was feeling was called *true love*.

The applause was thunderous as the congregation stood, touched by the music and the two women who performed it so beautifully. As Pastor Mark took the podium, he heralded the ladies while Ham escorted them to their front-row seats.

With an impish gleam in his eye, Pastor Mark cleared his voice. "Eleanor . . . Stephanie, never better! What a declaration of truth that God will never fail to sustain us as we move through the fire to even higher levels of achievement and perfection in him, for his purposes, and for his people. Every day is a celebration that God gives us. Yes, *this* is the day the Lord has made, and in it *we will be* glad and rejoice. And today is a particularly special celebration of triumph in Jesus' name."

Pastor Mark glanced for a long beat at Ham, Eleanor, Stephanie, Lauren, and Trace sitting a mere few feet from the podium. He paused dramatically, long enough for all to wonder what he was up to.

"We, as a congregation, had been asked to pray for the acquisition of Norros Diner for Stephanie, . . . and now that has come about with the partnership of Hamilton and Eleanor, we rejoice! As in all good things, when one belongs in the family of Christ, not only is the celebration for all, support comes from all. So . . ." On that note Pastor Mark lifted an envelope held fast with a beautiful, shimmering ribbon. "Trace."

Surprised at being called out, the boy jumped from his seat. "Yes, sir?"

"Why don't you come up and take this envelope to Mr. Ham."

Trace was on the stage in one leap but took his time walking down the stairs in an effort to regain his composure, handing the envelope to his mentor.

Pastor Mark and Ham exchanged a steady look; Ham hadn't felt such excitement since he was a kid at Christmas. The whole congregation was hushed in anticipation as he slowly unsealed the envelope. And with the sense of humor Pastor Mark was known for, he announced, "And the winner is . . ." Ham stared at the check he held in his shaking hand; it was made out to *Norros Diner* to the tune of close to two thousand dollars "from the congregation, with love."

Ham was so touched he pressed the gift close to his chest; he needed a moment to get his breath. Finally Eleanor couldn't stand it anymore and grabbed the check, sharing its contents with Stephanie, Lauren, and Trace. The women began to giggle while Trace simply stared in amazement.

From the podium came another one of the pastor's cute remarks. "Oh just a little 'fun money' that your church family wanted you to have as you all start your new venture. Following tonight's sermon, we will be praying over the diner for its covering and its success. We all know your hearts and your purpose for the endeavor, . . . that is to glorify God. Also, we will be praying for Tonya and Bobbie and their move to New York City. I've chosen a sermon that will be particularly appropriate, I hope. Although Tonya's adventure is born of hope, change usually comes from pain, and all of us in this flock have experienced times of adversity and loss. Nonetheless, as we stand together, we remain staunch and victorious in Jesus' name, no matter how bleak our circumstances may appear. . . . And on a personal note, I'd like to say once again how honored I am to be your pastor and your friend. You all are truly a wonderful group of godly men and women."

As Pastor Mark fought back his emotions, Trace thought, *I guess, real men cry, real men feel, real men love.*

Having managed to hold his seat at the diner's counter long enough to enjoy the double-dipped chocolate fudge brownie covered with Häagen-Dazs ice cream that Stephanie was serving up to the entire congregation, Trace told his mom that he was going to head out to Nashville and listen to some music; he'd meet her back home in a little while. Stephanie noted to herself that this was probably the first time ever she didn't feel worried about her son's leaving. No doubt Trace seemed to be growing up like a willow tree in the spring.

And the icing on the cake was when her boy held up the remnants of his brownie as he stood precariously on the swiveling stool at the counter, demanding everyone's attention. "Hey! Listen up!" And with his call to order, the glasses stopped clinking, the plates stopped clattering, the chatter simmered down, and all the attention was focused on Trace.

"I want to thank y'all for the support you've shown my mama and Ham and Eleanor." The boy paused to gather his thoughts; he hadn't planned to speak, but then again, Trace was always impetuous. "I don't know anyone who deserves the best more than my mom." He glanced at Stephanie, who had already lost her mascara from crying.

"I haven't been around family in a lot of years since my dad's been gone and we moved here. And I know y'all have been kind to my mom before I understood what your sort of kindness was all about . . . church stuff." He looked at Ham and Eleanor. "Well, I just want to say thanks for your support and . . ."

Stephanie knew her son so well; she could see the flush on his cheeks rise and the knot in his throat when he swallowed just like he'd always done whenever he felt uncomfortable or emotional.

Despite his awkwardness, Trace forged ahead. "That's it, really. . . . Thanks." And then he stuttered for a moment, "And thanks to God for bringing us to this town." By then, everyone was on their feet with jubilant applause.

Jumping down from the stool, Trace hooted, "Whew! OK, well, . . . I'm gone."

As he started to go, Stephanie reached for him. "Not without a hug, big guy." Everybody clapped even louder, whistling their support while the boy took out of the diner like a rabbit.

For a Wednesday night, the café was pretty packed. Trace claimed his usual spot at the end of the wall with his steaming cup of coffee about ready to burn his lips on contact. The café was the only place he wore his cowboy hat, a black one with a silver band that his dad had given him when the young man had made his first full-time ride on a bronc.

Trace told his father right off that he wasn't much interested in horses, so he felt silly wearing the hat. His dad just laughed,

"I drive trucks, and I wear a cowboy hat. It's good shade for the sun!" Then his daddy winked at his boy sitting up in the front of the eighteen-wheeler rig.

"But Dad, you like baseball better than you like horses. How come you wear a cowboy hat instead of a baseball hat? For shade, that is, sir."

"It's practical in nature. A cowboy hat keeps a lot more rain off my shoulders than some cap would, World Series winner or not."

But as Trace got older, he wore his cowboy hat out because it always worked better with the girls. Yes sir, he'd put on that hat, real low, so no one could see his eyes. Then he put on his jeans and his faded shirt and adopted a pose against the café's wall that would pull in everyone's attention; he had learned early on the mastery of mystery.

Now, Trace hadn't learned that strategy from his mom; she didn't have a lick of that kind of approach in her personality. She was just straightforward, pretty, honest, and spunky; and for the life of him, Trace didn't understand why she was still single. But then again, that was fine with him because, in his mind, there was no replacing his dad.

After leaving Norros, Trace had taken time to go home and put on his outfit to go listen to music. Yup, he was just in the mood to be a fly on the wall and release some tensions with the sweet sounds of guitars meeting lyrics. Little did he know that he was in for a sure shock at seeing Chelsea on stage performing for open-mike night.

Mind you, Wednesday night's entertainers weren't usually the caliber of record label's showcases for which the café was renowned. Still, in the three years since Trace had moved to Centennial, he'd never once had the nerve to get up on open-mike night. He had rationalized in his mind that he laid it all out with the best of them on the basketball court, and that was enough competition for him. And even though he had shared with his mom since the time he was ten that he wanted to sing and play his guitar, he knew music wasn't going to be his career, just his mistress.

Chelsea, on the other hand, was all about her career in music. So why was he so surprised when he walked into the café to find her on stage in all her glory only a month or so after her miscarriage. His breath was taken away. The lighting was incredible; she sounded like a pro.

Open-mike nights were designed to give up-and-comers a real chance to show their wares. And tonight was Chelsea's time to show off; backlit, her hair seemed to have grown a foot in his mind. She looked like an angel. He noted that she had lost a lot of weight, but it looked good on her. Real good, he thought. After all, the last time he'd seen her was in the hospital during the miscarriage.

He tipped his hat lower, making sure she wouldn't see that he was there until he decided his next move; part of him wanted to stay, and part of him wanted to run. Meanwhile, he was transfixed with her as she belted out "Red Velvet." She seemed so different. Who was he looking at? Certainly not the girl who had come to Centennial and bared her soul to him, spent the times in his car under the big evergreen—shy yet compelling, angry sometimes but never in a way that pushed him from her.

After staring at her for a while, it was obvious Chelsea was on to another part of her life and he wasn't in her script. He started to walk toward the door, but out of the shadows she spotted him.

As the music track ended and her last note trailed off, she called out to him. "Trace!"

Leaving the stage in a hurry, she hoped he would wait. He did. But when he turned to watch her approach, he wondered why she'd bothered to call after him; there was a guy by her side, arm around her in ownership.

"Hey, what are you doing here?" Her words sounded slurry.

Trace regarded the man next to her. There was an awkward pause until she introduced him, "Oh hey, this is uh . . . this uh . . ." Then she pointed at the guy, "Oh! Stephen, sorry. Trace, this is Stephen. Stephen, this is Trace, my friend." The man nodded, clearly a good ten years older than Chelsea. She giggled, waving her hands about. "He's my producer, manager. . . . Yeah, he's my manager. Isn't that cool?"

Trace dissected the guy with a look, then refocused on Chelsea. "That's great. So good to see you. You sound good."

Then after a beat, he tipped his hat and started to walk away again, but she grabbed him by the back of his shirt. "No, no! I've got another chance to get up and sing in, I think in two people.

So you want to wait? I've got some new material. Remember we used to play stuff . . . music with each other and . . ."

She was reaching out to him. After another awkward pause, he politely tried to pull her aside. "Excuse us, uh . . . Stephen. Mind if I talk to Chelsea alone?"

The guy stepped back, "No problem, man. Chelsea . . ." Then he nodded his head. "I'll be at the table."

"Oh, yeah, I'll be right there."

Trace escorted her toward the back of the club. "Hey Trace, you look really good. . . . I always liked the hat."

"Are you OK? You sound funny."

"No, I'm good. . . . I'm good. . . . I'm good. I'm sorry, ya know, when you called the hospital. I was really bummed. I was really whacked-out on meds and all. . . . Hey, with all that happened, I figured we better cool it." She swayed, unsteady on her feet. "Hey, maybe I was wrong. Maybe we could hang out some. . . . You know. Nothing heavy . . . or exclusive or anything like that."

Trace struggled with the part of him that wanted to protect her, that still loved her, but he was blown away with who she'd become. In fact, he didn't even recognize her get-up or the way she was talking.

"Chelsea, you know my number. So, whatever. I gotta go. I'm goin' to walk you back to the table. . . . You call me if you want to."

She was stunned, not used to having her invitations refused. One thing hadn't changed in the girl, her pride. "Fine, yeah. Take me back to the table. Actually, I'll take myself back to the table. You just go on back to your little town, Trace." And with that snipe, she was gone.

Chapter 11

Seeing Around Corners

The rain had been intermittent all day, at some points torrential; but now it was more of a drizzle that persistently
hazed up Trace's windshield. He'd promised his mom that he
would fix his wipers, but he hadn't had the time between school
and practice. And as he drove home that night from the café,
he regretted his procrastination.

Leaning over the steering wheel for better vision between
sporadic wipes, Trace strained to see the road ahead clearly. It
hadn't been so bad as he drove through town with streetlights,
but now he was on a dark, winding stretch heading up to his
house, and he was having trouble seeing.

He had to remind himself to pay attention because his
thoughts were randomly running since he'd laid eyes on Chelsea
again. He actually had to tell himself to relax his back and neck

muscles; he hadn't felt knots like this since he'd gotten slammed on the court and knocked out by the biggest guy on the rival team last fall. It wasn't so much his body ache that bothered him; it was his heartache. And more than that, the confusion he felt. Had he actually walked out of the café and not gotten her phone number? And if he knew how to reach her, would he have called her anyway? And what was wrong with her? How could she be with that sleazeball? Managers don't own you. They don't manhandle you. He wanted to smack the guy; he played the entire fisticuffs out in his mind as he drove.

Obviously Chelsea was inebriated on some level. Who knew from what, booze or drugs or something. She didn't even sound like herself. For a moment Trace hoped that she might be on some prescription medicine, maybe antidepressants. After all, she had been through a lot.

He flung his hat onto the backseat in frustration. Maybe he was being too harsh; maybe she just needed some space. No, he seethed again, she couldn't even unglue her tongue from her teeth she was so dry mouthed. Trace had seen some kids at school on coke looking the same way she looked—pupils dilated, thin, running at the mouth.

He thought about so many of the conversations he and his mom had had over their regular breakfast time since Chelsea had lost the baby. He tried to count how many times Stephanie had reminded him, "You can't help somebody who doesn't want to be helped." She warned him that he needed to be prepared for the possibility that Chelsea might not come around to him again.

Trace shook his head. Wait a minute. There Chelsea was, flirting with him, asking him to get back together with her a half hour ago! He felt that familiar heat going up his neck, hitting the top of his head like it was going to explode. What did she say? "Nonexclusive"? What does that mean? Now he was totally furious. He was betrayed. No! He couldn't allow his feelings to go there anymore. He'd rather be angry than devastated. Why did she have such a hold on him anyway? He smashed his fist against the dashboard, accelerating down the road, suddenly not concerned about the weather. He was consumed.

Something like an alarm clock or an overheated warning gauge went off in his mind. He knew there was a curve up ahead and that the road was slick; he had taken these short-cuts for years now. He told himself to slow down, even though at the moment he didn't care much about anything. But despite his inner warnings, he went around the corner faster than advisable.

And there it was, a magnificent buck. A ten-pointer flashed across his vision. The beast came barreling out of the woods on a straight track to the road; it exploded from the wet foliage as if it were racing for a collision with Trace. His trajectory was dead-on with the speeding car.

Trace had always heard the term, "a deer in headlights," but now he was seeing it lived out firsthand. Many of his friends had run over wildlife while driving at night, captive victims stunned by a car's headlights. But never Trace. Yes, he had hit a dog once when he was driving on a back road with his dad, learning the ropes before he got his license. The incident was so devastating to the fourteen-year-old that Trace didn't even want to get in a car for months following. His dad didn't really understand the soft spot Trace had for animals, but his mom did; they were cut of that same cloth.

Trace wasn't unhappy that he had to leave Alabama and the bubbas, friends, and family who always wanted to take him hunting. The boy flat-out hated the prospect. He didn't want to look like a wimp in front of everybody, but he didn't see any purpose in shooting something so beautiful, even if they said they "ate it." Bottom line, Trace didn't want to be one of the boys sitting behind blinds, chewing tobacco, cussing, and drinking hooch, hoping that their aim was good enough to nail the four-legged creature without having to track down their wounded carcasses.

His mind raced to present time just as the buck caught the reflection of Trace's headlights. And as it seems so often in times of peril, slow motion kicked in.

Thankfully, no cars were coming from the opposite direction that rain-slicked night. Trace slammed the wheel to the right, and in a split second he began to skid to the left side of the road.

He remembered his dad drilling into his head as a kid, "When a car starts to slide, take your foot off the brakes. . . . Take your foot off the brakes! . . . Take your foot off the brakes!" But Trace's reflexes didn't obey his dad's words; his foot simply would not release the brake. He felt the car start to hydroplane, hitting a pothole filled with water in the road. He also felt like he had traveled three miles by then, but it could only have been a few feet since the impact with the huge buck was inevitable. Yet they still had not hit.

And then something absolutely amazing happened. Like Rudolph or, better yet, the yearling, the buck took flight! Trace focused on every muscle movement, strain, and resource the animal called upon to catapult himself in a high jump over the car, so high the deer managed to totally avoid the moving vehicle.

Once Trace realized that the animal was out of danger due to its physical expenditure, Trace's car was still traveling a path to destruction. His relief for the animal's fate was fleeting, now recognizing that he was facing his own demise.

During the few seconds before the inevitable crash, Trace thought about his father again, about the accident that claimed his life. How long did those few seconds called an accident seem to take for his dad? Because for him, Trace's whole life was slamming across his mental screen. The visions came quickly and randomly in a surrealistic directive style while the sound of the squealing tires resounded in real time heralding the danger ahead.

The massive tree must have seeded over one hundred years ago to withstand the blow of Trace's car barreling toward its trunk. And as Trace screamed, "Oh my God!" a peace showered over him, like a comforter on a cold night or the breakfasts his mom always made for him. The final image Trace conjured up before coming in full contact with his fate was the time he held Chelsea in his arms—quietly, sweetly, lovingly, both gazing up at the stars through the looming branches of their favorite evergreen tree. And that was his last conscious thought.

The boy had been in a coma, but not for long. It was as if he had been sucked out of his place of disembodiment by sheer love and purposeful prayer. When Trace finally woke up in the hospital the next day, all were amazed, especially the doctors.

Stephanie had been told the worst by the medical team; there was no clear information on when, if ever, Trace might recover from the impact of his car accident. In fact, Stephanie knew when she had identified the remains of his totaled car— no one should have survived such a blow.

As Trace blinked hard to make out the foggy figure standing before him, he wasn't sure where he was or where he had been. All he knew was that he wasn't afraid. After a few moments he recognized his mother's face and slowly smiled. His lips were parched as he tried to speak; she hushed her boy, comforting him with loving prayer.

Stephanie's utterings and whisperings were joyous and uplifting. "Don't talk, just rest. . . . I love you so much. Praise God, praise God. You're going to be fine, son. You're going to be fine."

Two days later the doctors felt comfortable enough to release Trace from the hospital. His motor skills seemed normal; in fact, he seemed amazingly well considering the force of the car wreck. He had a slight bruise across his chest from the seat belt;

his mother thanked God over and over that her boy had buckled up before his journey. And he had one cracked rib. Even the nasty cut on his forehead was easily covered by his tousled blond hair; one would have thought that the boy hadn't even tripped over a log.

But it wasn't until their drive home from the hospital that the most amazing, supernatural part of Trace's whole near-death experience was to be relayed to his mom.

It was a bright and sunny spring day in direct opposition to the weather that surrounded the scene of Trace's accident. Stephanie had been so insistent since her son had come out of his coma for him to be still and recuperate. But by now he was about to explode with his need to explain what happened to him that night, even though he hadn't made complete sense of what actually occurred in his own mind.

Actually, Trace was hoping his mom could shed some light on the turn of events that night. His focus was not on how frightened he was at the time or even how lucky he had been to survive. What he wanted to know was what actually happened as he was about to crash into that tree. And although none of what he had seen or felt made any logical sense to him, the memory of it was as real as his hand that he now held in front of his eyes, as if he were looking to find some physical evidence that he was actually still here on earth.

Disheveled, Stephanie looked like she had been struck by lightning as she drove gingerly down the street toward home. She forced herself to adopt a positive lilt to her voice that had been strained from nights of no sleep and constant prayer.

She glanced at her son quickly, then back to the road. "How are you doing? You're going to be just fine. Are you dizzy at all? Why are you staring at your hand?"

Trace dropped his arm down to his side and laughed, "I'm good. I just can't believe I'm still here." Then he grabbed his side, protecting his injured rib.

Stephanie stuttered, "Trace, what's wrong? Should I go back?" She started to pull the car into a U-turn.

"No, no, no. I'm fine. It's just my rib. It only hurts when I laugh."

"So don't laugh. What are you laughing about?"

"I'm laughing at you, Mom. You look like somebody poured Silly Putty on your head."

"Well, that's nice, son. I haven't exactly had time to go to the beauty parlor while you were in the hospital."

"Sorry. It's just . . . I haven't seen you look like that since Dad died."

"Well, you're not Dad, thank God! I'll wash my hair as soon as I get you home safe and sound."

"It's OK, Mom. It's no biggy. It's OK to laugh."

"What do you expect me to do? I've been through this accident thing before, and it didn't turn out as well, so I've been a little tense." Suddenly, she pulled the car over to the side of the road, threw her arms around Trace, and burst into the tears that she had held back for days.

"Hey, Mom. I'm OK. Promise. Come on; it freaks me out when you cry." He patted her on the back. Stephanie pulled herself over to the driver's seat, wiping her tears on her sleeve.

He said matter-of-factly, "Life really is a roller-coaster ride, isn't it? One minute you get the diner; the next minute I'm in the hospital. You just never know. But you're right, Mom; everything's going to be OK." Stephanie gave him a weak smile as she started to pull onto the road once more.

"Mom, just listen to me for a minute, OK? I've got to tell you something. It's a good thing."

Putting the car in park again, she leaned over and brushed off her tears that had now fallen on his shoulder. "Just let me get you home, and we'll talk there."

But Trace was insistent, "No, Mom. I've got to talk to you now. Maybe you can help me figure this thing out."

Worry arose yet again in Stephanie, "The doctor said you were fine. Everything's OK. You'll be able to play ball by the time you go off to college. Everything's alright . . ."

Trace interrupted her with an authority she'd never heard from him before. "Mom, I've gotta talk to you about something really important. I've got to talk to you about what happened the night of my wreck and who I met."

"Look, I know that you were babbling something about seeing Chelsea when you were in and out of consciousness. . . ."

". . . No, Mom. It's not about Chelsea. It's about Jesus. I met Jesus."

Stephanie sat motionless behind the steering wheel as her son relayed his harrowing experience of just a few days prior. Despite the fact that she was trying to listen intently, his former statement kept ringing in her ears, "I met Jesus. . . ."

Trace was half out of his seat with excitement as he wove his tale. "So this big buck came flying out of the woods. We were a collision waiting to happen! I took my eyes off the road cause he startled me. Mom, he came out'a nowhere, and I started to swerve, and everything started going in slow motion. And then, I swear, he flew. . . . This ten-pointer flew! I remember he looked right at me. I mean, our eyes connected when the headlight flashed in his face. And WHAM! All of a sudden, he exploded over my car. He jumped the whole thing. . . . It was impossible, but I drove underneath him. . . . Then he vanished."

Now Trace was pressed back against his door looking at his mom for some reaction. His eyes were on fire with excitement, but his mother just stared at him, dumbfounded by the story that was being spun.

"OK . . . then, once the big guy disappeared in thin air, I realized that I was spinning across the road heading for this giant tree. I couldn't even take my foot off the brake! I know Dad told me a million times, but I froze there. It was all happening so slow, but I knew it was going really fast. And I remember thinking about a billion things. About Dad and you . . . and Chelsea and the tree that kept getting closer and closer. And just before I hit it, I screamed. I remember hearing it someplace in the back of my head 'cause I could hear the noise of moving fast. . . . And at the same time, I heard myself scream like it was another person in another room, in another space. I yelled, 'Oh my God!'"

Suddenly Trace's eyes welled up with tears. "And when I yelled, 'Oh my God,' Mom, *there he was*! I never felt anything bad, I swear. I didn't feel any pain like I should have when I hit that tree. I didn't even hear or feel the hit. I just . . . looked into his eyes . . . into Jesus' eyes right after he appeared. . . . After I yelled, 'Oh my God,' he was standing there with his arms open, calling to me. I didn't hear actual words or anything like that. But I wanted to go to him. I wanted to go to that amazing, blasting light that surrounded him. It didn't even surround him, Mom; it *was* him! I don't know how I knew it was him, but I knew; I knew as sure as I'm sitting here. . . ."

The boy stuck his hand in front of his face again, ". . . Just like I'm looking at my hand and you sitting there. And ever since I woke up, I keep thinking that I'm making it all up or something, but it doesn't feel like a dream. I felt so chilled, and I wanted to go with him. I wanted to go with him because I felt safe and so good. Like real love that doesn't leave. Protected. . . . Mom, when I hit the tree, I wanted to go with him."

By then both were in a heightened emotional state. Before Trace continued, Stephanie allowed herself a thought of her own. She recalled how many times she had cried out to God. Yes, in one way or another, he had always answered her prayers in his timing. But she had never experienced meeting him the way her son was talking about. And that was OK, of course.

Stephanie had most always felt Jesus' love and covering, even at her worst times of loss. Somehow in the end those tests always brought her closer to her Lord. More reliant on him. But suddenly her mind went off on a tangent, *OK, if that's what happened*

to Trace, why didn't Jesus rescue her husband? Yes, he was saved, but why hadn't Jesus saved him from dying so young, leaving her alone to raise a son and all? And at that thought, she zoned back into Trace telling his story.

". . . and it was right then that I saw Dad standing behind Jesus. He was happy, Mom. And there were other people with him, but I only recognized Dad. He looked perfect, not messed up from his accident. He looked like I remembered him. He wasn't banged up or old."

Stephanie's thoughts trailed off again. Everything that she had always told Trace, everything she had assured her son, he was now telling her was all true. Trace was an eyewitness to what she had known in heart, but he actually had lived it out. And again, as his story unraveled, she was drawn back into its details.

Trace's voice was calming. "I remember asking Jesus if I could come with him, and he said, 'Not yet.' He said I had some work to do for him back here. I couldn't believe it. I didn't want to come back. Not even with the scholarship and all. Not even missing you or Chelsea or anyone."

Stephanie shook her head in utter amazement, instantly torn between the assurances she was hearing of her son's eternal soul and the thought of Trace not "coming back." That thought was surely unbearable to her. Selfish, she admitted quickly, but still unbearable. And then she reviewed his commentary; who wouldn't want to stay where he had described. It was all about who was left behind to grieve, she recognized, and she thanked God in her spirit, right then and there, that he had not taken her boy home yet.

"Mom, . . . are you alright?" Once again Stephanie was drawn back to the reality of the interior of the car that spring afternoon where her son was telling her that he had met Jesus. . . .

By then he was whispering. He leaned over to her, imploringly, looking deep into her eyes. "It's true, Mom, isn't it? Tell me! It's all real . . . everything you always told me. I saw it. Why did I get to see it? What's it all about? Do you think I'm just making it up in my head somewhere? Was it some sort of weird dream?"

She studied the different planes of light now hitting her son's face. The colors of his eyes, magnificent. The sunlight danced through the window behind him, or was it some other glow? Yes, his expression was different. And yes, he looked like her son, but now Trace looked like she could see Jesus in him—faint and flickering, youthful and undisciplined, but on fire nonetheless.

What a blessing in disguise; the accident was actually a gift. Yes, Trace had met Jesus.

Chapter 12

RSVP

So much had happened that week, the *circle of friends* prayer meeting at Norros was postponed until after church on Sunday afternoon.

Tonya had called Pam in the middle of the night on Saturday to confirm she'd arrived safely in New York City with Bobbie. She asked Pam to tell the girls "hi," and that she was with them in spirit. Oh, and she had had a lot of time to think in between snacks and meal stops with Bobbie but mostly while he'd nap, and she wanted to let everybody know she was determined to make her change of venue a positive adventure. Yes, this was a defining time in the twenty-year-old's life; everyone seemed to be having defining times lately. And her prayer for her girlfriends and sisters was her confirmation as the "young'n" in the group that everything would be turned to good for those who loved the Lord!

Yet, it wasn't until Stephanie had called Tonya to give her the update and good news about Trace that the next cover girl felt a comfort in her bones that God really was in control. Oh, how Tonya loved when he would send a big ole confirmation slip across her mind when it was about to wander. She had already booked out of the agency for her visit back to Centennial in the summer so Bobbie could see his friends. Did she ever need to see hers too, and she had only been gone from Centennial for four days.

As Bobbie played in his room (the only place in their tiny Manhattan apartment that didn't have boxes piled everywhere), Tonya unpacked and thought about her *circle of friends* who were meeting just about that time at the diner.

"Under new management!" Stephanie billowed in delight as she hooted 'n hollered. "My son and the diner are both *under new management!* How sweet it is!" And with loud and victorious "amen and amen!" the ladies invaded Norros' back booth.

As usual, they had set up their parade of sweets and goodies to feast on before their prayer meeting started, scarfing down the various delights with zeal. Miraculously, Eleanor had kept off the weight she'd dropped prior to her reconstruction after breast cancer. Yes, to the amazement of all, she had learned to eat little portions of all her favorites, and Miss Eleanor looked like a million bucks.

"Less is more; less is more!" was her mantra, and the results were liberating. Every time she showed restraint, she'd do a little twirl, like a mannequin in a toy store display window.

Finally Eleanor settled down, then pointed at Pam, "But not you, girl! No, 'less is more' for you. You'd blow away, as Tonya would say. You go on with yourself and eat everythin' up for all of us."

Stephanie poked, "What are you saying? I'm fat? That I've got a little poundage coming on around the girth here?"

Eleanor regarded Stephanie up and down as if it were the first time she'd noticed her friend's figure, "You're an hourglass. I am a pear. Pam is a feather. . . . So what do we care?" Eleanor glanced at her watch. "So, where is Lauren?"

"She had to drop Tucker off at the shelter and check on some dog or cat or something, and then she's coming over. Do you want me to call her?" Pam proudly exhibited her new cell phone.

"Sure," Eleanor nodded. "You have her in your phone?"

"Somehow that sounds like science fiction."

"Go on, don't be afraid of your new toy. It took you long enough to get modern." Eleanor took a thimble of her favorite pie and put it on a plate. "I don't want to rush Lauren; I just want to make sure she's OK. . . . But if she doesn't hurry, I'll eat the rest of this pie!"

⚜

Lauren's cell phone was stuffed in the side pocket of her purse on her desk as it rang incessantly. The moment she heard it, her body tensed, but she remained transfixed in Brian's embrace.

He had wanted to kiss her for the longest time, virtually since days after they had been divorced. He had told himself he didn't want her anymore, that they obviously clashed; but every time he saw her he realized the folly of his thinking. Yes, he wanted her back in his life. He wanted the pain and loneliness to stop. He wanted to be with her again, to be a family for Tucker.

Brian also realized that until their move to Nashville he hadn't discovered his real feelings and desires for Lauren. And those weren't revealed until he had come in real relationship with his faith. No, it wasn't about simply attending church again. He had done that most of his life. Lauren had always talked about a personal relationship with Jesus, not religion. He thought she was criticizing him somehow, that she had something he didn't. Her encouraging him to want more of what God had for his life actually had driven Brian away from her and church.

Brian had always considered himself a Christian. He attended Sunday school as a kid, and he went through confirmation at thirteen with his class. He thought he was a believer. But not until recently did he understand the difference between sitting in a pew and surrendering his life to his faith.

Whenever he thought back on what actually changed his spiritual viewpoint, he had to laugh. It was a combination of the influences of two women and one man that had finally steered him in the right direction. And once he actually started reading the Word of God for himself instead of only listening to a Sunday sermon and performing denominational rituals, he finally began to have that personal relationship with Christ and shared accountability with another believer, Michael.

Mike worked as an art director at the same advertising agency with Brian, and they had become fast friends. Although Mike was ten years his junior, he had a work ethic and a marriage Brian truly admired. But beyond those successes, Mike had a deep and abiding faith that shown in every aspect of his life—as a leader, a friend, a husband and a father of two. In fact, he was the one who had asked Brian to church the first time in Nashville. He also introduced Brian to Mrs. Strickland, Lauren's benefactor.

What a small world, Brian thought at first, but he was soon to recognize that God had a hand in setting the stage for Brian's transformation.

Since Brian had asked Jesus into his heart as his Lord and Savior a few months ago, everything seemed to have taken on a different hue.

He thought back on the fact that Lauren had followed him, unwillingly at first, to the Nashville area when he was transferred. Knowing how hard she had worked to create her veterinary practice in California and her deep connection with Suz and her church family, he now recognized how much she sacrificed to keep Tucker close to him as a father. So many other issues had been revealed to him in the short six months since they had all moved across country, but the most challenging was his desire to make things right with Lauren. Instead of pushing her out of his heart, he wanted to let her in; he really loved and admired so much about the woman. And when he got on his knees every night, he prayed that somehow God would make a way for them to get back together. He couldn't believe the change that had come over him. It seemed almost sappy as he reviewed his life of late. His attitudes were so unlike him. He was the one who always played hard to get, who criticized to win the upper hand. But now it was different, and it took everything he had to contain his desire for Lauren.

Still, he was cautious of their volatile sides; both shared a past filled with explosive anger and combative behavior. And both were equal players in those destructive tendencies. Yes, he was gun-shy. That's probably why he hadn't had the guts to sit down and tell Lauren his real feelings for her. He couldn't deny he still had questions: had they repaired enough of their personal as well as collective wounds to broach a new start? They both seemed afraid of failure; maybe it was safer just to share parenting and remain civil to each other.

Brian knew that Lauren was just a little girl at heart who wanted to feel safe. He also knew that he needed to be respected and feel he could take care of her and Tucker. But most importantly, he wanted to sort out all his feelings before he shared them with Lauren.

But there they were holding each other. It happened when Tucker left to play with the kitty cats in the kennels when Brian simply couldn't stop himself. He looked at Lauren standing next to him in her office, and all of a sudden, he saw no barriers. He simply had to express his passion for her, his love for her. So when she turned to say something to him, he kissed her. Just like that.

Although Lauren's cell phone annoyingly continued to ring, neither Brian nor Lauren seemed able to move from their locked embrace. Yes, it had started with a passionate kiss at first, but their desires quickly turned to tender affection. They had always shared an ease with each other; they were familiar to the touch. So much so, Lauren had allowed herself to be taken in his arms.

She couldn't believe the depth of her emotions; she was lost within his simple hug. She tried to call upon her rerun reality list, but her warnings seemed to vanish the moment he kissed her. Somewhere in the back of her mind, she knew Tucker could walk in at any second, and then what would she and Brian say? She also knew that they had crossed a line now that would have to be addressed, and Lauren wasn't even sure how she felt, let alone what she would say. And of course she knew that, given their circumstances and divorce, if they actually intended to get back together, they should take conservative steps to that end. But that certainly was not what they were doing at that moment. She also knew that she was loving every second of his embrace. Oh, she had missed Brian.

Her femininity responded to him physically and emotionally while her practical side stuffed away the thoughts that were flooding her mind in some distant compartment. Yet somehow she managed to allow herself simply to be in the moment, regardless of the annoying cell phone ringing in the background.

Thank goodness Lauren heard the knob of her office door jiggle as Tucker returned from his playtime with the animals.

Lauren practically threw Brian across the room as she pushed herself away from him, madly attempting to straighten herself up. Brian's effort at a casual look was to sit on the corner of the large desk and appear normal for little Tuck as he entered the room.

Oblivious to his parent's ongoings, Tucker was yammering a mile a minute about the gray cat that batted at the toffee kitten, even though he was bigger. "Isn't that being a bully, Mom? How come cats are allowed and we're not?"

Lauren exhaled while she thought of a response, "Well, it's kind of like they don't intend to be a bully; they're just like that naturally."

Brian furrowed his brow, realizing he should step in with a more cohesive answer for his son. "Tuck, animals work off of dominance. If they're bigger or older, they usually take the lead role."

Now Lauren piped in, trying to support the conversation, which was quickly falling apart in her estimation. "It's a 'survival of the fittest' deal. Like when the Hulk gets mad and turns green and big and then stomps the bad guys."

Tucker looked confused.

"OK, sorry, sorry." Lauren fished for a better answer. "Do you know why a horse runs a race? He doesn't know there's a prize waiting at the end of the track. He just runs for the sheer joy of it!"

"What?" Brian shook his head.

"OK, OK. . . . Because he can?" Lauren offered.

Tucker jumped up and down like a contestant on a game show. "I know! Because he's bigger than the other horses. He's a big old horse bully!"

❧

As Lauren hastily made her way to the prayer meeting, one thing was certain: she was sure that she wasn't sure whether she'd tell the girls what happened with Brian. But she was sure she needed some help in sorting out her thoughts.

As she slammed through the diner's doors, Stephanie was just clearing away the plates from the back booth. Pam and Eleanor were on their feet at Lauren's arrival.

"Where have you been? You didn't answer your phone." Eleanor scolded.

"Sorry, sorry." Lauren dashed to the back of the diner, halfway pausing to grab a doughnut off the counter, "I'm late, and I left my phone. I must have dropped it in the kennel someplace."

She sat down and proceeded to stuff her face with the chocolate delight she'd confiscated. The other three women joined her to observe her behavior, giving Lauren the once-over. With chocolate sprinkles stuck to her face, Lauren suddenly stopped chewing and gazed individually at her three friends.

"OK, I lied. My phone is in my purse. First, you have to give me a minute to eat my doughnut because I don't know what I'm doing and maybe a sugar rush will help."

There was dead silence as the ladies allowed Lauren her munch break. But when she finished, she had to 'fess up.

Lauren looked at her friends sitting across from her like a jury panel. "Now, you know we're not supposed to judge one another . . . lest we be judged." Lauren offered up a sheepish smile.

Eleanor raised her brow higher than Lauren had ever observed before. "Girl, are you drinkin' or somethin'?"

A flush covered Lauren's face. "Ah . . ." she officially stammered, "I am. . . . It's just . . . we didn't . . . OK?"

"What is that supposed to mean?" Stephanie leaned in as if she could understand better if she were a few inches closer to Lauren's face. "Did something happen to you?"

Lauren just sat there like a silent lump. Finally, Pam insisted, "What happened?!"

"I . . . uh . . . ah . . ." Lauren was shocked into omission. "I didn't get blitzed; I got kissed. Yes, I did. I actually used my lips for something other than talking, lipstick on occasion, and eating food."

"If you don't tell us what's goin' on, I'm going to smack you, girl!" Eleanor was getting annoyed.

"OK, OK. . . . Remember Pam, I told you I was going to take Tucker over to the shelter, and Brian was going to pick him up after church, and I had to check on a dog, which . . . I forgot . . . to do. . . . I have to go back there now!" She started to get up, but all three women pushed her back down into the booth.

"Give it up," Eleanor ordered.

Lauren faced off with Eleanor, "You can be so mean. And bossy. I didn't know that about you."

"Lauren, *please* give it up. Now!"

"OK, OK. So, anyway . . . By the way, I did check the dog. I don't want you to think I'm irresponsible. I'm a responsible person and a good veterinarian."

The women responded in unison, "Now!"

"Right. So Brian was there, and Tucker went to play with the cats, and I walked into the office, and I didn't do anything. I really didn't do anything. I know I didn't do anything. I didn't give him any particular signal. I didn't . . ."

"What did *he* do?" Pam said slowly.

"Well, he . . . out of the blue . . . kissed me."

"With no warning?" Stephanie looked confused, "Just like that? You just walked in, and he kissed you?"

Lauren couldn't help but grin slightly. "Yes! That's exactly what happened." She looked at her friends. "And it was really nice. And now I'm totally and completely confused. I know it felt good, but I don't know what it means. I don't know what he's thinking because Tucker walked in right in the middle of the kiss-hug thing. And nothing else happened by the way, although, obviously we've been married and . . . OK, I know we're not supposed to . . . And I don't know what I'm supposed to do! I just know that I have all these feelings like I'm twelve years old again. I thought all those parts of me were put in a trunk someplace and stowed away for Christmas or another lifetime, or never to be again, more likely. And then *whack*, he kissed me, and I'm out of my mind in love with him! . . . Or in *lust* with him again. I don't know. That's why I'm telling you all. But before you all advise me, remember we're not supposed to judge, lest we be judged."

After a beat the voice of wisdom was first to speak, "Sweet girl, no matter what we think after we finish gossipin' 'bout all the good juicy stuff and how exactly, with every detail, it happened. . . ." Eleanor caught herself. ". . . Oh my, I feel like I'm in the middle of a romance novel someplace." She cleared her voice. "What I was sayin' was, no matter what we think, it's what you're feelin' that matters. . . . Oh and girl, I don't watch soap operas, but you just made my week!"

Now everybody looked at Eleanor as if *she* was on something.

"Stop it. I just know what it was like after my operation and the mastectomy and all. Not feelin' like a woman anymore. And now that I do again, it's exciting! I understand what you're feelin', Lauren, and we're here to support you. And God's Word is here to guide you specifically and spiritually. Lord knows, if there's any possibility of you and Brian reconcilin', that would be pleasin' to God. But he does have steps that are sure, and if any of his children go about marriage his way, it will be the right way. After all, God designed it . . . the sex and all that good stuff."

Pam giggled, "Have you been reading Song of Solomon again, Miss Eleanor?"

"Why yes." Then Eleanor leaned across the table to Lauren, who already felt better given her friends' silliness. "So give us all the details, and then we'll open the Word and pray. Amen?"

All the ladies said, "Amen."

"Hey, Suz!" Lauren chirped, staring at her cell phone as if she could make the static in the connection go away with merely a look. "Sorry, sorry, I can't hear you. I'll call you right back. I'm going to pull over."

Night had fallen as Lauren pulled her truck into one of Centennial's bigger shopping centers to find a better connection for her call. She dialed her friend back while she jumped out of the truck, walking the perimeter in front of some buildings to find her signal. "Oh Suz! Hey, how are you doing?"

Sitting on their porch, Suz and her husband were enjoying the setting sun in the warmth of a California breeze. As evidenced by every nook and cranny of her surroundings, Suz was a home-maker; hand-painted signs were stuck in plump, lush plantings flourishing along the edge of her bead-board, wrap-around porch. Fred was reclined in his wheelchair, always at half tilt, his serene expression captured in the afternoon light.

Suz rocked back and forth in her favorite chair as she spoke with Lauren. "Hold your horses." Suz sipped on her ever-present cup of coffee. "You're telling me that in one week's time, Ham, Eleanor, and Stephanie bought the diner, Trace was in a car wreck and met Jesus, Tonya took off to New York, and Brian kissed you?"

"And that's your local news, folks." Lauren continued to pace the sidewalk as if she were in a footrace. "Isn't it all cool? Except maybe the kissing part, which I'm not sure about, but that's why I'm calling you—to get your opinion. It's amazing how you can feel like you're sitting on a pause button with God for what feels like eternity, and then all of the sudden, WHAM, he lets everything loose."

Suz laughed, "Oh, how God of him. His timing is so dramatic."

"And romantic!" Lauren suddenly stopped under a street-light to consider whether she really wanted to continue their conversation. After all, she'd been over everything with the girls at the prayer group. But this was Suz she was talking to, her mentor, the person that really knew her better than anyone. Plus, Suz had been there through the whole Brian fiasco the first time around.

"Lauren, did I lose you?"

"No, sorry. I'm here. I was thinking."

"Novel idea. So what's this new chapter with Brian all about?"

"OK . . . So we went to the shelter. I was dropping Tucker off, and he kissed me, and I went . . . ya know, nuts! I melted like a . . . a . . . snowflake in a frying pan."

"How descriptive. May I remind you that that reaction is nothing new for you when it comes to Brian. He always had that effect on you, or don't you remember?"

"Of course I remember! I was trying to forget, but he reminded me the second he touched me, and it all came back. I've been sitting here like a blithering idiot asking myself, 'What happened to my marriage?' and 'Why would I marry that man?' Now I know why. . . . He touches me, and I melt."

"So does a volcano." Suz's voice was compassionate but warning.

Lauren took a deep breath. "I'm ridiculous, aren't I? I sound like I'm Harriet High School, running to everybody asking, 'What do I do, what do I do, what do I do?' The girls prayed over me, and we looked in the Word of God for guidance and . . ."

"And . . ."

"And I know what I'm supposed to do and what I'm *not* supposed to do too fast. I'm supposed to take a deep breath, have a cup of coffee with Brian, and discuss his intentions and how we both feel. Then we should go to some marital counseling before we even consider taking a serious direction. We have to make sure we're on the same wavelength spiritually and that all our past garbage has been forgiven and forgotten. And if we don't have the ability to pray together yet, we can't stay together in any way, shape or form. I've got to know more about where he is in his walk with the Lord and vice versa. And it's OK if it's not exactly the same, but we have to share the same direction. We have to figure out whether we're still trying to control or change each other. We have to learn to put each other before ourselves because when we were married before, we weren't all about God. We were about my old pains and his old aches and my old insecurities and his old furies."

Suddenly Lauren stopped. "Ah, sometimes I think it's all too complicated. And when I really think about it, I don't even want to step into that arena again with Brian because it's so consuming, and I've got so little time and so much to do. Besides, Tuck's doing well, and I don't want to mess that up, but . . ."

Suz smiled, ". . . But when Brian touches you, you melt."

"Right! So what am I supposed to do with that?" Lauren started pacing again.

"Well, since you're not Harriet High School anymore, as you put it, I don't think you're going to fall hook, line, and sinker. . . ."

Lauren interrupted, ". . . From the mere flush of a man's touch! I got it, Suz! I'm an adult. Ha!"

"This is me hating to burst your bubble. You were *over forty* when you married him the first time. This time you have to be grown up . . . with spiritual maturity. And that's a tall order when all your hormones are screaming, '*Yes!*'"

"I hate it when you're so smart."

"Remember when we used to talk about Peter? All the disciples had different talents and capacities. Paul was a teacher, and Peter, remember, was a great starter, but he got sidetracked a lot along the way. He lost his focus. Remember when he was walking on water and he was doing fine as long as he kept his eyes on Jesus? But as soon as he looked at the storm around him, he sank like a rock. And then there was his denial of Jesus. . . . It goes on and on. My point is, Peter jumps in whether he's right or wrong, and you're kind of like him. But Jesus adored Peter. So in God's plan each of our own lives is made special by gifts from God. We are to use them well and temper them more often than not. So go ahead and fly in there with Brian like a Peter move, but just make sure you have the staying power. I'm positive the girls just told you the same thing."

"Yes they did. Almost verbatim." Lauren considered Suz's words. "I just get so excited at the thought that our marriage could be repaired. But OK, you keep a tight tether on me. I want to be accountable and to stand in agreement with you and the girls. I really don't want to get entangled with Brian physically . . . prematurely. . . ."

"Just stay an arm's length away, and you'll be fine." Suz nodded as if Lauren could see her over the phone. "Just because you had the easy access of marriage with Brian at one juncture does not mean you share that commitment right now. It's as if you've never been married as far as the sex department goes, so hands off till you two get your repair list in order. Actually, it's even more complicated because you have been married before."

"Oh, goodie. . . . If you were looking to give me food for thought, I'm *stuffed!* I'll be sure to carry along an electric prodding stick from the shelter anytime I'm going to be near Brian. Beyond that, pray for me, please."

"Always, my friend. Always."

Chapter 13

Fine Line

There was a lot of gray area in Chelsea's life; fuzzy lines of boundaries, decisions based on compromise, unsteady thinking, naiveté, and a boatload of bad advice being slung her way.

Trace had called it; Stephen was exactly ten years older than Chelsea in years but decades beyond her in terms of slick-living. The most disturbing part was that Stephen was an *unusual* suspect in the Nashville entertainment field, spawned by a family of managers working the LA area of show biz. Their type were a dime a dozen in Tinsel Town.

Stephen was to learn, after he had moved to Nashville a year before, that business was done a little differently in Music City. His first lesson of ethics happened at a label party where he ran into a well-respected individual from the business side of the recording world.

The gentleman was quick to chasten the young manager from la-la land with a story he told in passing, hoping that Stephen would gather his true meaning. ". . . So when she picked up her Grammy that year, we were all celebrating, and she introduced me to her family as her financial manager. I was quick to correct her and to give her parents the assurance that I was a CPA. Any Joe Shmo can call himself a manager, financial or otherwise. I had to go to school to become a Certified Public Accountant. Managers have no credentials other than their so-called integrity and their achievements." Then he looked Stephen square in the eye, "And I don't mean acquisitions or notches on their belts."

Stephen might have been slick, but he wasn't stupid. He knew that the playing field locally was a little bit different from what he was used to. Still, for a time, he was determined there was a place for him in Nashville considering his film contacts for some artist "wannabes" to cross over into his field of expertise, young ladies and film. Frankly, he'd never met a singing artist who didn't want to act or an actor who didn't want to sing.

Chelsea woke up slowly that morning despite the sun streaming across the room smack onto her face. Nothing much motivated her to move in the a.m., especially since she was out in the clubs every night with Stephen working her songs for whatever label people might be around.

She was most excited about the studio time Stephen promised to bankroll for her, and staying in his back bungalow no rent required and no strings attached, was a slice of real luck, she told herself. Yes, slinging hamburgers at that joint just off Music Row had gotten old quickly. But she was doing OK; she now *lived* off Music Row and was about to cut her demos. She was sure, especially with Stephen's encouragement, that she would soon be a star.

What she wasn't sure about, as she unglued her eyelids and took in the day with disdain, was whether she should take her meds that day. It was a coin-toss ritual every morning; should she limit her singing voice due to the dryness her medication caused, or battle with the anxiety that inevitably sprung up to haunt her within a day of not taking her prescriptions. Then again, the pills kind of calmed her down so that little nervousness in her voice vanished. On the other hand, the weed or the beer that Stephen would share with her before they went club-hopping helped chill her out. So what was a girl to do?

Chelsea told herself she could handle it. After all, Ford used to give her wine from the time she was ten. "Their little secret," he would whisper in her ear. Besides, in Europe kids grow up on wine, and he loved treating her, well, like a big girl.

Chelsea reached for her prescription bottle. No, she wasn't going to entertain those thoughts that day. She hated Ford. She was sure that by the time she became so famous everyone knew her name, she would have succeeded in erasing him completely from her mind.

She downed two pills without the aid of any liquid, then pulled herself up to the edge of the bed, catching her disheveled image in the mirror across the way. Her makeup was smeared under her eyes, her hair looked like a rat's nest. But she told herself, "That's OK. I can always pull it off, no matter how rough last night was." She was young, she was pretty, she was resilient, she was invincible, she was special, and she was going to make sure everybody knew it.

After her internal pep talk, there was a bang on her bedroom door. "Yo, little lady!" It was Stephen. "You up?"

Chelsea scrambled to her feet, grabbing her bathrobe at the end of the bed. "Yeah, yeah. Sure."

She staggered over to the door and unlocked it. Stephen gave her a long look, brushing her bedraggled hair away from her face. "I don't know why you lock that door. You're safe with me."

"Just a habit, ya' know."

She looked up at him for a moment and smiled. Yes, he was the most important person in her life right now, and she wasn't going to do anything to make him mad. Beyond her career, the thing that really interested her about him was that Stephen had never made a move on her. Yeah, he had put his arm around her in public, but that was just his way of branding her.

She had asked him once if he had a girlfriend, and his reply was revealing, "Chelsea, you and I are going places, and it's not going to get messed up with any kind of personal stuff. I've seen it go down bad too many times. . . . It's not that I wouldn't like to," he would tease her. "My job is to make sure you get everywhere you deserve. Nothing's going to get in the way of that. You'll thank me later."

Yes, he was seeing big bucks in this girl, and he was not going to blow it over emotional entanglements. She had already shown him some sides of her that he labeled, when he was in a kind mood, as "unstable." To counter his concerns, he made sure she stayed medicated, numb, and happy. Not being an entirely evil snake, he promised himself once he got her established, he'd also get her psychological help. After all, she wouldn't be good for the long run if she didn't figure out some of the messes in her mind that would come out late at night or when she was scared.

"I've got news that's going to blow your socks off."

She had never seen him look at her quite that way. "What is it? A label? A song? What?"

"A movie! And if they buy you, I'm going to make it part of the deal that you get to sing the title song of the film. Bingo!"

Her eyes were the size of golf balls. "A *movie* like in movie theaters!? Like a feature film kind of a movie?"

"Yes, ma'am. Like marquees, tickets sales, Oscars, Golden Globes, red carpet!"

She squealed with uncontained delight.

"Yo, I'm not saying you got it. We have to fly out to the Coast, and you've got to test for the part. It's an independent film, but the director's shot three before, and they were all good box office. This is the break of a lifetime, Chelsea. We've got to make the five o'clock flight. Pack for three days, don't overpack, and don't forget your red outfit. I left two suitcases in the hall. I'm going to go get you some coffee and food. I'll be back in an hour." She just stood there shaking her head.

"Hello? Earth to Chelsea?"

She suddenly jumped at him, giving Stephen a huge bear hug. He allowed the embrace for a moment, then set her back down on the ground.

"OK, you get going. And oh, don't forget your license. They need to know you're eighteen."

That comment caught her short for a minute. Why would they need to know if she was eighteen? He immediately sensed her concern, addressing it with one slick retort. "Lots of managers lie about their clients' ages. And this part is playing a sixteen-year-old. I told them you were eighteen and you could look sixteen. They don't want to deal with school breaks and stuff on set so bring your license."

Trace was scarfing down a burger under the big evergreen tree at the far end of the parking lot at Greystone High before going into basketball practice. Obviously, he was in no shape to play yet following the car accident, but that didn't mean that he didn't want to be there for his team.

His priorities had narrowed considerably since his recent experiences, and he found it difficult to maintain focus on his studies. His mind was so filled with questions and thoughts; his feelings and emotions had not all lined up yet. He recognized that he had a barrelful of questions, but the spiritual peace he'd received a few nights before had not left him. And, as is true with most new believers, he was bursting with an excitement that he could barely contain. In fact, that day at school, he was tempted to tell everybody he ran into about Jesus, but he controlled himself, not wanting to sound like some nut. His witness was still raw, to say the least. Besides, a lot of the kids that went to his school already knew what he now knew.

Sitting under the big tree where he and Chelsea used to park, his thoughts went to her. She hadn't called him, and deep down he wasn't surprised. Still, he had hoped she would, and now he felt totally helpless in trying to reach her. It was the first time he thought about how his mother's friends must feel—Miss Irene, Chelsea's mom, and Miss Lauren. How could they handle not knowing where Chelsea was? Yes, now he really understood how not knowing where someone you truly loved was. . . . Gosh! He said it again. Love. Did he really love Chelsea, or was he just infatuated with her?

Thankfully he spotted his friend Shooter lumbering to the side entrance of the gym as he passed, under the "Welcome" sign that carried another daily "Hamism":

"OLD ACTORS NEVER DIE, THEY JUST FAIL
TO PERFORM."—HAM

Trace got up carefully, still guarding his wounded side, and made his way toward the door to meet up with Shooter. He couldn't help thinking that, yes, he had been in the car accident, but Shooter looked like he had been in a train wreck. The fact was, the two hadn't had much chance to talk since Tonya left and Trace had been in the hospital. Shooter did show up to see his infirmed buddy, but Trace was still in a coma, and Stephanie had kept her son away from the phone until he was ready to go back to school.

"How's it goin', man?" Trace asked. He could see by Shooter's expression that he wasn't having a good time of it.

"It's goin'. You watchin' practice?"

"Yeah. I'll write a critique." He smiled, but Shooter didn't find the humor in the moment.

They were about to enter the gym when Trace pulled his friend aside. "I hear she's in New York." Shooter just nodded. "You OK with that?"

"She's got free will. The only thing that gets me is that she's also got Bobbie."

"Did y'all have a fight or something?"

"Look, man, we've talked about this with Ham. I don't want to talk anymore. I'm not ready to marry her; she's ready to move on. We're straight." The boy started for the door again.

"I saw Chelsea." Shooter turned around.

"Yeah, the night of the accident. At The Café. . . . She was singing at open-mike night. She looked pretty messed up."

"She is messed up, man. You should stay clear from that girl."

Trace didn't like Shooter's comment, but he decided not to take offense. "Well," he let the tension ease. "She knows where I am, and I don't know where she is, so I guess it's out of my hands."

Shooter nodded again, "Yeah, it's that way. You're straight, man."

She hadn't felt like this since she had won the equitation class on the A circuit with Gracie almost a year ago. Unleashed and exhilarated, Lauren was tearing across an open field on a big gray mare a friend from the shelter had loaned her for the afternoon. What was even better was that the mare was stabled right down the road from the piece of land Mrs. Strickland had committed for the shelter's use. So Lauren was going to get to ride the property, pray over it, and envision her wildest imagination at what it would look like when it was filled with life—recovering animals, riding for handicapped and inner city kids. Oh, how excited she was for those who had never had the opportunity or joy of putting their little hands on a sweet-smelling horse.

As she dashed across the ground, Lauren leaned forward, lying along the horse's neck, hugging her steed in utter childlike joy. The mare didn't seem to mind a bit, keeping steady as she dodged a few gopher holes along the way. The mare's owner had said her horse was tried-and-true, so even though Lauren hadn't ridden in a while, the mare was sure not to take advantage.

Lauren knew that she was in for some sore muscles the next day, but riding a horse was like riding a bike: once you know how, you find a balance you never forget. Of course, it's a more exhilarating experience on some horses than others, but that's what's so amazing about the sport. It is a union at its best. A horse is not a bicycle you can throw in the corner when you outgrow it. Boy, had she learned that with Gracie. Suz and she used to giggle about the show-stopper horse, brilliant in every way—she could jump the moon, but she was a moody beast; and if you got on her wrong side, or got on her on the wrong day, you were in for quite a ride. Nonetheless, when Gracie was on her best behavior, she was unbeatable.

※

Lauren had taken solace in the fact that when she sold her horse, the proceeds actually paid for the entire move to Centennial as well as their first six months stay and house down-payment.

And now, with Brian on the wings of her heart, Lauren felt like a cat on a hot tin roof, full of life and renewed dreams. Still she was almost afraid to embrace the fullness of all the potential her circumstances held—the shelter, her friendships, her spiritual walk, the thriving of her son, and the invitation to address the possible restoration of her marriage. Was it too good to be true?

She encouraged herself to take all the positive turn of events in her life to heart; it was OK to do so. And as she slowed the mare down to an easy walk, she breathed in the fragrant air and looked up at the sky.

Like the horse she was riding, for some time now she had moved through her life with her eyes glued to the ground, cautioning herself not to fall down some hole that could swallow her up. She was determined not to derail physically, emotionally, mentally, or spiritually. But amid her intense concentration to assure her survival, she often missed some of the glorious experiences each moment of life offered.

It had taken her a long time to let God guide her feet so she could look up and breathe deeply like she was doing at that very moment, taking in his creation with humility and expectation. Actually, she had learned to do the "letting God" part on her porch since she'd moved to Centennial, and now she was dedicated to moving forward. But that resolve suddenly railroaded her back to her trepidations; every time things seemed to get really good in her world, there was a period of enjoyment, and then the next labor pain would eventually come.

Suz had offered Lauren the metaphor of childbirth during her times of spiritual growth and graduation. She pointed out that the last three pushes before a woman births her baby is called "transition."

Her point was, some women have an easier time of childbearing than others, but most concur that it is an excruciatingly painful yet exhilarating experience. Being a veteran mother of six, Suz confirmed that *transition* pain never seemed to get easier. In fact, most women find the last three pushes of birth flat out unbearable.

Lauren always thought that Suz was sharing this information with her to make her feel better about not being able to birth her own children. But the truth was, Suz was trying to make a more profound point to her younger sister in Christ. Given Lauren's excitement about the Lord, she needed to recognize that there would be times of trials and tribulations for periods that sometimes felt never-ending. But just like childbirth, once one had gone through "transition" and the last push was over, a new life was presented.

Despite the pain, most every mother will tell you that she'd go right back and do it all over again to receive the blessing of a child. Clearly the reward overshadows the challenging process. And that was also true in one's spiritual life, as Lauren had learned by experience. Yes, God would allow certain threatening people, events, or circumstances to enter into his children's lives to mold and shape them. But in the end, they would grow and flourish on a far more purposeful level.

Suz enhanced her point by sharing with Lauren a story about one of her daughters; this youngster was curious about kitchen activities and always wanted to help her mommy cook. At her tender age, the girl was just tall enough to stick her fingers above the lip of the stove. She had been warned time and time again to stay away because the stove was hot; boiling water could fall on her; the pots and pans could spill over her; and there was a gas flame underneath all the cookware. But despite Suz's warnings, her daughter couldn't get the concept of "don't touch."

In an effort to protect her child by way of a lesson, Suz put a little hot water in a thin pot away from the edge of the stove. Then, from another room, she watched her little girl march into the kitchen knowing full well that she shouldn't be doing what she was doing. The tot glanced around to make sure no one was watching and then slowly stuck her finger up in the air and curled it around until it met with the metal pot; her fingertip burned upon impact. The little girl screamed as if she were innocent and some big bad thing had jumped out and bitten her.

Suz immediately came to her daughter's rescue, asking her what had happened. The little girl said that she didn't know, that it was the pot's fault. Suz pointed out that the pot was where it was supposed to be, but the girl's finger wasn't.

"What would happen if it had fallen on you and splashed down your arm or on your face?"

Her daughter cringed; lesson learned. Needless to say, the child never stuck her hand up on the stove again. In her recap to Lauren, Suz concluded that our learning curves are up to us. And how often we circle the same mountain is also up to us. "Sometimes God will allow us a little burn to avoid a skin graft. And as for my birth analogy, the end of the transition period, a new birth is before you. A new level of spiritual maturity. A personal surrender that is blessed by God in ways we can't even imagine. And that only happens when we let go of our own agenda."

Lauren sprawled herself across the mare's neck, once more enjoying the rhythm of her gait. She prayed, "Oh God. Everything feels so good right now. Please let it last a little while until my next 'stretch mark.'"

This was not to say that Lauren's life was without adversities; her concern for her unsaved family members and Irene going through the tortures of a lost child was a daily reminder of the dark side of trials. But Lauren had made a vow in her thanksgivings every morning with her Lord that she was determined to be more trusting of him and less fearful of circumstances. She rebuked the idea, "Well, I've tried everything, and so I guess all

I have left to do is to pray." No, prayer had finally become Lauren's first thought of the day and her last in the evenings.

⚜

Lauren persuaded the mare to move through an overgrown thicket, revealing Mrs. Strickland's farm property on the other side. From the angle she was entering, she was taken by the sweet atmosphere and pleasantly surprised with the structures already standing on the extensive acreage. Lauren had only driven by briefly with Mrs. Strickland after one of their lunches to take a gander at what the lady had so kindly donated to extend the outpatient services of the shelter.

Yes, everything about the Grace Shelter had been a joy in just the few months they had been open. In addition to the fulfillment of supporting homeless and hurt animals, Lauren had been impressed with all of her employees but especially Carla. She was beginning to consider letting this young lady take over the animal evaluation position that had yet to be filled. Carla was a bundle of energy and positive ideas. As a newlywed, she could have divided attention, but Lauren was thrilled with this twenty-year-old's level of expertise and dedication.

She didn't often see that kind of work ethic in the younger generations, Lauren noted, as she urged the mare on toward the little barn at the far end of the property. Yes, Carla came to work with an agenda; whenever it was slow at her reception desk, she either studied tapes or read books by professional animal behaviorists and trainers. But beyond book knowledge, she had an excellent demeanor with both pets and people alike. Yes, Lauren looked forward to promoting this diligent girl.

Thinking back on the few people who had supported her through some of the defining moments in her life, Lauren smiled, remembering the teacher that let her participate in the school play even though she couldn't sing her way out of a paper bag and one of her friends growing up who was a year older and slipped her a "grow bra" to help with Lauren's preteen low-esteem feelings. The self-realization that Lauren didn't seem to be developing as quickly as her peers had shattered her. Thankfully, her trauma was short-lived with the assistance of her friend.

Dismounting the gray, Lauren now stood transfixed before a little red-and-white barn that begged to be filled with pets and children's laughter. She imagined a potbellied pig and some chickens and dogs running all over the place challenging William and Bingo, who, in her imagination, were trying to hold court in the corner of the barn. And of course there were all those barn cats for Bingo to contend with.

Lauren's vision didn't include the bell collar around Bingo's neck. She had removed the collar that first night, never to be reintroduced. Her purpose in loving her pets was not to embarrass them, even if they had flawed manners. "Spoiled" came to Lauren's mind. And then she recalled Tucker asking about the "bully cat," giggling at her son's evaluation. No doubt, everyday at the shelter brought with it unique experiences.

Only yesterday morning, when the doors first opened, a small elderly woman from Nolensville came into the shelter holding her limp cat. There were no marks on the kitty, but her eyes were wide open in a terrorized death mask.

Lauren quickly escorted the woman back to an examining room where she went through the motions of examination, explaining that there was nothing she could do for the little kitty; she had died hours before.

The lady was beside herself at the loss, explaining that she had found the cat only six months before. She was a little feral cat weighing under five pounds at a year old. The woman went on to tell how she'd taken the cat she called Moto to the local vet once she caught it and wrapped it in a towel so she wouldn't get bitten.

Surprisingly, the wild kitty never tried to go after the woman. She just sat quietly in the car staring at her captor with her determined yellow eyes. And when the vet had said that they should put the young cat down because she tested positive for feline leukemia, the woman simply couldn't do it.

Lauren's heart was breaking at the story. In fact, even as a vet, she had rarely put an animal to sleep and never for frivolous reasons. When an owner couldn't afford medical costs, Lauren always footed the bills; and if she ran across people who just didn't care enough about their pets, Lauren would take the animals in, make them well, and then place them in loving homes. This was her heart, and she knew it was this woman's as well.

The lady explained to Lauren that she had gone to considerable expense to save the little kitty with IVs and oral medicines, and with that care the cat rallied. And when she took her home, she was able to nurse her back to health. She also told Lauren that her biggest concern for the cat was her two wonderful dogs that she had adopted from the pound. They were big, brawny, and playful mutts. And as Moto healed over the months, the dogs became accustomed to the feline as long as the woman kept a watchful eye on the three.

"I was strict that my dogs treat Moto with respect." She assured Lauren. "Actually the cat got quite full of herself when she hit almost six pounds. . . . She actually started to stalk and tease the dogs!" Lauren laughed relating to her own Bingo who did the same thing to the kennel dogs. Cats can be such a kick, she mused.

Suddenly grief overcame the woman, "I had never let the cat out of the house to roam because of her leukemia. It's transmittable, you know."

Lauren nodded.

"Anyway, my dogs go out and play. I had visitors over yesterday, and by accident they left the door open for just a second or two. Least that's what they told me when I called them from my car on the way here. . . . Moto must have slipped outside, being the ever curious one. I didn't realize she was even out until this morning when I found Moto lying there, cold. . . . The dogs were just staring at her. Oh my, they must have killed her! They didn't bite her, I don't think. Least there was no blood, . . . but they must have killed her. They must have trapped her in a corner somewhere and played with her until she just up and died. You know, the way animals play, like a cat and a mouse."

Lauren envisioned the scene and tried to turn her mind off the details, as did the woman who was horrified at the demise of her feisty little kitty.

"I picked her up," the woman's voice cracked. "I screamed at the dogs. I was so mad they hurt her." By now the woman was sobbing. "My dogs just looked at me, like they had no idea what they had done! . . . I'm sorry I'm so upset."

"It's OK. I really understand. You're fine." Lauren wrapped Moto in one of the shelter's towels. "Would you like to take her home, or would you like us to bury her for you?"

"No, I'll take her home." The woman finally decided. "I know a quiet place under my apple tree where she can rest." She carefully gathered the towel around Moto and began to leave the examining room when she turned to Lauren. "I'm sorry, I wasn't thinking. Do I owe you anything?"

Lauren just shook her head, "Of course not."

"Well, thank you then."

Just before she exited, Lauren stopped her; the woman half turned back, still unable to control her tears. "It's not your dogs' fault. It's just their nature, ma'am. They're not like people. They didn't plan to kill your cat. It's just an instinct on their part."

The woman slowly nodded, "I know. They're really sweet doggies." Then she looked Lauren straight in the eye, "I wasn't looking forward to resenting my dogs. . . . Not forgiving them, like so much of my life."

"Yes, ma'am." Lauren said in a consoling tone.

At the end of her memory, Lauren mounted her horse again; she perused the land before her knowing that she knew she was standing on blessed property—a place that would make a way for a lot of healing, hope, and freedom for both animals and people alike under the Grace Shelter banner.

Chapter 14

Passing in the Night

Never one to procrastinate, Irene had had just about enough
of sitting like a bump on a log in Centennial, Tennessee, not
knowing where Chelsea was or, more importantly, how she was.

After another festive lamb dinner with Sam and Margaret,
Irene declared she was finished sitting on the sidelines. "The
evening is still early," she announced with verve, whipping out a
piece of paper that had been scribbled over so many times that it
looked like a wet napkin. "I have a list here of all the music clubs
in the Nashville area, and I've decided to visit each and every one
of them until I find my daughter! Since I can't afford to hire a
private detective, I'll become one." And with her announcement
made, she snapped her purse shut; she didn't seem out of control,
just adamant.

Margaret looked at Sam in concern, "Irene, what are you going to do if you find her? You can't make her come back."

Defiant, Irene stood, then began to pace the small apartment, covering its full parameters with her lanky stride. "Obviously, I can't throw her over my shoulder like a cave man, but I can at least let her know face-to-face that I'm concerned . . . if she'll even talk to me. I just have to know if she is alright."

"Have you considered that chasing after her just might boomerang? She knows how to reach you. If you push her, she could just run from you and make matters worse," Sam cautioned.

"I know, Dad, I know. But doing nothing is simply unacceptable. Some interaction is better than none. It's not like Chelsea's gone off to college and I know her dorm number and address. She's certainly not out there on her own getting an education. At least not the kind I want for her." Irene threw her hands in the air for emphasis. "She just came out of the mental institution at eighteen with more problems than I have at fifty-two, and that's going some!" Irene defensively glared at her parents. "And I know, don't say anything. It's me. I'm sure it's all my fault. But, I'm not going to roll over. If Chelsea wants to look me square in the eye and tell me to get out of her life, then maybe I will. . . . But not when she's been through sexual abuse, a miscarriage, a mental breakdown, and is on more medication than the pharmacy can keep stocked."

Margaret was oddly impressed by Irene's behavior, "I never thought you had it in you to be so tenacious about your girl."

"What do you mean, you didn't think I had it in me?"

Margaret waffled, not wanting to exacerbate Irene's obvious angst.

"It was a compliment, Irene. All I meant was that you've never been the mother-hen-type."

"Like you, Mom?" Irene snapped.

Hurt now, Margaret was not about to back down. "Irene, you and I are more alike than you obviously want to admit. I might not have baked you cookies and let you have sleepovers, but I've always loved you."

"Never mind." Irene made an unusual snap decision move to the candy plate as she popped a double chocolate almond in her mouth.

Inadvertently, breaking the rising tension, Lauren, accompanied by William and Bingo, entered the apartment in a rush "Hey guys! I had the most amazing day. I actually got on a horse again, . . . which is why I'm looking a little bent in my lower extremities. Geeze Mageeze! I can't even walk, and I only rode for maybe an hour and a half." Lauren attempted to kick up her heels in excitement, but her expression of joy was immediately foiled by her rebellious inner thigh muscles. Instead, she crumbled to the floor. Once prostrate, Lauren was immediately pounced on by her dog in loving concern. Her parents and sister simply observed Lauren, the "loon" of the family, flailing around like a beached baby whale as she dealt with her challenged "sports muscles."

Margaret finally broke into the visual spell Lauren had cast on all present. "Have you eaten, dear? We still have lamb. I didn't know if you and Tucker were joining us, so I made enough for everyone."

Lauren wrestled with William for a moment of folly, then unglued herself from the floor with great difficulty, weaving for a moment as she secured her balance against the TV. "No thanks, I'm just crawling out to get Tuck. He's at Brian's. I wanted to touch base. . . . We'll be back in about three days at the rate I'm moving."

Now Irene pulled herself up from the couch, straightening her tailored suit. Stepping forward, she suddenly towered over Lauren due to her model posture and high heels. Lauren slowly looked up to her sister's face and then down to her Chanel shoes. "How the heck do you wear those things every day? And *why?* Rene, you should just throw on some sweats and relax!"

"Actually," Irene said with a tinge of sarcasm, "I'm going on the rounds of the Nashville scene to look for Chelsea, and I'm not club hopping like I'm running a 10K. I have the names and addresses of everywhere an eighteen-year-old would be allowed in to sing."

Concerned, Lauren regarded Irene, "You're going where to do what?"

"I'm going to find my daughter, and if she doesn't want to see me, I'll back off. But until then, I'm, as you would say little sister, 'On a mission.'"

"But Rene, driving around Nashville is a little tricky. . . . They have a highway 'inner loop' and an 'outer loop.' . . . Could you just wait until tomorrow night? I'll get Brian to watch Tuck, and we'll go together, OK?"

Since she was a child, whenever Irene set her jaw, everyone knew to watch out; there was absolutely no arguing with her. And, no, it wasn't difficult to understand her motivation; she had just finally hit the wall and needed to do something about her absentee daughter, advisable or not. *Complacency* was definitely not Irene Lee Patterson Williams's middle name.

⚜

Without warning and out of character, Sam stood, hiking his pants up in a gesture of firm resolve. "Irene, I'm going with you."

Margaret regarded her husband.

Lauren reacted. "Now, guys, hold on. Can't you just wait till tomorrow? I have to go get Tuck. . . ."

Irene started toward the door. "I'm going by myself. I just wanted to let you know what I'm doing, and hopefully I'll be bringing Chelsea home *tonight*!"

Lauren gave her a dubious glance, "When monkeys lay eggs."

Her sister's comment set Irene off, "Listen to me, I'm going. That's it, . . . and it's, 'when monkeys fly, not lay' . . . oh, never mind."

Sam stood fast. "Irene, I said I'm going with you. I'm not about to let you out there alone, unescorted."

The room froze; these were words Irene had longed to hear from her father her entire life but never imagined would pass his lips. And then there they were, his sentiments still lingering in the air like a sweet aroma. Had Sam really said what he said? The women were taken aback.

Sam's protective side was something completely new to this man, as well as to his female constituency, and as he took his stand, he felt a comfort and a resolve that surprised even himself.

"Margaret, you wait here, and I'll keep you posted by phone." She nodded at her take-charge husband.

Irene, Tucker, Sam, and Lauren's heads bobbed mercilessly set against the bouncing action of Lauren's tightly wound truck springs.

Lauren was at the wheel, navigating the aforementioned outer and inner loops around Nashville, illuminated spectacularly against a clear spring night. The BellSouth Building, better known as the "Batman Building" with its two spirals expanding into the higher atmosphere held true as Lauren's best frame of reference for directions. No, Lauren had not spent a lot of time dealing with the downtown intricacies of one-way streets and addresses of Music City's club scene; nonetheless, there they all were together on an adventure to find Chelsea. And despite the inconvenience when it came to Lauren's former plans with Tucker that night, the coming together of family overruled her personal agenda. Still, as Lauren was the head navigator of the evening's search party, she hadn't let go of the idea that she might have had an opportunity to have a conversation with Brian about all that had gone on between them in her office. Oh well. Clearly Irene needed her flanks covered by a loving emissary more than Lauren needed romantic confirmation.

The one that was particularly excited about the family's adventure was Tucker, despite the fact that he was told he wasn't allowed to go into the music clubs. Still, he was encouraged with pit-stops of ice cream, pizza, and strolls down the street to window-shop while Sam and Irene checked the various venues for Chelsea. And in Tucker's sweet little heart, beyond enjoying the evening of goodies, he was most excited at the prospect of seeing his older cousin.

Surprisingly, Chelsea had spent a lot of time with Tucker, unbeknownst to most in the household. She'd sneak in and play cards with him when she didn't feel the need to be withdrawn and defensive in front of her elder family members. Yes, she adored little Tuck, and he adored her.

No one could ever fault Irene for not being prepared for tasks she'd decide to take on, and tonight was no different. She not only had detailed maps to the locations of the myriad of clubs; she had flyers printed up with Chelsea's picture on it along with a reward for information as to her whereabouts. Lauren couldn't resist suggesting that if her big sister stapled the flyers to trees around the neighborhoods, her daughter would look like another lost pet. Irene didn't appreciate the comment, but in her own thinking, she had to admit that her approach was probably a little over the top. So, before she and Sam entered the first club, Irene acquiesced, folding one flyer over to hide the reward section and decided to subtly show her daughter's picture around to the club owners and clientele.

Nashville nightlife offers a unique blend of performers and audiences; the overflow of musicians, songwriters, and singers often outnumber the audience. And, as all gather at the array of establishments to entertain, at the end of the night, the songs remained the stars of the shows. This fact was apparent even to Irene who had noticed when she was watching the CMA awards with Chelsea last fall in New York City that, almost without exception, the winners gave God the credit for their amazing talents. Irene had never dared ask Lauren about that observation, although she was curious. Still, since Irene wasn't looking for one of her sister's lengthy dissertations about God, she let the question fall into their default category of unsolved points.

As Irene entered the first music establishment on her list, she couldn't help but be taken by the song resonating from the stage. Performed by a young woman playing a guitar, she presented her soulful rendition of an original song with lyrics that literally stopped Irene in her tracks. Even Sam took a beat, pausing in response to what was happening on stage. The words told a tale about a girl feeling abandoned. And although Irene quickly moved toward the seating area to scan the rest of the room for Chelsea, she couldn't escape the effect of the song. And as Sam perused the club, both father and daughter were drawn in by the words that rang true with profound meaning:

You were my weekend father since I was ten.
Nothing much felt right after then.
Mom said you loved me; Mom said you'd be by.
But when you left for good, you had tears in your eyes.

Father in heaven, bring my dad home.
It's not right, your children are alone.

Mom went to work to put food on the shelf.
She said, "Call the neighbors if you need any help."
I got in some trouble; oh, I made some mistakes.
I started to do whatever it takes.

Father in heaven, bring my mom home.
It's not right, your children are alone.

Now I talk to my Father who lives in the sky.
His Holy Spirit's in me; His Son never lies.
I know he loves my mom and dad
Even though they couldn't stay.
He loves us all, even when we turn away.

I had this place, deep in my heart
Never satisfied; it was tearing me apart.
But Father God, he never lets me down.
I was lost; now I am found.

Father in heaven, bring love to our home.
Without it our children are alone.
Father in heaven, make your presence known.
In your arms your children are never alone.

As the song concluded, Irene struck up a conversation with the club's manager, Norman, who quickly recognized

Chelsea's picture. But Irene's spark of hope fizzled when the manager reported that Chelsea hadn't been in the club for a few days.

Irene didn't take umbrage at his comment, "Now there's a girl that's not going to go unnoticed." No, Norman didn't make his comment in a demeaning fashion—it was more complimentary than not, especially when he mentioned what a great voice Chelsea had.

Irene and Sam thanked Norman, leaving a note with him to give to Chelsea if he happened to see her before they found her.

"Is she in some kind of trouble?" Norman wasn't being nosy.

Caught in a vulnerable moment Irene was momentarily speechless when Sam intervened for some man-to-man communication with the manager. "Chelsea's just eighteen, and she shouldn't be out and about on her own yet, even though she thinks and looks like she should and could. We're just trying to check on her without calling the police." Sam gave an intense look of protection, one Irene had never seen before. "I don't believe my granddaughter is a missing person. . . . She's just failed to communicate with her family. And, of course, that makes all of us worry."

The man exchanged a knowing nod.

As Sam and Irene walked out, Irene had a sliver of comfort in the fact that she had envisioned these places of music to be much more sleazy and dangerous than they in fact were. No, this establishment was not a pickup place; it was about the music.

After father and daughter got back into the truck, Tucker was most of the way through a Nutty Buddy ice cream as evidenced by the chocolate smeared all over his face. Irene immediately pulled a tissue out of her purse and started to clean her nephew up as well as the seat and surrounding area affected by the aftermath of his treat. Lauren, on the other hand, seemed perfectly content just to allow the boy to be a boy, enjoy the ice cream, and not fuss at him until he had finished.

Observing, Sam wondered, "How did I spawn such different daughters?"

"So?" Lauren had waited long enough for some report from the two.

Sam took the front seat, "There's some good news and some bad. . . . " He paused for a moment of drama before continuing. "Chelsea's been there. They know her. But she hasn't shown up for a while, and she wasn't there tonight. Irene left a note."

"Oh, good, Rene. That's a good start. When did they see her last?"

"I think he said a couple days ago. Right, Dad? He did say that she comes in pretty regularly, though."

"Oh, this is going to work, Rene. This was a good idea! We'll just keep going to the other places. . . . Maybe she's somewhere else tonight." Lauren flashed her biggest smile. "So what did you say in your note?"

There was another pause, when suddenly Irene's look of determination shattered into a deluge of tears. Drawn from his feeding fest, Tucker considered his aunt; he had such a tender heart for a young boy. "What's the matter?"

"Oh, I just had something in my eye." She dabbed the corners of her lashes with some tissues while her makeup ran down her cheeks.

"We'll find her. Don't cry. If I ever get lost, I'll just stand in one spot till everybody comes and gets me, OK?" Then the boy looked at his mom, chomping into the end of his ice cream cone.

Emotions swept the interior of the truck. "Oh that's good, Tuck. That's good." And although Lauren started the engine, everyone sat in silence for a minute before she put the truck in gear.

And after what seemed to be an eternity, Irene answered Lauren's question in a small voice. "I just wrote, 'I love you and miss you. Please call so we'll know you're OK. Love, Mom.'"

"Perfect, Rene." Lauren took a breath, checking her rearview mirror. "OK then, point me in the direction of our next rendezvous."

Eleanor and Ham sat at the back booth of Norros sipping on their coffee while Stephanie did her last round of cleanup. The diner was empty aside from the three.

Stephanie yelled over her shoulder from the end of the counter, "Now, you two don't have to close with me every night just because you're my partners. . . . Or are you watching to make sure I don't dip into the till?" The three enjoyed a hearty laugh, something they cherished more than profits.

Finally coming up for air, Hamilton turned, giving his wife a wink. "Steph, we're gone . . . it's past out bedtime."

"Oh, you two should be locked up somewhere." Stephanie rolled her eyes.

Lauren's headlights flashed across the front of the diner, pulling the threesome's attention to the door. After a beat, Sam, Lauren, Tucker, and Irene entered looking rather bedraggled from their night's excursions. As they proceeded, there was a sense of defeat and frustration in Irene that was clear not only by her expression but her body language as well.

"Are you closed?" Lauren guided Tucker under her arm as the boy walked along in a near zombie state of exhaustion. But upon seeing Eleanor and Ham, he perked up and ran down to the end booth, crawling across Eleanor's lap for a snooze.

Ham stood up to greet the rest of the weary travelers. "Looks like some coffee is in order."

"On its way." Stephanie immediately adopted her waitress mode while Irene, Sam, and Lauren moved toward the back. "How' does everybody like theirs?" Stephanie had a fresh pot brewing in nothing flat.

"None for me," Irene was barely audible. "I thank you though."

"Black for me, Stephanie," Sam smiled. "Appreciate it."

Lauren suddenly made a U-turn to join Stephanie behind the counter, "I'm just going to have some water, and Tuck's probably already asleep."

As Irene and Sam continued down to the end booth, Lauren whispered to Stephanie, "We've been out looking for Chelsea. I think we've hit every music club, at least all the ones I've heard of. I don't know why I'm surprised that there are so many; after all, it's *Nashville*."

"Why are you whispering?"

Lauren considered the question for a moment. "I always whisper when Tuck is sleeping. . . . Silly, huh?" She adopted a regular tone. "I forget he's not a baby anymore."

Stephanie smiled, "I still do that with Trace. . . . So any luck with Chelsea?"

"Nope. We couldn't find her, but one thing's for sure, everybody knows Chelsea. Isn't that amazing? But where she is tonight, I can't figure. . . . Rene left her sweet notes, so I'm sure she'll call. She has to." Suddenly Lauren's exhaustion got the better of her. "We're all whipped. I was hoping we could pray, and I figured this was a good excuse to get Irene and Dad in here."

"Sounds good." Water and coffee in hand, they headed toward the back booth. As polite as Irene was attempting to be, she was clearly depressed at her failed effort to find her daughter. Everyone settled into the booth in silence for a moment until Lauren broke in. "Hey guys, since we're all here, is it OK, Rene and Dad, if we pray? It's very powerful when two or more pray in agreement. If that's OK, I really think it would be a good idea."

Suddenly Irene felt trapped and duped for coming into the diner for what she thought was a simple cup of coffee for her dad. Her discomfort was escalating by the moment along with Sam's who was, to say the least, unaccustomed to public prayer.

But Hamilton seized the moment before it went sour. Stretching his hands out, he took Eleanor's and then Lauren's. Lauren held Irene's hand, who hesitantly took her father's while Eleanor claimed Sam's other one; the circle was formed without much ado as Tucker snoozed on Eleanor's lap.

Ham's voice was compelling as he began. "Father God, we come before you in your Son's name to pray for Chelsea. You have such a heart for all of your children, and Father we ask you to release the heavenly angels to put a hedge of protection around Chelsea. Father God, she may not know you right now, but you know her. You long for her to turn to you so she can experience your unconditional love, grace, forgiveness, joy, and peace. It's so difficult for us here, Father God, to watch our young ones go astray. I pray for Chelsea's whole family, and Irene in particular, that she might rest in you and know that you will cover her child if we come together and ask. You say in your Word that when two or more gather in your name you are in their presence. So, you are here Father God, and you are hearing the cries of a mother for her child. Show her your grace, your power, and your majesty. And speak to Chelsea's heart through the power of the Holy Spirit, even though it may be hardened at this time. Yes, we ask the Holy Spirit to soften her heart. You say in your Word that our prayers will be honored . . . prayers of agreement in your will; and we know Father God, your will is to woo and pursue this child and bring her back to her family. And Father God, you know the heart of a father and a grandfather, so we ask you to encourage Sam to rest in you. As men and as fathers, our desire is to make things right. And when things seem out of our control, it creates a unique dilemma within us, so I ask that you ease that in Sam and let him know that he can also rely on you . . . trust you because you are his father in heaven, and everything that he desires for his family, for his daughters and grandchildren, you've put in his heart. I ask you tonight, Father God, to meet Sam, and if he would meet you, then right here and now, one of your children will have come home. We ask that all in Jesus' mighty name, the Son whom you sent as full payment by sacrificing for each and every one of us. He took our place so we can know you God, you who knows all our needs. We praise you and lift up your name and give you all the glory! Amen, in Jesus' name."

By the time Ham finished, there was not a dry eye in the group; there was also a spiritual presence that was undeniable. As Lauren lifted her eyes to meet her sister's, she saw the slightest hint of softness in Irene that was encouraging. But when she looked at her dad, she had never seen him look so vulnerable. For his entire life, Sam faced the world with a rather stern demeanor. He rarely, if ever, allowed his tender heart to reveal itself. Even with Margaret, he seemed to need to maintain a level of authority. But now, as Lauren looked at her father, he seemed emotionally available. Maybe it was because he had heard a man pray instead of just Lauren talking about God. Surely he had felt the passion in Ham's words that perhaps he had previously considered to be more of a "girl thing." Whatever was going on, Lauren could feel the presence of the Holy Spirit. And no one moved for a moment. No one said a word. They all just continued to hold hands and take it all in. It was truly awesome; it was God in their midst.

Chapter 15

Mad Dash

No doubt Tonya had raised a resilient child in Bobbie. She had just dropped her son off for his first day of school at the brownstone down the block from their new apartment, and although the boy showed slight apprehension, no tears escaped his determined expression. Bobbie marched right in and joined the class of kids who had known one another all year. Not only that, he immediately fit in.

As Tonya chatted with the teacher while she watched her son, she couldn't remember being more proud in regard to the rearing of her child. Surely his confidence had come from a feeling of belonging and being loved; and despite all of the trials and tribulations she had experienced as a teenage mother, she had managed, with the help of her *circle of friends,* to raise her boy with a strong sense of security. Even the teacher commented that she'd never seen a child engage in new circumstances as quickly as Bobbie had.

"Thank you," Tonya cooed. "But I can't take all the credit; Bobbie has a wonderful daddy." And with that said, she suddenly was speared in her heart with sadness.

It was rush hour, pouring rain, and Tonya was not adept at flagging down taxis. She had come to New York City with a modest amount of money in her pocket. So she swore she would leave herself enough time to take the subway to work once she learned the ropes of underground travel. But this morning there was no option other than to try for a yellow chariot to take her to her modeling agency on Fifty-eighth Street and First Avenue.

After unsuccessfully chasing down several cabs, Tonya quickly learned that first day that there really was an art to cab hailing. Defeated, she decided to run into the corner drugstore to buy an umbrella. She asked if the lady behind the counter would mind giving her a big bag so she could protect her modeling portfolio against the weather. The woman sweetly complied.

Tonya had heard so many bad things about New Yorkers, and she chastised herself for assuming the worst. Yes, she needed to remember that drugstore and the kindness of the elderly Asian lady. Still, Tonya wondered if she'd ever embrace a feeling of "neighborhood" where she lived now.

Navigating the sidewalk was a task unto itself, something that Tonya was also unaccustomed to. The Manhattan foot traffic was almost as dense as the street cars, which seemed to be crawling up First Avenue. She quickly concluded that she would be able to walk the twenty blocks to work far more quickly than if she were ever lucky enough to get a cab. As she stretched her long legs in a committed stride down the street while dodging oncomers, she consoled herself as she went that she was saving herself a pretty penny and getting exercise to boot. Unfortunately, her jaunt took its toll on her hair—frizzing from a sleek look to an afro within the first block of her adventure.

When Tonya finally made it through the agency's door, the waiting room was wall to wall with beautiful girls all vying for a spot in front of the camera or on the "catwalk." Still, everyone paused at her entrance. Even the bookers all lined up at their desks in the back room stopped and took in Tonya's image. No doubt, the girl was absolutely stunning. There wasn't a person, male or female, young or old, who cast their eyes on this lovely work of art that didn't at least pause in admiration and often jealousy, as Tonya was soon to learn from her new career.

Tonya had been used to attention all her life. Her gray-blue eyes set against her brown skin had especially made her beauty stand out; and when she finally grew into her almost six-foot dancer frame, there was no question that she had cornered the market in the looks department. But despite her beauty, the most compelling thing about Tonya was her heart.

As she digested the impact she had just made by simply walking into the agency, she thanked God that she had taken her time to get where she now stood. Yes, raising Bobbie, finishing high school, starting college, spending time with her *circle of friends* and church family had given her the stability she innately knew she was going to need to make it her way in *the business.*

⚜

Denise, as she was affectionately called by the fashion world elite, burst out of her private office, arms outstretched awaiting an embrace with Tonya, her newest superstar. The head of the agency greeted the girl as if they had known each other their entire lives; a quick peck on each side of the cheek without messing Denise's lipstick was part of the ritual. And although Tonya stiffened for a moment, feeling all eyes on her concerning the attention she was receiving, she felt relieved to be welcomed with such warmth and fanfare. You see, no matter what Tonya looked like, basically she was shy.

Eleanor would always say to Tonya since she was a teenager, "Your looks can be a passport or a folly. The choice is yours, girl. A lot of people will be takin' your shyness as your bein' aloof, and that's one thing you're not. . . . Although, I'm not sure their thinkin' you're aloof might not be a good thing—you don't want to over-do it and have them city-slickers considerin' that you're difficult to work with. So always remember to put on your armor of God 'cause God's got your back. Yes Missy, he painted a beautiful picture when he made you. . . . My, oh my."

Before Tonya could recover from their air-kiss hello, Denise shuffled her into her private office and closed the door behind them. The girl took in the expansive room, its walls covered with models gracing one magazine cover after another; legends of the business over the last twenty years to the present. It was a catalog of exquisite frozen moments. The collage on the back wall behind Denise's marble and carved wood desk appointed with orchids and crystal carvings was entirely of Denise's photography work. No words needed to be spoken; the stills made the statement that Denise had reigned as one of the top models of all time. It also made it clear that the legend knew the ropes of the fashion world from beginning to end, and that gave Tonya comfort. Still, she sat nervously on the edge of her seat while Denise reviewed her photos in her portfolio, now spread open across the prodigy's desk.

"Yes. . . . No, get rid of that one." Denise was totally engrossed in her editing process as she dramatically flung one of Tonya's prized pictures into the wastebasket.

"Ah, now . . . this one is divine!" She focused on a picture of Tonya looking sultry; eyes straight into the camera, skin glistening from sprayed-on dew. And by the time the procedure was over, Denise disregarded over half of the photos Tonya had acquired from years of amateur photo sessions in Nashville and the one-day shoot sponsored by Denise last month in New York.

Tonya had only been accepted into the Denise Modeling Agency after being mercilessly scrutinized over a period of time. Yes, it was a ruthless process to become a "Denise model." The process started when Eleanor had mailed the agency one of Tonya's pictures and a home video that she had shot of the girls' last birthday. In short order, Denise called Eleanor personally about Tonya coming to New York for an interview.

And the timing was perfect since Tonya probably wouldn't have considered the offer to test in New York if she hadn't just had her fateful fight with Shooter. But given the circumstances, she decided to consider other horizons since her future looked bleak with the love of her life. And as always, Eleanor and Ham were at the helm of encouragement for their spiritually adopted daughter.

Denise zipped up the portfolio and smiled at Tonya with intensity. "You're going to be just marvelous!" This legend was magical when inspired and ruthless when threatened, and it would take the girl from Centennial a while to get a handle on the players who were about to influence her life so profoundly.

Denise shoved a set of contracts at Tonya, which she happily signed having already reviewed a copy with Ham. In fact, he and Eleanor had sent the contracts to their son in Washington just to make sure there weren't any loopholes. No doubt, The Denise Agency was the top tier in the New York fashion world, and Denise had no tolerance for any type of monkey business concerning the girls the agency represented.

Tonya quickly noted that The Denise Modeling Agency was a whole world apart from the smaller Tennessee agencies Tonya had experienced in the past who would work the Nashville area.

Tonya's heart would break for the girls (and guys) who were sold bogus tickets to stardom—the "aspiring" who wanted fame and fortune but clearly had, in reality, no chance of making the big-time. Sadly, there was almost as much to be made in the modeling business by taking gullible young people and their money *nowhere.*

Show biz could be, and often was, a seriously nasty business and Tonya was already in the big leagues. She hadn't really had to pay her dues, something she reminded herself of anytime she entertained a moment of cockiness. Clearly, balance was the name of the game for her to survive this world unscathed.

Denise changed accents as often as outfits, but they all sounded enticing to young Tonya. "I believe you're going to do as well at the fashion shows as you will in photography. That used to be unique but not so much these days. When I was in my heyday, you either were a fashion model, or you were a runway model, and one never crossed over. In fact, I remember the first time I was photographed for the collections for Vogue in Paris when I was fifteen."

Tonya was astounded, "Fifteen?"

"Yes, darling. Believe it or not, you're considered old starting out at twenty, but you have such exquisite skin, and models of color end up having longer careers. Genes, you know."

Tonya couldn't imagine what it would be like to be told she was over the hill at twenty. Still, she knew that it happened all the time to others.

Denise's eyes gleamed as she recounted her past experiences to "the new girl." "We shot the collections all night with Avadon because the clothes had to be on the runways during the day for the buyers. *Vogue* would *never* have accepted a runway model for their fashion spreads." She mused at her memory. "Mind you, I certainly made a pretty penny in my day, but not compared to what has happened with models in the last ten years. They are international stars! They can walk the runways, do the photos, do commercials, and often move right into acting. The world is your oyster, Tonya darling. It's your call. But I would suggest the following. You have an *exclusive* agreement with this agency; and although we'll find you just the right acting agency once we get you started, I want you clearly informed that we will be covering all your activities by way of commission. We will oversee who to align you with in respect to representation . . . accountants, lawyers, agencies, press, etc. I will take care of you, and I expect that we will be together for a long time. There is a lot of scavenging out there. There will be agencies that will offer you services for less percentages or a chunk of money in advance to coerce you away from me. But, as I have stated from our first meeting, we are family, and I expect loyalty. Are you that kind of woman?"

"Yes, ma'am." Tonya confirmed without hesitation. "I signed the contract. But my word is better than any contract."

Her statement surprised Denise as she took a moment to consider the young lady before her. "I almost wish I had a Polaroid camera right now to take a picture of you sitting there at the starting gate of your career. As I said, I will take care of you, Tonya, and protect you. But ours is a tough business, and if your word is better than the contract, you're going to run into issues with people and their attitudes that probably won't be to your liking . . . given your background. When last we spoke, of course you told me about your son, Bobbie. By the way, how is he acclimating to his new school?"

"Very well, ma'am. This morning was his first day. He didn't even cry. He's a good boy. I'd like to have you meet him sometime."

"Delightful," Denise returned a sincere smile, "I would like that. I know it's hard to believe, but I have some grandchildren around your boy's age. After I turned fifty, I decided I didn't have to hide how old I was anymore—I just had to look magnificent and amaze people."

Now she laughed heartily. She was still stick thin and always dressed to the nines. "You also told me about your faith, and although I don't share your beliefs, I do believe they are important to you. I tell all my girls not to compromise their standards, but their standards are different than I sense yours are."

Tonya hesitated for a moment, "I'm not going to be doing anything that will be displeasing to my Lord."

"And who might that be?"

"Jesus Christ, ma'am."

"We have girls in the agency who are Scientologists, Cabalists, Buddhists. . . . The list goes on. And I can't say that I understand all their parameters, so you just need to keep yourself on your own trolley track. But if anybody presses you to do anything that is outside of your comfort zone, you call me, day or night." And with that Denise pulled her personal card out, sliding it across the marble table; it stopped magically in front of Tonya as if directed.

"Thank you, ma'am. But I'm sure I won't have any problems. You're not sending me to Playboy or anything like that."

Denise gave her a wary look. "Please note, my dear, that people do a lot of things in the name of art."

"Well, I thank you, ma'am, for your support."

"Of course, darling. Now Robin presides at the first desk on your right as you leave, and she will give you your bookings for next week. One of the catalog companies is going to try a runway show for the first time, so that will be a nice launch for you." Denise became suddenly effusive, "And then you'll have your DuPont shoot! Congratulations! That's a big one for someone who is just starting out."

"Yes, I'm so grateful, ma'am." Tonya stood and started to extend her hand to shake with Denise, but the woman rounded the desk with three long steps, embracing Tonya once again. "Only hugs here, darling, only hugs. And never call me 'ma'am.' In the fashion world those are words of death."

Tonya was shattered. "I'm so sorry. To me, *ma'am* means respect, ma'am."

"Fine, I'll try to take it as you mean it." And with that, a unique bond between these two was forged for the future.

It was hard for Chelsea to believe she was actually driving down Sunset Strip in a convertible on a glorious sunny day next to her manager on the way to read for a movie. Yes, she had grown up in Manhattan and had a level of sophistication to her that was head and shoulders above most of the girls she'd met in Centennial. But Hollywood wasn't about sophistication; it was about fame and fortune, stardom and celebrities. And as much as Chelsea loved to sing, the prospect of acting really "floated her boat." Being impetuous, her dedication to one aspiration was easily overturned for another at that stage in her life, and now all she could see was her name on movie marquees.

❧

She had received the pages for her scenes (she quickly learned they were called "sides") to read the morning after they had arrived in LA from Nashville. Stephen had gotten Chelsea her own room, courtesy of the production company. It even had a little minibar inside, which Chelsea managed to avoid other than for a candy bar and a half bag of chips. Yes, she was determined to be on her best behavior. Considering the important "go see" looming before her. She knew that salt made her eyes puffy, hence the half bag of chips. She had also decided to take her medication diligently since, she had to admit, they did keep her on more of an even keel emotionally.

"How come they didn't give us the whole script?" She asked Stephen, her hair surrounding her face like a mummy blown from the breezy open-topped car.

Sporting hip sunglasses, Stephen gave her a side glance as he maneuvered through the traffic. "That's what they always do. Remember, you don't have the part yet. But when you get it, and I say *when*, we'll get the script in plenty of time for you to learn your lines."

Chelsea stared up at the billboards along Sunset Strip, transfixed. She could actually see herself up there. *Starring with . . .* she thought as she started to review her favorite actors, *Sean Penn, Robert Downey Jr. . . .*

She pulled out her compact to check her makeup; some of her hair was stuck to her lip gloss. "Are you sure I'm going to have time to get ready when we get there? My hair is all messed up."

"Don't worry, sweet-cakes." Stephen smiled, "I'll take care of everything."

She straightened her red, low-cut dress and checked her stockings for any runs. Satisfied, she admired her high-heel shoes, a perfect color match to her outfit. Not only that, she had topped off her look with the same tone of red lipstick. *Yes*, she thought, *I'm rockin' today.*

Chelsea pulled out the "sides" to take one more gander at her dialogue as they neared the casting office.

Irene had gotten the numbers of each and every manager or head waiter with whom she and Sam had spoken with a few days earlier. Not one of them had seen Chelsea come in at all. Irene was surprised at how kindly they had handled her numerous follow-up calls; most were happy to report what they knew, understanding Irene's concern. Just when she was beginning to feel totally frustrated with no leads, Norman called.

"Mrs. Williams?" Irene had picked up the phone on the first ring in anticipation.

"Yes!"

"Hey ma'am, this is Norman over at The Café. You came a couple of nights ago looking for your daughter?"

"Yes! Yes, that's me!"

"I know we just talked on the phone, and I said I hadn't seen Chelsea . . . is it?"

"Yes, Chelsea, my daughter."

"Yes, ma'am. Well, like I told you, I haven't. But I was thinking about it, and maybe I can do a little research about the guy she always comes in with that she calls her manager. I only heard his first name . . . Stephen, I think."

Irene was so excited she was about to burst. "That would be incredible! I could pay you for your time. Whatever it would take. I just have to know where she is. And now I'm really worried because I've called all the other places and no one has seen her either. It's like she's vanished. In fact, I was considering calling the police."

"Don't do that yet, ma'am. Let me ask around. Our Saturday night's are big, and most everybody who's anybody makes it by here. We've got a good headliner tonight, so I'll ask if anybody knows who this Stephen dude is. I've seen him around for a little over the last year. Somebody must know who he is in the business."

"Oh, thank you so much. I cannot tell you what this means to have some kind of lead!"

"I understand, ma'am. I happen to have a couple of kids myself. I know right where you're at. My boy pulled the same thing on me as soon as he graduated high school. Course, a boy is a little different from a girl. I can't even think how worried you are. I'll do my best."

"Thank you, sir. This is my cell number. I'll have it with me constantly, so don't hesitate to call . . . any time! Again, thank you."

Irene hung up and leaned against her dresser, meeting her gaze in the mirror. What was happening to her life? She looked so haggard and worried. How could it all turn so badly so fast? No, she told herself, you can't fall apart now.

Suddenly, a voice raised up in her, a wail from the pit of her very being. She looked up toward the ceiling. "God, if you exist, let me know. Show me. Help me, now! I can't do this anymore by myself. I have no place to go and . . ." Suddenly she stopped as quickly as she had started, as if some outside force reigned her words back in. Calming, she regarded her image again in the mirror. "What are you—nuts? What are you doing? Talking to the ceiling. Get a grip, Irene."

She grabbed her cell phone and stormed out of the room and down the hall. "Lauren!"

There was no answer from her sister, but William practically tackled her. Then almost tripping over the cat, Irene banged on Lauren's bedroom door; again, no answer. Frustrated, she moved on through the house. "Lauren!" She headed for her parents' apartment and pounded on their door.

"Come in." Her mother yelled from the other side.

When Irene entered, both her parents were on the couch watching TV. "Is Lauren in here? Do you know where she is?"

Margaret shook her head. Without taking his eyes off the TV, Sam answered, "I think she went to the movies with Tucker. She didn't ask you to go?"

"Oh, yes, that's right. She did. I've been calling all the clubs for feedback. Dad, there's some good news. No one's seen Chelsea, as I told you, but that Norman guy from The Café—the nice man called me back. He hasn't seen Chelsea, but remembered when she hung out at his club, she would be with some guy. Oh, Dad. This is so scary!"

Margaret clicked off the TV, realizing her daughter needed their full attention.

"Norman said the guy's name is Stephen. He doesn't know the last name or what he's all about except that Chelsea said that he was her manager . . . a *manager*. She has a manager?!"

Margaret got up to hold her daughter, an affectionate gesture rarely experienced in their family. Suddenly the two women were joined by Sam and the three stood in the middle of the apartment hugging. After a few moments, they all came up for air; tears streamed down Irene's face.

"Norman said he knew how I felt. He has kids, too. He knows what I'm going through, and he's going to try to help find this Stephen person. But if he doesn't find out soon, I'm going to call the police."

"I hate to say this, Irene." Sam hesitated. "I don't think they can do anything except make sure she's not hurt . . . That sort of thing. You know, check the hospitals, etc."

"Oh, Dad! Don't even say that!" Now another layer of terror assaulted Irene. "If she were hurt, she had an ID, and they would have contacted us. So I'm not even going to think about that, Dad."

"You're right. I'm sorry. I didn't mean to upset you more. I just . . ."

Now Margaret spoke up. ". . . Your father was only trying to be logical. There is no way to prove where she is. She could have left town for all we know. That's all he meant. This is a good lead that you have with this Stephen fellow, and it will work out. We'll find her."

"I'm canceling my trip to New York on Monday. I just don't feel good about any of this. I'm not going to be gone when we find her. I don't care about the legal meetings."

"That's right, Irene. Just let your lawyer handle the Ford case. You don't have to be there every minute," Sam concluded.

Irene whirled around, "Yes, I do because those *step*children of mine will fabricate circumstances that could affect the outcome. I'm the only one who knows what Ford really said or promised to me, and to them!"

Margaret tried to soothe her daughter, "Sweetheart, you were married to the man. He cheated on you. He sexually abused your daughter, and then he died before he divorced you. You have rights. They are legal rights, and they are going to stand up. Just let your lawyer handle it. This running back and forth is going to wear you out. You have to stop it."

"Your mother's right. You need to focus on Chelsea. Besides, you still have this legal circus going on here in the local court."

Although Irene felt defeated, she knew her parents were right. Moreover, their display of care truly touched her. "Thanks, Mom . . . Dad. I agree."

"Good girl." Sam patted her lightly on the back.

"Try to get some rest, and let us know the minute you hear anything."

"I will, Mom."

As Irene headed back down the darkened hall flanked by William and Bingo, she thought, yes, she did need to stay someplace where she felt loved, even if she didn't want to admit it. She had been on her own and alone for so long. She never felt she could go to her parents like she had just moments before and expect to get any real support. It always seemed as if they wanted to stay at arm's length from her. She had always rationalized their behavior with the notion that whatever her past dilemmas had been, they really couldn't fix them because they always seemed to revolve around "men problems." Sam would simply throw up his hands at her traumas while her mother flat out couldn't understand how Irene could keep picking men who didn't treat her properly. And she made no bones about saying so.

Although Irene had only been married twice with both unions turning out to be disasters, she had also been engaged many times. All ended up breaking apart amid great drama. But beyond men, Irene had finally realized after years of therapy that there were other roots of her pain, namely from her relationship with her parents. And on rare occasions when those divides were addressed, the family exchanges only ignited furious and hurtful words and accusations that further split and conquered the fallible relationship between this daughter and her parents.

As Irene gazed into the empty living room that night, she slowed her pace to a standstill. And for the first time she recognized that the strides in healing that had been made within her family had all happened since they had moved in with Lauren—despite all of the horrific events that seemed to plague them recently. Irene also realized that she really should embrace the good parts of Lauren's vision for their family's reconciliation. And now it seemed it was not only Lauren who had changed, but their parents as well, most notably, Sam. Irene had never seen her father more tender, more protective, more available.

Irene smiled, slightly thinking of one of Lauren's twisted sayings she'd shared the other day. "Now, Rene, don't look a gift horse in the eye. He might blink and miss you."

Actually, your version makes more sense than "Don't look a gift horse in the mouth." What would that mean? Irene had laughed.

"Exactly . . . that's why I like mine because, if you look a gift horse in the mouth, he might bite you." Then Lauren went on one of her diatribes. "Rene, have you ever seen a horse get its teeth floated? Let's start with the term itself. It doesn't make any sense. What does that mean, floating? Actually, what they do is put this giant metal thing in the horse's mouth to force it open. They usually have to tranquilize the poor beast because, after all, what horse is going to want half a metal crow bar in its mouth? . . . The dentist or vet steadies the horse by holding its neck up with a rope like they're hanging it. It's the most horrifying vision you've ever seen!"

With that, Irene shut off her mental dialogue with Lauren and proceeded to her bedroom. It was definitely time to wind down, if that were at all possible.

Chapter 16

The Real Deal

Stephanie had been receiving rude messages on her answering machine for several days now.

The first couple of "postcards from hell" she listened to all the way through, trying to discern who might be the bearer of such disturbing language and content. But she didn't recognize the voice; its timbre sounded rather female to her. In her concern, Stephanie considered that the messages might be from somebody trying to reach Trace, but each recording was specifically addressed to her, not her son.

After the third round of verbal abuse, when Stephanie heard another message begin, she immediately erased the tape, unwilling to digest the disgusting sentiments of the mysterious voice. She also erased the messages because she never wanted to chance Trace overhearing the disturbed ramblings. And that actually made her sick to her stomach, then the fear snuck in. No, they weren't threatening messages, per se, but they were rude and lascivious, an invasion of smut in her home. And once the recorded words were registered in Stephanie's mind, it was so hard to take them captive and not have them pop in her dreams or, for that matter, her thoughts during the day. Clearly, whoever was trying to disturb her was doing a good job.

Stephanie finally decided to confide in Eleanor and Ham, not sure exactly how she would even describe the verbal abuse that had been left for her to ponder.

After closing that night at the back of the diner, Stephanie, Ham, and Eleanor were in deep conversation concerning the phone messages Stephanie had received. Eleanor couldn't remember seeing Ham so worked up, not for years that is. Eleanor knew full well the warning signs Ham flagged when he was entertaining a bout with his temper. Yes, he had conquered his post-traumatic stress disorder after his stint in Vietnam years ago, but that was not to say the man couldn't be incensed. Eleanor recalled when she had recently gone through her breast cancer; her husband was well able to maintain his decorum, handling his feelings of being out of control better than she'd imagined he could for a man who insisted on making things right for the ones he loved. But now, as she watched Ham digest what Stephanie had shared with them, he looked like he wanted to punch someone—now!

"Have you changed your number?" At Ham's suggestion, Stephanie felt ridiculous. *Why hadn't she thought of that?* She guessed she hadn't been thinking. She was just reacting. She sheepishly shook her head no.

"Make it unlisted!" Ham continued. "But don't do it until you get one of the calls on tape . . . because if the sicko persists, we're going to need that proof—voice, words, innuendo if we're going to nail the creep. We'll take the tape to the police and see if they can track it down somehow."

Feeling more trapped than ever, Stephanie stuttered, "What if they don't call again?"

Eleanor took Ham's hand, which was beginning to ball up into a tight fist. "If they don't call again, then you don't have a problem, do you, Steph? It'll be alright."

Finally, Stephanie took a deep breath, "I have just been so shook up about all this."

"Girl, you've been through your son almost dyin' and taking over the diner. . . . I'd say you've been under a little strain lately." Eleanor gave her friend a reassuring smile.

But Ham was not about to be sidetracked by supportive chatter; he was totally focused on understanding the situation that was happening to his friend. "You say it sounds like a woman?"

"Yes . . . That's what's so strange. Why would a woman say those kinds of things to me? To another woman?" Now Stephanie was visually shaking.

Ham reflected for a moment, "Maybe a woman's saying them, but a man's behind them. And the only person I can think of that would be looking to hurt you would be Norro."

Stephanie shook her head, "But he's left. He's left town with his tail between his legs like a beat dog."

"My point exactly. You don't think he can oversee this kind of garbage long distance?"

"Oh, you're really scaring me now."

Eleanor slid over closer to her friend. "Ham, I think you're gettin' carried away."

"My purpose is not to scare you." He glanced at Stephanie. "I'm just trying to evaluate the situation from all possibilities." Now he turned to his wife, "We haven't had any calls, have we? You're not keeping anything from me are you?"

His intense expression caused Eleanor to pause. "Ham, I would never do that. But I surely don't like seeing you gettin' this upset."

Ham was clearly struck in a sore spot. "I won't be taking from either one of you not telling me what's going on just to keep my blood pressure down! Something doesn't feel right here, and I intend to get to the bottom of it." And with that, the ladies held their tongues knowing Ham had just put the period at the end of their conversation.

❧

Brian, Lauren, and Tucker made their way through the crowd as all dispersed from the evening movie.

"Well, that was dumb." Lauren casually commented to Brian as they headed toward her truck.

"No it wasn't, Mom!" Tucker seemed almost offended. "I thought the mole had a cool hairdo."

"Sorry, sorry, Tuck. I actually thought it was cute, too." She glanced at Brian. "At least it didn't have any bad words . . . But it also didn't have a moral to its story. . . ."

"Whatever happened to Superman?" Brian said lightly.

Lauren shushed him, whispering, "He fell off a horse."

"I didn't mean the actor. I meant the kind of character Superman was . . . is. Why don't they come up with a new hero a bit more dynamic than a mole?"

"Dad, I like the mole!"

"Well, it's not much to aspire to, son."

"What's *aspire* mean?"

"To look up to."

"Well see, you're silly. You can't look *up* to him—moles are little. I would have to look down on him."

"Exactly my point, son. Who wants a hero you look down on?"

"And why don't they make movies that entertain the whole family. I think they dumb down the message to you kids a lot. You're smarter than they think, you know?" Lauren encouraged her boy.

"Smarter than some big people you know, Mom."

"Uh, Tuck, I said 'smart,' not 'smarty-pants.'"

"Sorry. . . . Can I open the truck?"

"Sure, when we get a little closer. . . . No disappearing between vehicles OK?"

Tucker nodded, recognizing rules were not going to be bent that night despite the fact that it was the first time he'd been out with his mom and dad in a long time.

He watched with curiosity as his mom's attention turned back to Brian. "No, but I mean it, Bri. Remember we used to watch things, at least I did growing up with my parents . . . *The Honeymooners, Lassie Come Home.* . . . What's wrong with that? I don't understand Hollywood. I read an article yesterday in the newspaper that stated that G-rated movies, across the board, make tons of money. I think it said the most money of all releases, and yet the bozos keep making the "R" and "X" rated garbage. You don't even have to be rated X to be X-rated anymore. You can be rated R and be X-rated."

"Like the X-Men?" Tucker piped in.

"No, no. The ratings give you an idea of what's in the movie so you don't get surprised with bad things when you think you're just going out for some family entertainment."

"Bad things like what?"

"Well, like violence or other things. Bad words, bad behavior."

"Oh . . . Mom, can I do the keys now?"

"Sure, buddy." Lauren pulled her truck keys out of her purse and tossed them to her boy as soon as he was in safe proximity to the truck. And as he entertained himself by clicking the automatic door opener on and off, Brian and Lauren finally had a moment to themselves.

"That was kind of fun to do that together. The movies and all." She looked at Brian with a silly smile.

"Yes, it was. I enjoyed it. Thanks for inviting me."

"Sure." There was an awkward pause.

"Listen, Lauren. About the other day . . ."

She wasn't thrilled with the expression on Brian's face, and became suddenly embarrassed at all the imaginations she'd had for their future following their kiss. Maybe she had read the whole thing wrong. Not the kiss; no one could deny that he had kissed her. But maybe he was just being a guy. Yes, that was what she decided before she cut him off. It was just a "guy thing."

". . . Don't worry about it. I understand . . . A quick stroll down memory lane, that's all. It's fine."

Brian studied her for a minute. "Well, that's not all it was for me. Is that all it was for you?"

She stuttered for a moment. "I . . . uh . . . no. . . . I don't know. What was it for you?"

Brian laughed. "OK, I'll show you mine if you show me yours."

"You sound like a kid . . . or a pedophile."

"That's not funny."

She decided to try to corral the conversation into a more meaningful direction. "What were you going to say before I so rudely interrupted you and said it was nothing when it was something?"

Brian was enjoying watching Lauren flounder, "I was going to say it was 'something' before you said it was 'nothing.'"

"How about a few more adjectives?" She prompted. "Like, what *kind* of something?"

"It was a start, I think. At least I'd like it to be a start. If you would."

"What's a start? The kiss, the intent, the 'show you mine,' or the 'about the other day.' How am I supposed to answer that unless I know what the finish line looks like?"

"Well, you certainly have not simplified since our divorce."

Lauren glared at him, "Was that a compliment or a complaint?"

Brian glanced at Tucker who was still totally involved with the keys, the truck door locks and his power over them. "Neither. It was a request. Are you saying we can't take this one step at a time and see where it leads us?"

Rarely speechless, Lauren allowed herself a moment to regroup before she tripped over her own words. And, as logical as Brian's sentiments sounded to her, and as much as Lauren wanted to say "sure" to his suggestion, to be honest, she was scared out of her boots about getting involved again. Still, she hadn't been able to keep Brian out of her thoughts or her heart. No! She also knew that his was not the right approach to rekindle—if that's what they were trying to do.

Suz had coached Lauren about the possibility of this very moment in terms of healthy boundaries and intent. And as much as Lauren just wanted to fall into Brian's arms and "play it by ear," she knew that wasn't going to get them any farther than where they had been before, which was a divorce. No, she was convinced, the playing field has to be identified before the courtship begins!

"Brian, I'd love to say 'sure' and act really casual and cool about this whole thing, but I don't think that either one of us is up for games at this point in our lives, especially considering Tuck. I don't want to get hurt, you don't want to get hurt, and we surely do not want to hurt our boy."

"No, you're right. I'm sorry." Brian said with an unfamiliar maturity she had never heard before. He gathered his thoughts carefully before continuing. "I intend to make this family whole again, and it can take as long as it needs to make it right. . . . But that's my finish line. That's my goal."

Lauren was dumbfounded. As much as she had dreamed about hearing him say that, once his words were delivered, she felt like she was in some sort of fantasy world.

And there was more to delight and surprise her as Brian continued. "I let you down before, and I can't promise you that I won't let you down again, but I think I have a better handle on it all now. Who I'm supposed to be to you as a man, and as a father to Tuck. I think I'm finally beginning to understand what you were always trying to drive me to as far as my faith—my relationship with Jesus and the headship of my family."

Lauren flat out could not believe what she was hearing. Who was this man standing before her? Did he actually just say "Jesus"? . . . "Headship"?

"What . . . ?" Was all she could muster in response.

"Now . . ." Brian regarded her, amused by her incredulous expression. "Do you mean, did I actually say *Jesus*?"

She nodded like a puppet on a string.

"I had to practice for a while, even in the confines of my conservative church."

Lauren immediately offered an apology. "Bri, I didn't mean to be rude about . . ."

". . . No, listen. I've learned a lot from my men's group . . . guys that I really respect, starting with my buddy at work who makes me look like a child, and he's my junior! But when we meet, it gives us a chance to talk about the real deal. About our fears and our aspirations, our anger and frustrations, and what's important and what it really means to be committed and to deal with what I have to change. Lauren, I was always telling you what you had to change. . . . That's up to you." Suddenly Brian fumbled in what seemed too big a transformation in character. "But hey, don't get me wrong, it doesn't mean you don't have things to work on."

Lauren laughed, "Let me count the ways."

They both enjoyed a moment of vulnerability. "We both do, OK? And I'm just going to work on me. The point is, I couldn't bury the fact that I love you under the pile of things that I didn't like about you."

Lauren hesitated. "OK, I think that was very romantic. Although it kind of came out a little harshly . . . As in, you hate me?"

Brian put his arm around her. "Of course not. . . . Listen, if you want to pursue this, I just want you to know that I do." He glanced again at Tucker who was now inside the truck, flashing the headlights on and off, amazed that he hadn't been curtailed by his parents as yet.

And when Brian and Lauren looked into each other's eyes, they knew the direction of their relationship had been clarified.

Chapter 17

Ready or Not

To Pam, it was clear that morning why Centennial was what one might call a "Specialty Boomtown." Even though she had lived in the sleepy southern suburb her entire life, she could never take a walk down Main Street without noting the postcard perfect architecture, plantings, and quaint shops that made up Centennial, Tennessee.

And although she was fully aware of the shadows of the oppressed that remained, and the deceit of the wheelings and dealings that constantly transpired behind the scenes of this lovely town, she had to admit, on the face of it, Centennial offered a charming, 1950s "Father Knows Best" existence.

Her strolls were a good diversion, Pam told herself, since she recognized that she was virtually obsessed with the areas of need and repair in Centennial; specifically, racial reconciliation and equal education for future leaders. Oh, how many times had she expounded on these sentiments over the last two years as she, Ham, and Eleanor knocked on various corporations doors in an effort to sponsor their Hope School.

Pam had continued to struggle with their lack of success at raising funds as well as what she considered to be her personal failure in counseling Chelsea.

Still, as she neared Norros Diner to grab a quick cup of coffee, she set her thoughts on God's promises, determined not to succumb to negativity. After all, she had to set a good example for the girls attending the abstinence class she'd taken over at the high school now that Tonya had moved to New York. And as she purposefully recited Scripture along her way, she actually felt God's words lifting the heavy coat of frustration off her back.

Yes, Pam was coming through what had been a long, dry season. She realized that, finally somewhere deep down she had been questioning God's timing and she was ready and willing to trust him wholeheartedly.

Ham and Eleanor had been especially sensitive to Pam's frustrations as they had become partners with her in the dream of the Hope School. And it was due to, for the most part, their understanding her pain and the wise counsel they offered that finally began to release the stronghold over Pam.

Just last night at dinner at Ham and Eleanor's home, a revelation happened; Pam had cleaned her plate of Eleanor's fried chicken, mashed potatoes, grits, and collard greens with relish. It was a known fact that the food at Norros and Eleanor's home cooking were the only two places Pam would overindulge, her slight frame unaccustomed to mountains of vittles. But, it always seemed worth it at the time, like a Thanksgiving dinner.

So there Pam was, leaning back in her chair in an effort to make a little bit more room for the apple pie that sat before her, when Ham let her in on his idea.

"If you agree, Eleanor and I think it would be prudent to hire a professional fund-raiser for the Hope School."

At first, Pam took his suggestion as another failure on her part; her reaction was her cross to bear as an "overachiever." Eleanor knew immediately where her friend was going in her mind and tried to sideswipe her thoughts before they traveled to a not-so-pretty place.

"Pam, God gifts every one of us with different talents. Clearly, you are not designed, nor am I or Ham, to raise funds. We're teachers. . . . Ham and I have been prayin', and we've been watchin' your angst over waitin' on the Lord to do somethin', when maybe we've been just tyin' his hands. Ham did a little research on some people who are effective in fund-raising and work off a commission."

Ham interjected, not wanting the flow of information to slow down. "Bottom line, it won't cost anything. If they don't come up with the funds, we're not out anything, and they don't make anything. And Miss Eleanor and I have figured it doesn't get any better than that. I don't know about you, but I'm tired of looking for money in all the wrong places. I say, 'God, take this from us.'"

Pam's face finally exploded in an expression of release. "Amen!"

Yes, Pam felt about two tons lighter since last night. Her frustrations had actually taken over to the point where it hurt when she breathed, she had been so tense. But now, every time her old negative tapes would creep into her thoughts, she'd rebuke them and renew them with God's promises, and her peace would return. What a relief!

Lauren lingered on Brian's professions of intent from the other night during her afternoon break at the shelter before Tucker got out of school. She marveled at how she had successfully made it through the last forty-one hours and twelve and a half minutes without calling Brian, determined to let the man take the lead in what promised to be a new chapter in their lives. Of course, she was anxious over the fact that Brian hadn't called her. Why he hadn't made the next move toward their renewed relationship? But then she caught herself, recognizing her old "control" patterns. "Pushing" was exactly how she married him the first round before establishing a healthy spiritual foundation on which to base their union.

At the "union" thought, her mind wandered back to their kiss. Oooo, she swooned. What a nifty thing to look forward to. But before she could continue on down that path, there was an anxious bang on the door announcing her sister's arrival.

To say Irene looked agitated was an understatement. Lauren was immediately on her feet in concern. "What's up?"

"I found her."

"You found Chelsea!?"

"No, I didn't find her, but Norman found that guy Stephen's contact."

"What do you mean *contact?*" Lauren had moved around to the front of her desk where she now faced Irene. "*Contact* sounds like some kind of drug ring."

"No." Irene dismissed Lauren's notion as quickly as it popped up. "*Contact*, as in a phone number. He's not responded yet, but we have it. It's his cell phone number. And I left a message. He actually has an answering service. He's a real person. . . . But whether he has Chelsea remains to be seen." Irene started pacing.

"What did you say?"

"I said, 'he's a real person,' and . . ."

"No, I meant, what message did you leave him?"

Irene whirled around and stared at her sister like she had three heads. "I said who I was and that I wanted to speak to my daughter. . . . What do you think I said?"

Lauren paused for a second, worried about Irene's level of agitation, "But you said it nicely, Rene? Didn't you?"

"*Nicely?*" Irene mocked her words. "What do you mean *nicely?* Like inviting him over for dinner and promising to smother him with gifts so he will tell me *where my daughter is!*"

"Rene, calm down. You don't even know if Chelsea is with him. Did you get an address?"

"No. Norman said that he had heard he lived near Music Row and that he used an answering service that a lot of the professionals in town use. So I was able to call up and act dumb." Again, she glared at her sister.

Lauren quickly responded, "Which, of course, you're not."

"Of course," Irene continued. "I acted like I was a label executive looking for talent. I guess that's what you call them . . . Or clients? Anyway, it seemed to work. I told the service that I had misplaced his last name. Stephen Garrison, they said. That's when I left a message."

Lauren looked at her sister for a moment, "What if it's the wrong Stephen?"

Irene's frustration was escalating again. "I don't care if it's the wrong Stephen—I only care if it's the right Stephen! If it's the wrong Stephen, then he won't return my call, and if it's the right Stephen . . ."

Lauren finished the sentence for her, ". . . He still might not return your call depending on what Chelsea says."

"Who are you, the *grim reaper*? I came in here to tell you that for the first time I feel I at least have a lead! You're the optimist between the two of us. Why are you dashing my hopes?"

Lauren pulled up a chair and invited Irene to sit. "Sorry, sorry. You're completely right. I hate when you do that to me. I hate it. I hate it. You're totally right. One lead is better than no lead at all. How long ago did you call?"

"On the way over here. Frankly, I wanted to be with you if he calls back."

Lauren wagged a finger at Irene, "*When* he calls back. Not if. We will be positive. You were right, and I am busted. He will call back, and we will find out what's going on."

Just then Tucker burst into the room delivered by Clive. "Hey, Mom!" He jumped into her arms, his backpack smacking Irene as he sailed by. "The eggs hatched today in school, and all the little chicks are cute. Except one got smushed in the grating."

Irene muttered, "How disgusting. We didn't have to go through that scenario until high school biology."

Lauren put Tucker down, "Give your Auntie a hug."

Tucker promptly complied, always happy to see Irene. "Why are you here? You never come here."

"Nice to see you, too, Mr. Tucker." This boy was magic to Irene. Somehow, no matter what kind of mood she was in, he could always divert her attention. "I'm waiting for a phone call. What are you doing here?"

Tucker squealed, "I'm here to help Mom with all the animals. You wanna come?"

Irene melted at the boy's invitation, following him like a puppy on a leash, her cell phone clasped firmly in her hand. No, she didn't want to miss the phone call about Chelsea, but she also didn't want to miss this time with Tucker. And that melted Lauren's heart. *Sweet,* she thought as she followed her sister and her son out the door.

※

The ladies' room at the casting agent's office was crammed to the gills with young actresses, all prettier than the next.

Yes, Chelsea was experiencing her first taste of real competition, all in a five-by-eight square-foot area of primping as the girls vied for a sliver of mirror space over the sinks.

In Nashville, Chelsea had heard some amazing talent on open-mike nights, but the LA scene was a new animal to her.

She didn't have any idea what caliber actresses these girls were who were infesting the ladies room that day; all she knew was that she was barely holding her own in the looks department. Yes, it was a crash course in reality for this eighteen-year-old, and by the time Chelsea got back out in the waiting room, she practically dragged Stephen toward the front door in a panic.

"I can't do this. I don't know what I'm doing. I've never read 'sides' before! Sides to me is a side of a cow. . . . They're all in there, a bazillion beautiful girls talking about the last movie they made, what kind of push-up bra they have on, the last surgery they had, who their boyfriends are, how many times they've read for this company, blah, blah, blah. It's scary, Stephen. I don't know what I'm doing. At least when I sing, I know the lyrics, I have the voice. . . . I have some of the moves."

Escorting Chelsea outside, he put his arm around her, then walked her around the corner so no one could see her come apart; Chelsea didn't like all the competition of the "cattle call."

She expected Stephen to soothe her concerns; he was always so liquid in his answers when dealing with her insecurities. But as they rounded the corner, and Stephen leaned her against the stucco pink wall of the building, she looked at him, realizing he was angry and serious as a heart attack.

"Get a grip!" He thundered. "Figure out how to use all this fear you're feeling and put that energy into a role. Remember, the character's supposed to be vulnerable. This character wants to run, just like you want to run now. Use it. But just stop whining in my face, Chelsea. You wanted this break, and I got you this break. I'm standing here with you. . . . I put everything I've got into you in a short period of time, and I've delivered. Now it's your turn to deliver!"

His tactics worked; she sank into submission, "OK, I'm sorry. . . ."

He cut her off, "Don't say you're sorry; just go in and do it!" Then he softened slightly. "Do you want me to run the lines with you again?"

She shook her head, mortified. "I know the lines. . . . I just . . ."

Now he grabbed her by the shoulders, ". . . Listen to me. I believe in you. That doesn't happen. Maybe you need to be out there longer, blowing around in the wind looking for somebody to give you direction. I'm here. You're lucky you've got a shot. Get it together."

Mesmerized, she shook her head like a rag doll, which seemed to incite him all the more. He pressed her back against the wall harder, then let her go as if he were walking away.

"Stupid me," he mumbled to himself. Then he turned back to her, furious. "You told me you had what it takes! You pulled me into your little sob story, and you had me believing in you. It's not about me, Chelsea, it's about you. Do you really want it, or do you just want to play games? You just want to stay on your meds and have your little 'breakdowns.' Listen, the best actresses are usually the most wounded ones. As far as I can tell, unless you've been lying to me since we met, you've got a lot of drama to pull from. Acting is just being real in an imaginary circumstance, and all I can see in you is a girl having trouble being imaginary in a real circumstance. It's called right now, right here. Your shot. You blow it, I'm gone."

Her makeup wasn't perfect; she had eaten off half her lipstick by the time she walked in the room to face the casting agents. Yes, there was a group of them—five men to review Chelsea's talents. Not just her acting, but from the bottom of her red high heels to the top of her blonde hair, they scrutinized her.

Stephen wasn't allowed to go into the casting room and Chelsea felt like she was in a den of wolves. Having never been through a "reading" before, she was totally out of her element and totally off balance from the lashing Stephen had given her in the alleyway. But one thing sustained her—her anger.

No doubt Chelsea would have walked away from the whole scene if it had not been for her total desperation to make her own way, call her own shots and have her own power. Yes, that was it, she wanted her own power. She had been under everyone's thumb for so long and she was sick of it.

When she sat down on the chair in the center of the room, it was hard, cold metal; not an ounce of comfort did it afford her as she quickly decided how to cross her legs. Suddenly shy, she tugged at the hem of her skirt. Her mind raced. Her outfit wasn't anywhere near as provocative as those worn by her competition in the waiting room, yet she could see by the men giving her the once-over, somehow it was working for her.

Her anger pulled her voice up out of a place she didn't know existed as she made a bold move. "Gentleman, I'm Chelsea, and if it's alright with you, I'd like to sing a song first . . . because I'm a singer. My manager tells me if I can show you I'm an actress, too, I'll also be able to sing the title song for your film."

Chelsea actually managed to surprise the hardened veterans in the room; they had never heard such an approach, such presence and determination. The bald fat man on the couch finally answered, "Sure, sweetheart. . . . Show us what you've got."

Chapter 18

"Take Two"

Bobbie hadn't stopped talking for the past three days about his new friends at school. In fact, Tonya had already made plans for him to have a boy named Cooper over for a playdate on Saturday. "Oh my," she reveled, "God is so good!"

Tonya was also full of news. After putting her boy to bed, she spent her evenings on the phone with Pam and Eleanor for catch-ups, prayers, and strategies.

"I can't believe it, Pam! I'm shaking just thinking about tomorrow. It's the real deal! All week I've been on 'go-sees,' and they went fine, but now I have to do that runway show for the catalog people, and I'm nervous as a cat."

"Tell me again what a 'go-see' is?"

"It's when you *go* and they *see* if they want to hire you. The photographer or clients look at my book . . . *my pictures,* and give me a radical once-over and book me . . . Hopefully."

"OK, I wrote it down this time. Promise I'll practice the jargon. Hey, and about tomorrow, you'll be great. You're a gazelle. What are you worried about?"

"I'm not a gazelle in high heels. I think I've worn them four times in my entire life. Actually, I've been practicing at home and feeling pretty stupid in the process. Bobbie walked in on me once when I was strutting across the living room like an *attitude on stilts.* I looked so weird, he actually asked if I had broken something."

Pam giggled. "I miss my boy."

"He misses you, too."

Pam looked at her watch, "Wow, it's late. What time is your call in the morning? Hey! Listen to me. I already have the 'lingo' down . . . 'call,' 'go-sees.' I'm a regular jet-setter!"

"I wish you could jet-set yourself over here *now*! I miss you, and you're right, it is late. I have to take Bobbie to school at eight sharp, and then I go right over to the show."

"Well, you better get your beauty sleep. Not that you need any. You're going to be great."

"Speaking of sleep, how are you doing in that department?"

"Oh, I feel like a new person. Not all the time, but I'm just glad I don't have to think about raising funds for the school anymore. I've been on cloud nine, especially while I'm sleeping. I'm actually having sweet dreams! Can you imagine?"

"No . . . and I'm definitely jealous. Listen, you get some sleep, and we'll talk tomorrow."

"OK . . . Love ya. Bye-o." As Tonya hung up the phone, she felt a surge of excitement about her first real modeling job the next morning. And then her nervousness set in; there wasn't going to be much sleep for her, she concluded.

Tonya had checked the address three times and had even splurged on a cab, but she was still having trouble finding the entrance to the showroom.

She had been reminded by the agency that very morning that this was an unusual booking because the catalog company was trying something completely new; they were going to photograph a runway presentation of their fall line to use in their catalogs to revamp what had been their "stilted" photography look. It was a bold move on the company's part, and they were paying a pretty penny for some of the top models to do their show.

Tonya had asked if there were going to be rehearsals or, at least, some way she could get on the runway before the actual event, but the answer kept coming up "no." She had only been sent to a fitting with a seamstress, her location having nothing to do with the actual site of the show.

Tonya decided to wear her one pair of high heels to arrive at the shoot so she would at least look the part, but as she pounded the pavement on Sixteenth Street on the lower West Side of Manhattan, she was sorry every step of the way for her fashion decision; her heel was already suffering from a blister. Nonetheless, her pain was immediately overcome by the relief she felt when she finally found the entrance to the showroom. She had envisioned the building to look completely different— elegant, Fifth Avenue chic. But in reality it was an old warehouse and with an iron grate in front of an open freight elevator that

Tonya had to navigate and conquer before it would deliver her to the sixth floor of the building.

The elevator opened into a huge reception and showroom filled with lights, photographers, buyers, and catalog company employees scampering about. Tonya was surprised there wasn't a separate entrance for the models, and at that instant she decided she had made the right decision to wear heels because, as she stepped into the room, all eyes were on her.

A pencil-thin, bobbed-haired woman in her sixties rushed over to direct her; the woman had a pad filled with scribbles from top to bottom. She checked Tonya's name off once she could finally hear it above the escalated conversation of the mingling crowd.

Looking above her horn-rimmed glasses, she regarded Tonya a moment before pointing her to a side door. "You're new."

"Yes, ma'am."

"Tonya, you say? No last name?"

"No, ma'am. Miss Denise advised that I only use my first name, ma'am."

The woman giggled in demeaning fashion, "Yes, single names are popular these days." Again, she looked Tonya up and down and then pointed. "You better be good. Go back there and ask for Juan."

Tonya was a bit rattled by the woman's rude approach, but chalked it up to the New York demeanor she'd noticed in so many people in the fashion industry. No, there had been absolutely no friendly greetings put forth when she had walked into the various studios for her "go-sees"—not by the photographers, their assistants, or receptionists. There were no "welcomes," no "hello," no smiles, just attitude. It was a consistently painful experience for Tonya, the aloofness making her feel about two inches tall. In a short three or four days, the new girl in town had more uncomfortable confrontations with her shyness than she had survived her entire life. On her "go-sees," Tonya was having to force herself to speak up and ask someone passing by where she should "go"; she was treated as if she were completely invisible. It was hateful.

Oh, how Tonya was ever thankful for the lovely lady on the first day in the drugstore who had at least smiled at her and, of course, Denise's enthusiasm upon her arrival at the agency. If she had not at least received their brief expressions of kindness, Tonya figured she would have simply shriveled up and died of embarrassment by day two.

She actually had shared her feelings with Eleanor who innately seemed to be plugged into Tonya's sensitivities since she had turned a teenager. Of course, Miss Eleanor was there with good advice for her young friend. "Rise above it, sugar. They obviously had bad rearin'. Give 'em a sweet smile and a sweeter prayer, and know that they're better to have met you."

So it was, that first morning of professional work, that Tonya forced herself to sport a pleasant smile instead of expressing what she really felt, which was terror, as she entered the side door.

If she had thought the front showroom was a cacophony of sound and mass movement, the back area where the girls were preparing to begin the show was nothing less than mayhem. But what caused Tonya to freeze in her steps was what she was soon to learn was normal fare in a runway fashion show; half-naked girls with curlers in their hair—makeup people, male and female, running around gluing eyelashes on the models—hairstylists blowing "dos," and dressers pinning and shaping the clothes onto the girls who seemed totally oblivious to all the poking and prodding. It was as if they weren't even in their own skin, distant and unfazed that half of them weren't even dressed!

Communication was curt between all, delivered in different languages and various accents when English was actually being spoken. Two French girls were chatting in the corner while Juan, the head hairdresser, was barking instructions to his assistant in Spanish. And once again Tonya stood there as if she were invisible, wondering who she might ask for directions.

Thankfully, Juan noticed Tonya stuck in her place of confusion and screamed across the room, "You girl! Are you Tonya?"

She stepped forward, tentatively, "Yes, sir."

"Sit." He pointed to a chair next to a blonde, blue-eyed beauty from Sweden. "You're late." he snarled.

"I'm sorry, sir. I couldn't find the entrance."

He laughed with his assistant, "You can drive a truck through it. . . ."

As Tonya started to take her seat, Juan grabbed her hair with his hand like he was yanking on the scruff of some dog's neck.

"Extensions?"

"What, sir?"

"Is this your hair, or do you have extensions? And if you do, are they synthetic or real? We wouldn't want you to melt, dear."

Tonya was at a loss for words for a minute. "It's my hair, so it's real. . . . What I mean, sir, is that I grew it. It's natural."

All the while Tonya was trying to answer Juan, it seemed impossible for her to unglue her gaze from the Swede sitting next to her in a totally see-through camisole. She might as well have been wearing nothing at all; and although Tonya didn't want to look at her, she had never seen such a thing. It was like she was passing a car accident on the road, and as hard as she tried not to stare, she simply couldn't help herself.

Juan twirled around pointing to an assistant, "Put her in hot rollers." Then he was back in Tonya's face, "As soon as they get the rollers in, go over there to Mark, and he'll dress you."

The assistant pulled off Tonya's jacket to get better access to the girl's hair while Tonya dumped her belongings at the foot of her seat. The only thing she could think of as her hair was being rolled was, "Go over to Mark, and *he will dress you.*" She was petrified.

She had been careful to wear nude-colored underwear as suggested by her agency; Tonya had invested in full under-pants and a bra bigger than any bathing suit since the 1930s. Nonetheless, she couldn't get past the idea that she would be standing in her underwear in front of a man who would be "dressing her." She had been embarrassed enough at the fitting with the seamstress who finally had to ask Tonya to stand still so she could pin her clothes without stabbing her since the girl was wiggling so much in discomfort.

And as her concerns mounted, it happened; horrors of hor-rors, as the last roller was being put in Tonya's hair, she looked in the mirror and saw that her mascara was pouring down her face.

She was actually crying, just like she had done with Shooter there last night, and she simply couldn't stop.

The model next to her finally shifted her stare, eyeing Tonya with curiosity as if she was some alien. Tonya smiled sheepishly, grabbing for a Kleenex. "I've got something in my eye."

Hearing her comment, the makeup girl working on another model to her right threw some eye drops Tonya's way.

"Why don't you get dressed first, and I'll put your lashes and lipstick on over there at the wardrobe side when your eyes dry out," offered the makeup guru who couldn't have been much older than her early twenties. She was oriental, beautiful, and had a soft expression to her, unlike any other person in the entire room.

"Thanks," Tonya said gratefully.

"I'm Sue," the girl nodded. "It'll be OK. There's a lot of lint floating around here. I get it in my eyes all the time."

Tonya looked down at the Visine and grabbed for the hand mirror in front of her. The fear of feeling so exposed physically and emotionally brought on the involuntary tears, but now the fear of being unprofessional override Tonya's discomfort. Although she did decide that she wasn't taking off her underwear, no matter who pressured her—and she was never going to do a "runway" again.

Then, as that thought scampered across her mind, she considered the fact that she might have just experienced the shortest modeling career in history.

Chelsea couldn't believe the paparazzi actually singled her out, flashing their cameras at her like fireworks on the fourth of July. The entrance to The Bistro, the hottest restaurant in "La-La Land," was like walking the red carpet on Oscar night. Everyone who arrived in their limos, BMWs, Lamborghinis, or Mercedes had to be "somebody," Chelsea thought. And if they weren't somebody in the film business, they were somebody who made a heck of a lot of money.

Chelsea was dazzled and speechless at the whole scenario. Yes, she had been in many a fine restaurant with her mother and Ford over the years, but this was different—glitzy glamour, she noted. Every woman looked like she was cut out of a fashion magazine. Nary a hair out of place, Chelsea thought as she was being escorted by Stephen and Mr. Brandon, the heavyset man who gave Chelsea the go-ahead to sing. Craig Brandon ended up being the producer/director of *Stash*, the movie she was now going to star in.

Every woman sported what Chelsea would call a "gym body." Tight, fit, and athletic—but one would wonder what sport they played. They were consistently full lipped with long locks and a frozen, wide-eyed expression, clothed in some of the smallest outfits she had seen in the hippest fashion magazines. And although it was early springtime, everyone was evenly tanned; quite different from the New York crowd she'd been accustomed to. Not only that, some of the men were just as pretty as the women, although notably older than their female counterparts in most cases. And everyone seemed available to anyone else in the room who happened to glance their way.

Stephen put his arm around Chelsea, guiding her through the maze of tables in his typical "ownership" fashion; he looked like a strutting peacock. Yes, he had landed his client the lead in the next "Brandon Film," and he was going to use it as his ticket-to-ride. Although, he wasn't allowed to go in when Chelsea had read, no one was going to keep him out of one second of the rest of the saga of "the making of a star."

Earlier that afternoon, Stephen had decided to take Chelsea out to a local restaurant for some lunch while they sat on pins and needles waiting to hear how her reading went compared to all the "Hollywood beauties." As they sipped on their double-latte-frappé-coffee in the corner booth, Stephen grilled his client. "But did they say anything when you finished reading?"

"I told you, they said, 'That's fine. Thank you. We'll get back to you.'"

"How did they look? Happy? . . . What?"

Chelsea tried to imagine the reading as she reran it for the fifteen millionth time since she had left the office. "OK, I walked in . . . I sat in the middle of the room on the chair. And then I asked them if I could sing a song first. And the fat guy in the corner . . ."

Cutting in, Stephen rolled his eyes. "Mr. Brandon. He's the director and producer."

"OK, Mr. Brandon. Well, what do I call him if I see him again?"

"You call him 'Mr. Brandon' until he says you can call him Craig. If you ever see him again. I'm just not getting a sense of how you did."

"Well, they let me sing the song, and I knocked it out of the box. It sounded incredible because that's what I do. I think they were really impressed."

"Why? Did they say *anything*, Chelsea?"

"No. They didn't say anything. They were kind of like . . . speechless. And then one of the other guys, the skinny guy, just picked up the sides and read the first line so I just went right into the scene. And I remembered all the words even though I was nervous. And I remembered you said to use that nervousness, so I did because I had to do something with it, right? But it worked for the scene, just like you said. My voice was perfect when I was singing, and it was shaking when I was talking because I was so scared. But that's what the scene was about, just like you said."

Satisfied, Stephen leaned back, "Well that's good, good girl. I just wish they had given you some indication but. . . ."

". . . They said when I finished reading that it was very nice and 'we'll get back to you later.' That's all they said."

Chelsea was becoming visibly more and more insecure, so Stephen patted her hand. "You did good. You did good. It was your first time. And the singing thing, I wouldn't do that again, but if it calms you down, why not. Actually, I think you made a good move. But don't do stuff like that without talking it over with me first. Maybe it worked this time, but these guys usually don't like surprises."

"But isn't it good to be different from everyone else? . . . Stand out, you know?" Chelsea had a little foam mustache on her mouth that she licked off as soon as Stephen pointed at her. "Sorry."

"Yeah, they like different. But not cocky. Cocky just reads to them like you're going to be a pain to work with as soon as you figure out how good you are." He winked at Chelsea who finally relaxed into a smile.

"Stephen, I really think I was good."

"Well, we'll see. They said they'd call by five, which probably means seven. We can't sit here all day, I'll jump out of my skin from the caffeine. Let's just go back to the hotel and wait. You want anything else to eat?"

"No, I can't eat anything."

"That's good. They like them 'lean and mean' out here."

Chelsea instantly fell back into feeling insecure again. "Do you think I'm fat?"

"Did I say that? No, I don't think you're fat, but I don't want you to put on any weight either."

"I won't. Promise!"

"Good girl." He patted her hand, then waved to the waitress for the check.

❧

Chelsea sprawled across the couch reading *L.A. Magazine* while Stephen paced the length of the hotel room. He was proud of the fact that he was able to talk the production company into giving Chelsea a mini-suite during her stay in LA. He explained to Chelsea that he wanted to establish that they respect her talent right from the start.

Chelsea was surprised that Stephen was fine with his single room, but he said he wasn't the star, she was. Yes, he did have a way of making her feel special. Still, all afternoon she kept having flashbacks of how intense he got with her before she read for the part. It kind of scared her, but then she told herself to chill out. He was right. What he told her to do worked for the scene. If he hadn't yelled at her, she probably would've just chickened out and gone home. Yes, she concluded, she was happy he was in her life, and she was happy he was managing her.

As Stephen walked back and forth, she noticed he was now the one who looked like a nervous wreck. "You're going to make a hole in the rug. You're making me nervous again."

"It's seven and a half minutes after five, and I want these people to call." The phone rang as if on cue, but Stephen didn't respond. It rang once, twice, three times.

Chelsea was up on her feet squealing, "What are you doing!? Answer!"

"I don't want them to think we're too anxious here."

"I am anxious! Answer!"

He waved her off and finally clicked on his phone. "Hello?"

Stephen didn't say another word, he just listened. He also didn't give any indication by his expression as to what he was hearing; he was totally deadpan. His closing words were simply, "Seven o'clock."

He punched off his phone and looked at Chelsea, maintaining an uneventful expression.

"Seven o'clock what?" She screamed. "Do they want me back to read again? Did I make the cut? Is it seven tomorrow morning? Tonight? What's going on?"

Stephen shook his head, "You're not on a basketball team. It's not about making 'the cut'."

Chelsea collapsed on the couch, sure that she had been rejected. He let her suffer for a moment longer, and then a smile exploded across his face. "No, you don't have to read again. You got the lead!"

It took her a moment to digest what he said, and then she shot off the couch like a jack-in-the-box, jumping into his arms. He twirled her around like a slow-motion love scene until they finally slowed and her feet touched the ground once more. She stood there shaking like she had been shaking that morning, but this time it was from excitement not fear.

"He told me you were spectacular! He said there was no negotiation about your fee. You're a newcomer, and you're working for scale. But you're still going to get your SAG card off of this show, girly! Did you know that only 2 percent of members of the Screen Actors Guild make over $5,000 a year? You've already passed the 2 percent mark! . . . It's a six-week shoot. You're on call the whole time."

Chelsea had never seen Stephen so excited, and it was contagious.

"We have to be at The Bistro at seven. Craig's going to give us the full script then, and you start shooting tomorrow, as in thirteen hours from now! You'll be up and at makeup at six-thirty in the morning, you little Starlet!"

Stephen had pulled the chair out for Chelsea like she was a princess as she sat at the white-cloth table set for four in a choice location in The Bistro.

Craig Brandon took a few extra minutes to negotiate his chair; there was not enough room for his robust physique between the wall and the table. The young man who had already arrived to round out their foursome was up on his feet pulling the table back without having to be asked.

As Craig settled into his seat, he introduced the Rob Lowe-looking actor to Chelsea and Stephen. "Reis Lawrence, Stephen Garrison and Chelsea Lane." Enthralled with the young man's good looks, the magic of their meeting was broken by Chelsea's confusion over her introduction. She looked at the director. "It's 'Chelsea Patterson.'"

He smiled as he waved for the waiter to service their table. "No, Chelsea. It's Chelsea Lane. It's prettier, better for the marquee. Is that alright with you?"

He leveled her with a look, but before she could answer, Stephen spoke up. "I like it. Chelsea Lane."

Chelsea experienced a flood of mixed emotions about her life being manipulated once more without her input or permission, but she had to agree; *Lane* did sound better than *Patterson*. And besides, she was determined to leave her past behind. She had never taken her father's last name since he had abandoned her as a child, and even though Ford Williams had adopted her, she refused his name for obvious reasons after she'd left New York City. Chelsea had told her mother she wanted to go back to using the Patterson family name, which Irene found to be very sweet. Obviously, she didn't understand her daughter's true motives behind the switch. But now, "Lane." Yes, "Chelsea Lane" sounded good to the girl.

She nodded approval as the waiter arrived. "Yes, Mr. Brandon?"

"We'll have a bottle of Clo de Bois Chardonnay and Merlot." He threw Chelsea another scrutinizing look. "Your manager here says you are eighteen. Is that right?"

"Yes. I have my driver's license if you need to see it."

He laughed, "Well, if you want to show it to me, but you can buy one on just about any corner on the Strip. Stephen here wouldn't lie to me though, otherwise we'd have some serious business issues right off."

It was the first time Chelsea had seen Stephen challenged, and she was happy to observe that her manager did not back down—or at least he didn't act like he was intimidated.

He simply replied, "She's eighteen, like I said."

Mr. Brandon acknowledged Stephen's response. "Reis here is . . ." He looked at the young man, ". . . twenty-two. Right?"

"Right on."

"The good thing is that you both look younger than you are. . . . The two lead characters are supposed to be seventeen and sixteen. I'm sure my director of photography's soft lighting will keep you looking like little cherubs through the whole picture. Reis is a veteran of two of my films. The last one was *Redline*, right?"

"Yeah, *Redline*, and then *Exquisite*."

Chelsea was clearly impressed. "Wow, I've heard of them, I think."

Stephen covered for her. "We've been recording a lot. Not much time to go to the movies."

"Sure." The director looked at Chelsea. "You can call me Craig. 'Mr. Brandon' makes me feel like my father." When he laughed, his face turned red. "I work a lot with young people. Reis here is a good actor, and he'll show you the ropes. He doesn't mind running lines early if you need to while you're both getting your makeup done."

"Great." Chelsea was finally beginning to believe she wasn't dreaming; she was actually going to make a movie. And when Craig handed both the actors scripts, she knew it was the real deal.

Brandon's voice turned smooth. "Now, Chelsea. Don't feel like you're late in the game here as far as getting the script. We just finished rewriting last night, and no one has gotten the final script till now. Tomorrow will be an easy first-day shoot. Not a lot of dialogue. Get to know everyone on the set, and get to know each other. After all, this is a love story. Course, that's all about acting, Reis is taken."

As the director patted his leading man on the back, Chelsea wasn't sure whether she was disappointed or relieved at the news that Reis was unavailable. But as Brandon continued, she didn't have time to ponder her feelings.

"We rarely shoot in order. Actually, never. And that's what's going on tomorrow. All the bungalow scenes will be up first, and they run throughout the script. After we wrap the bungalow scenes, we'll be going on some locations toward the end of the week for the night shoot fight scenes and bar scenes. We'll be on nights for about two weeks, then we'll turn around again."

Craig nodded at Stephen. "I'll give you a full shooting schedule in the next two days which will probably be 90 percent accurate. So, like I said, tomorrow we're starting with the bungalow scenes." He now turned his attention back to his "leading lady." "Chelsea, I know you haven't read the full story line, but you know your character. At least you seemed to when you read your sides. Good job, by the way. Your character is young. She's innocent, she's naive, and she's also like a duck out of water. She's from the Midwest, which is why I've called in my dialogue coach to work with you to make sure you sound the part. You say you're from Nashville? You don't sound like you're from Nashville."

"Actually, I grew up in New York."

"Good thing it wasn't the Bronx."

"We were just about to get Chelsea a record deal," Stephen interjected, "when this opportunity came up. We were working in that direction for her image, anyway."

"And what direction would that be, Stephen?"

"Like you said, innocent and beautiful. The country music audience likes a country accent and feel, so we were moving away from the New York edge to more of a Nashville look and sound, which is what you said you wanted for Chelsea's character in the film."

"That's exactly right, Stephen."

"I'm originally from LA," Stephen added, "so I've called in an acting coach friend of mine to work with Chelsea full-time while she's shooting."

Craig regarded Chelsea. "You're going to be a busy girl." He nodded at Stephen. "Good choice. I think she's a natural. If she can just stay out of her own way and take directions, she'll be fine." Then he was back at Chelsea. "Reis here will tell you that I'm pretty much a first- or second-take director, so you won't be tortured with having to do a scene over and over. I don't believe in it, and the schedule won't allow it. I move fast. You just have to come to the set knowing your dialogue and trust me. I'll make you look good . . . I'll make you sound good."

Chelsea already felt like a star. "I'm real excited for the opportunity."

Craig nodded, then he looked at Stephen again. "We're going to be wanting three options. If Chelsea does as well as Reis here has . . . Or some of my other young discoveries, we're not going to be held up with highway robbery fees. You can go make your millions off of some other producer once we get your girl here launched."

"I'm sure we'll be working up from scale after the first picture." Stephen questioned, knowing what was being offered for his client was a fair deal and he didn't have much negotiating power.

"Does she have an agent? Of course, you know you can't negotiate for her as manager. I work with a sharp woman over at CMO Agency who would love to sign Chelsea. I called her about it this afternoon."

"With all due respect, Craig, I oversee all of Chelsea's business. I work with a lawyer, which, of course, is a perfectly kosher way to negotiate any deal without an agent. So why don't I just have our lawyer give you a jingle after dinner, and we can firm up the details before she starts to shoot in the morning. I put him on notice this afternoon to be available."

Craig studied his opponent for a moment and then nodded. "Sure . . . We want to do well, and we want everybody else to do well. Just so you know, the three-film option is not up for discussion, but we do increase our star's salary in increments of a hundred thousand dollars with each film, which ain't no peanuts for a newcomer. We do the same deal for every actor that ends up working good box office for us. . . . But I'll be happy to run those numbers by your lawyer so he can sign off on the deal."

Chelsea was out of her skin with excitement, kicking Stephen under the table to back off. And he did after one more comment. Yes, Stephen was a good poker player, able to maintain a calm demeanor during what, in fact, had been an intense negotiation. "I'm sure these three options of yours don't have any kind of 'loan-out clause' attached."

Craig smiled at Stephen. "I like you. Of course not. We don't sell our talent—we use our talent. And we hope that our talent remembers us when they're making big studio movies and we want them to come in for a cameo here and there."

Stephen nodded. "We won't forget."

"Done."

And with that, the wine arrived. And as Craig swirled the merlot around, he gazed at Chelsea over the rim of his glass. "We'll be doing wardrobe after wrap tomorrow. All the bungalow scenes the first week are played in a bathrobe. The setup is that you've followed your boyfriend out to Hollywood, and you've taken up residence in a small house behind the restaurant where you are a waitress. So," he finally took a sip of wine, nodding at the waiter with approval, "we have a one-size-fits-all bathrobe that you'll be working in tomorrow."

"I have one, too, if you want me to bring it." Chelsea didn't like the sound of "one size fits all."

"We need doubles to shoot. So, unless you happen to have three of the exact same robe, we've got you covered."

"Oh, . . ." Chelsea suddenly felt stupid.

"The robe is pretty, Chelsea don't worry. . . . I always . . ." Stephen's phone ringing interrupted the director, which clearly annoyed him. Yes, Craig Brandon was a man who definitely liked to hold court at the center of everyone's attention.

"Excuse me," Stephen stood and exited the table, not wanting to irritate his new relationship with Craig. Nonetheless, he was not about to back off from looking like a busy and important manager.

And as he stepped a few feet away, he listened to his message service for a few minutes before he replied into the phone, "Save that one, yeah, that one . . . Who? Irene Patterson? Urgent? No, erase that one. Yeah, and that one and what else? No, that's not important. Just keep the first two. Thanks."

He ended the call, then observed Chelsea at the table who was now in a deep conversation with Reis. No, it wasn't a hard decision for Stephen to ignore Irene's phone call; he wasn't about to let anything or anyone get in the way of his plans for Chelsea. Besides, she could call her mother whenever she wanted to, he rationalized, as he made his way back to the table.

Chapter 19

Spring Fever

Settling into Brian's sports car, Lauren was thankful he didn't have the top down. She noted he normally would have, but this spring evening, her ex was on his best behavior, obviously remembering that Lauren hated having her hair batted about her face when he would go topless. He had also remembered exactly how she liked her steak cooked and what her favorite dessert was.

Oooo, can all of this really be happening? she thought. *This rekindling stuff is fun, so far.*

"Thanks for dinner, Brian. It was way too good! You're going to have to roll me up my stairs."

"That sounds interesting." He gave her a sexy look. "By the way, I think it was a good call on your part not to bring Tucker.

We really do need to make sure that we can work all of our 'whatevers' out before we present a united front."

"You make it sound like a war tactic."

"Well, since we spent most of our marriage warring, I think you and I both want to build on the good and let the bad go." Brian pulled his car out onto a double-lane road as Lauren leaned back against the door to observe him.

He felt her gaze, "What are you doing?"

"I'm looking at you . . . I don't think either one of us is up for another round of disappointment. . . . Not that I'm saying I was not an equal opportunity destroyer."

Surprised, Brian glanced at her. "Well, that's a big confession for you. Obviously we both have our issues, but there was a lot of good, too, and that's what I'm interested in."

Satisfied, Lauren leaned back. "Well, good. Me too, Bri. I just think it would absolutely shatter Tucker if we were not successful the second time around. I tell you, the more I've learned, especially from Eleanor and Ham, the more I want the real deal. I can't wait till you get to know them better. . . . They have the coolest relationship. They're respectful and supportive and passionate. They're totally there for each other. See, that was my problem. I was expecting you to fill me up. I was expecting you to make my world whole. . . . That's between God and me. And even though I had my faith when we met, I fell right back into my old patterns of 'needy, needy, needy.' I used to get so shattered and hurt and disappointed. And I don't think it even had anything to do with you . . . much. Well yeah, there's that temper of yours, but I've really thought about it a lot. The hardest part was when I didn't feel from you or from myself that there was a level of commitment that would last. And I guess we didn't. . . . It's called divorce."

Brian started to say something, but she cut him off.

"No, no. I really want to get this all out. I want to let you know what I've been praying about. I do want to go and get some counseling. I know there are courses in remarriage, and I'll go to your church. . . . You pick whomever you want to counsel us. I'm a bulldozer sometimes . . . I was so excited about my faith, and I know I spent a lot of time with Suz talking about that, and I think I cut you out of it. I mean, it's a personal thing, Bri, I know it is. And I've seen a change in you since you've been here in Tennessee, since you have been able to go to the church *you* want to go to. I do. I really see a difference. And I know that I'm always going to be more 'shout from the rooftops' about my faith than you . . . Hey, women talk 30 percent more than men, but that doesn't mean that you don't have real faith. And it doesn't mean you don't care, and doesn't mean that you don't want an intimate relationship with God. . . . And it doesn't mean that you don't want to step in as the head of the household. And because you don't talk so much about Jesus doesn't mean that you're not committed to his ways no matter what happens, does it?"

"Good one, Lauren. You've managed to verbally present an application sheet for me to check off and sign in blood."

"Are you mad?" she couldn't read his expression. "That was a joke, right? Hey, I can't be afraid of being me."

"I'm not mad. But you said it yourself, you're a 'bulldozer'."

"I didn't mean it that way. . . . I was just asking about where you are these days. I know I'm aggressive, but that's who I am.

And I need to know who you are, and I have to accept and love who you are, where you are right now. Not where I need you to be later after I fix you or you fix me. I can't feel like I've got a dream in front of me that I can't be excited about it. Does that make any sense?"

"No."

Lauren looked shattered.

"I'm kidding. . . . I know that. But sometimes you just have to take a breath and smell the coffee and be satisfied with where you are. I can't plot everything out for you."

Lauren wasn't exactly sure what he just said, but she wasn't about to give up. "I want to feel good more than I want to look good. I want to be kind because I want to remember how it felt when my heart was broken. I don't want to blame my new husband on the things an old one did to me. Even if it's the same husband. I don't want something cloned. I want a fresh, new start. I don't want to be in denial like the dead cow that was hit by a truck a week before with her legs sticking up in the air in rigor mortis and have someone go over and ask, 'How are you?' and the cow says, 'I'm fine.'"

Thankfully, Brian was accustomed to her zaniness. "Lauren, you are always, as you put it, on a mission, and no, I don't like to move as fast as you do or make fast decisions. Is that going to be alright with you?"

"As long as we're not ninety-five by the time you ask me to marry you again."

"I wasn't talking about that decision. I'm sure we'll know, soon, with a lot of help, professionally and spiritually, whether we're going to make it as a couple. I'm just saying that I agree with you. We have to approach 'us' as not what you have to change in me and what I have to change in you. I don't have to answer to you, Lauren; I have to answer to God. I know that's what you've been trying to tell me since the day we met, and I'm receiving it now. I'm understanding. Not because I have to, not because *you* said so, . . . because I desire to be the man God had in mind when he created me."

Lauren was dumbfounded, impressed; Lauren was in love again.

"OK," she finally responded. "So what you're saying is that we're not going to do, 'when this gets fixed, I'll be happy' anymore, right?"

"Right."

"But the fact that you have received Christ, . . . Ooh, I've always adored you as a man, and now you've knocked my socks off spiritually!"

Amused, Brian countered, "Now that's an interesting visual."

"Ha!" She pointed her finger at him. "See, I can still make you smile. Remember, laughter is the shortest difference between two people. And I admit, I want a belly laugh, not a belly bulge. . . . Hey! How about a little humor 'bout aging?"

"Shoot." He threw her an encouraging smile.

"OK . . . The *opposite* of Alzheimer's is remembering things that never happened!"

Brian nodded, "I'll give you an eighty-five for content but only a seventy for delivery."

Lauren poked him hard on the arm. "OK, OK . . . how 'bout *stages of life*. First you believe in Santa Claus, then you don't believe in Santa Claus, then you look like Santa Claus, and then you believe you *are Santa Claus*! OK, I'm done; don't grade me."

"Where do you get these things?"

"I don't know, all over the place. They're not mine. I don't make them up. I just hear them and remember them for some reason. They tickle me. I like things that tickle me or touch me. Or make me think. Like you. I'm just silly, but you were always saying one-liners that were thought provoking."

Brian enjoyed the compliment.

"So, your turn. . . ." Lauren pointed at Brian. "Oh my, you're actually blushing."

"No, I'm not!"

"Yes, you are. Your earlobes get purple just before you get profound. That's one of the things I love about you."

Brian leaned back in his seat, trying to come up with something to impress Lauren. "Fine . . . alright. So when I was moving here, I remember thinking: 'Rarely do I think about what will happen if I succeed. I usually think about what will happen if I fail.'"

"Oooo, that's good! Kind of like the 'glass half full or half empty' gig."

"Sort of, although I thought it was a tad more lyrical. My point was, I realized that I tended to be a little bit of a negative thinker, which, by the way, you always used to point out."

"Sorry, sorry."

"'Sorry' accepted. Incidentally, it's much better to discover our personal flaws on our own. Believe me, one tends to work on self-realization instead of defending our bad habits."

"Wow, another good one. You're on a roll here, Bri."

"OK. . . . Another conclusion I have come to recently is that I think frustration is probably one's avocation. . . . *And* trials complete me, not defeat me."

Lauren squealed with delight. "Oooh, a doubleheader! Bri, those are the two most positive things I've ever heard you say."

Brian took a breath of satisfaction. "I'm getting there."

"Yes, you are."

As they continued their drive home, Brian sweetly took Lauren's hand; she gazed at him, feeling all warm and fuzzy. "Did you know that 80 percent of relationships on TV are illicit?"

Brian glanced back at her, "Did you know that silence is a virtue?"

She looked straight ahead for a moment. "Do you know how hard it's going to be to control ourselves. Physically I mean? Since we already know each other. That way, I mean. While we try to know each other in different ways."

"Uh-huh."

"I'll help you if you help me. Let's promise that one of us will keep us on the straight and narrow because I do not want to go down this road again without it being pleasing to God."

Brian looked over at her again; their eyes met. "Neither do I, Lauren. Neither do I."

"I love you, Bri."

"I love you, too."

Trace honked three times as he pulled up outside of Shooter's house in the projects. His friend was at the car in about three giant steps as he piled his books in the backseat and jumped in the passenger side. "Thanks, bro."

"No problem." Trace glanced at his watch. "We'll make it before the bell." He glanced at Shooter who looked as disgruntled as he had ever seen him. "You OK?"

"Yeah, man. I just wish I had a car that hadn't been owned by three of my friends before it landed in my sorry life. That thing breaks down more than I break out."

Amused, Trace winced slightly from a shooting pain from his broken rib. "You'll be buying some big, gaudy mega-machine soon enough."

"Hey, man, is that a racial slur?" He feigned anger. "We 'black boys' don't always invest in the big white Cadillacs with dripping chrome and pink dice hanging from the rearview mirror."

"OK, fine. Tell this 'white-trash boy' what you've got your eyes on? If you could buy your dream car, name it and claim it."

"Makes no never mind to me as long as Tonya'd be sittin' in the front seat next to me and Bobbie-boy in the back."

Shooter's disclaimer surprised Trace. "That sounds like a family portrait to me."

"Sounds like wishful thinking to me." Shooter looked away. "I spoke at Bobbie the other night."

"How'd he sound? He OK?"

"Yeah, the boy sounded good."

"That's good, isn't it?"

"Yeah, man. It's good. I guess I was hoping he'd be missing me and Tonya'd be homesick, and they'd both be back here by now. But no, man; . . . it's all good. Tonya says Bobbie likes his school. He's even having a kid over to play on the weekend, and she was goin' to do her first modelin' job."

"Well, at least you know where she is." Now it was Trace who looked out the window as they approached the high school parking lot.

"Yeah. I know where she is, . . . and I know where she's not."

"I thought you said you were cool with that."

"That's what I tell myself. But I miss my son."

"Yeah, and what about Tonya?"

"Yeah man. I miss my girl, too."

"You can do something about it. Right? If you asked her to marry you, don't you think she'd come back?"

It took Shooter a while to conclude, "I don't know, man. I need to feel like I'm in charge of something. Now that I've got my opportunity, she takes off. I want to have it straight in my mind."

Trace parked underneath the high school sign which read:

HAVING SIGHT WITHOUT VISION IS WORSE
THAN BEING BLIND.—HAM

Chapter 20

Eye Witness

Tonya sat across from Denise at her elaborate desk as if await-ing a criminal sentence. Yes, she had tossed and turned all night in fearful anticipation of what she needed to tell her boss about the booking yesterday for the catalog company. And yes, she realized that her left eye was actually twitching from nervous-ness as she sat before "the queen." Oh, how she had prayed for guidance. She also had spent most of the night on the phone with Eleanor and Pam for moral support about the decision she was now going to share with Denise.

The modeling matriarch looked at Tonya with concern. "Are you alright? You appear to be sitting on a porcupine."

"Yes, ma'am. I mean, no ma'am. I'm just a little nervous. Or a lot nervous, to be honest."

"Well, if you're concerned about whether you did a good job yesterday, everybody at the company said you were fine, beautiful, nice to work with, and not to worry about the trip on the runway. It happens, and they realize you're a tad wet behind the ears, as we say."

Tonya just stared at Denise, mortified.

"A little green . . . new at the runway. My point is, don't you worry, darling. Besides, that's why I wanted you to start out with that booking. It wasn't a situation where it would make or break you for the future because it was their first round, too. They were as out of sorts and nervous as you were. That's what I call good casting!"

Tonya swallowed hard, her voice was weaker than she wished, and yet she didn't seem to be able to muster any more volume. "It's very kind of them, ma'am."

Denise shook her head, "Darling, call me Denise. Everyone does. Especially my girls." She offered Tonya a warm smile.

Unfortunately, Denise's kindness just seemed to make Tonya all the more nervous considering the message she needed to relay. "Denise," Tonya paused again. "Oh, that feels so funny, ma'am. Denise. Sorry. OK, well, that's nice of the catalog company to be so lenient with me. I don't think I did a very good job, but I tried." She cleared her throat again. "But the reason I called to come in this morning is that I've made a decision. You said that I could let you know if there was anything that rubbed me wrong, and I had a hard time . . . Well, . . . it was difficult because, what I . . ."

Gratefully, Denise cut in, realizing Tonya couldn't even finish her sentence. "Did somebody offend you in some way or treat you incorrectly? If so, I'll clear it up immediately!"

"I don't think there's anything you can do about it, ma'am
. . . *Denise*. I think it's about what my friend Eleanor would call
. . . 'the spots on a leopard'."

Tonya paused, thinking Denise would understand her
meaning, but instead she just stared blankly at the girl.

"Alright, Tonya, . . . could you elaborate a wee bit?"

"Sorry, I don't know why I'm having so much trouble with
this. I've been worried about it all night. I couldn't even sleep
because I don't want to let you down. You've been so nice to
me, and I really do want to do a good job and have a future in
the business, but I'm not sure that runway work is going to be the
right place for me."

Again, Denise tried to reassure her. "Darling, if I could tell
you how many times I had tripped over my own shoelaces during
shoots, you'd feel like a million dollars right now. I actually broke
my own nose while doing a shoot with Penn in a rowboat."

Tonya's eyes widened.

"Oh yes, my darling, I totally lost control of the oar, and
in my deep desire to appear that I had everything under control,
I grabbed at it. And instead of realigning the little monster in its
metal thing on the side of the boat, the oar flipped over, smacked
me in the face and broke my nose. And it wasn't even at the end
of the shoot day! So, not only was I injured, Irving Penn was out
a model, and I was positive I would never be booked again. But
thanks be to the longest legs in the business at the time, everybody got over it. Certainly faster than my nose did. And as soon
as my black eyes were makeup erasable, I was working nonstop
with Penn and every other top photographer. So, my point is,
don't worry about a teeny-weeny little trip on the runway."

"Oh, I'm so sorry. . . . It's not about that, ma'am. It's about what happened before the trip. Actually, from the second I walked in."

"Oh good heavens, what was wrong?"

"Well, they didn't have any clothes on."

"Who?"

"The models. And there were people running around . . . *men* and hairdressers and people who put the clothes on the models. Men and women . . . and MEN!" Tonya emphasized. "And the girls just sat around and let these people do their hair, or put their clothes on, and half of them weren't even wearing underwear. . . . The girls, I mean. The models." Tonya took a well-deserved breath. "The models weren't wearing anything most of the time."

"Well, darling, that's good that you got it all out." Denise knew she had to be careful in respect to Tonya's feelings, which she viewed as overblown. Nonetheless, being the professional that Denise was, she realized that it could well be a shocking event for an amateur to be in the backroom of a runway show.

"Tonya, it sounds like you were working with a lot of veteran models and a lot of *European* models."

Tonya shook her head, "There were a lot of languages being spoken, but there were some American girls there, too."

"Well, what I mean to say," Denise tried to reroute her thoughts, "in Europe and South America . . . places like that, it's common to go to the beaches and girls don't wear bathing suit tops. So they're very accustomed to no undies. . . . And they're definitely not shy about their bodies. Nudity doesn't embarrass them. Frankly, they don't think twice about it."

"Yes, but that's my point . . . I do. And I'm not embarrassed about my body. It's not that. God gave me my body and . . ."

Again Denise cut her off. ". . . And a beautiful body it is, I might add. No one asked you to be photographed nude, did they? Or wear anything that was inappropriate on the runway."

"No, ma'am. They did not. But I had a battle on my hands just to let them know that I was not removing my bra so they would need to dress me in clothes that were not strapless. It caused quite a fumble because I had to change outfits with another girl. I was positive they would have reported that to you. I think I made them mad, but I just didn't want to do it. I didn't have to take my bra off while I was at the fitting . . ."

". . . Well, I'm sure it didn't matter at that point. But I'm also sure you can see that you can't walk down the runway with your bra strap showing. So next time I'll see to it that they put you in something that's not going to require your taking off your bra . . . And you make sure you wear a strapless bra."

"I'm sorry, ma'am. Thank you, but that won't work. It's too frantic, and it's too fast. Really, nobody does care about their exposure, but I do. I just don't want to start feeling comfortable about standing in front of a bunch of strangers undressed. I don't believe in it. My friend, Lauren . . . she's a veterinarian. She always says that 'animals don't blush.' Then she goes on to say, 'Of course, who would know really if they do, we can't see their skin under their fur.'"

Denise began to look at Tonya with curiosity. ". . . Forgive me; clearly I'm not following you."

"I'm sorry, ma'am. That's just the way Lauren talks. Her point is that we see so many things on TV or wherever, that we've gotten to a point that we don't blush anymore. I just don't want to get to that point. I guess what I'm trying to say is, my values are not something that I want to 'get over.'"

Denise quickly recognized that she was not going to convince Tonya to deny her upbringing. "Well, I appreciate your candor. We simply will not book you for any runway work."

"Thank you, ma'am." Tonya's eyes fell in disappointment. She took another breath, pausing before her next question. "Denise, does this mean that I can't model? Is it the same way at photography sessions?"

"No," Denise replied quickly.

"Seriously, ma'am? Because I really do want to do a good job."

"You said it yourself, Tonya. . . . The fast pace of a runway show simply leaves no time for modesty, and if that doesn't fall within the parameters of your comfort zone, we can work around that. Certainly, it would be your call. See how you feel on a photo shoot. You're booked to do your DuPont ad in a few days, correct?"

"Yes, ma'am."

"Well, you're working with one of the top photographers. I will definitely give everyone a heads-up about your feelings."

Tonya shrank at the thought, "I'm sorry, ma'am. I don't want to sound like a baby, and I don't want to sound unprofessional."

"No, no. It's fine. I can't control everything, but I can certainly let them know to be respectful of your privacy. Even on photo shoots, quite often hairdressers think they have free access to the dressing rooms. Because frankly, most of the girls don't mind. But if you do, just stand up for yourself, and we'll see how it goes, alright?"

Although Tonya felt embarrassed, she knew, for her, she was drawing a good line in the sand. Still, she was concerned that she might have made her bold move to New York, and she wasn't, at the end of the day, going to fit in with the scene.

Her first morning shoot had gone surprisingly well, even though Chelsea hadn't slept a wink the night before. Between learning her lines and worrying about the next day's work, she was exhausted.

She had tried to call Stephen with some questions about the script when she realized it was three in the morning by the time she had finished reading. Needless to say, he didn't answer his phone. She had been tempted to take something extra to help her sleep, but between what she had had to drink at dinner and her normal meds, she thought she'd never get up in the morning to make her call time if she indulged further; so she just sat there, a bundle of nerves wrapped in a comforter on her bed as she practiced her lines into the mirror across the room.

On their ride over to the set as the sun rose, Chelsea asked Stephen about the bedroom scene scheduled to shoot that afternoon.

"Don't worry, Chelsea, they're not going to start with that scene. We'll have plenty of time to talk to Craig about how he's planning to film it."

"But it says that Cathleen and Alan are in bed, and they're making love, and . . ."

". . . That's the operative word, Chelsea, they're making *love*. Cathleen loves the boy, and she's determined not to lose him by not standing by his decision to become an actor. There is nothing raunchy in their relationship. The two are committed to each other. They've been in love since they started high school. She knows him. I'm sure Craig will create a very sweet scene."

"But what you just said is not what I get from the script."

Stephen was starting to get annoyed. "Oh good. And exactly how many scripts have you read, because I've read thousands? But never mind, what did *you* get from the script?"

Chelsea was silenced by his answer; she didn't want to ignite the anger she had experienced the other day from him, and still, she was concerned.

"Look, trust me, or forget it. I'll be right there with you. I'm not going to let anything happen. Just remember how lucky you are to get this break. I don't want you walking in there with an attitude. Let's just see how it goes, . . . OK?"

Chelsea nodded, realizing that she'd better drop the subject.

Chelsea made it through the morning scenes with a lot of help from Stephen and the script girl as well as a lot of patience from her director and encouragement from her costar.

Thank goodness Stephen had brought in his friend and acting coach, Krissy, who worked with Chelsea every second she wasn't actually on camera. It was a lot for Chelsea to take in; a lot of "hurry up and wait." And the budding actress quickly became grateful for any time she was actually not on camera. Yes, Chelsea recognized, by the end of the morning, that perhaps only fifteen minutes of footage was actually shot per half a production day. All the rest of the fourteen hours on set was spent setting the lights, laying tracks, rehearsing and hitting marks.

And while Chelsea was having a crash course in acting, she was momentarily thankful for the dancing lessons her mother insisted she take in New York because she was quickly able to conquer the difficulties of landing in the lighting "sweet spot" for the camera. Reis had also given her tips on how to walk backward out of the scene so she could count her steps as she entered and wouldn't have to look down for her mark. He also suggested she take in landmarks around the set that she could reference to help her end up where the camera expected to find her.

She was amazed at how well she remembered all her lines, having only been able to work on them the night before. And she vowed to herself that she would be doing a lot of studying at night for the next day's work to prepare. Yes, Chelsea wanted to be taken seriously as a professional actor, and she was grateful for all the help she was getting. Krissy had also given her a trick of the trade by explaining that actors need to know their lines so well the words naturally come out of their mouth while the emotion of the scene motivates them.

After flubbing her entrance for the second time, Chelsea wished she could be transported to a music studio right about then since she was adept at not popping the microphones and matching her vocals with harmonies, something that had taken her a lot of practice. But she told herself she'd get there with this acting thing, and she was feeling pretty confident when the first assistant director called a forty-five-minute lunch break.

Stephen opted to eat outside under the tent with the crew, reminding Chelsea how fortunate she was to have her own little trailer for her first film. "Most first shows, actresses, if they're lucky, get a slot in the honey wagon."

"What's a 'honey wagon'?"

Stephen pointed over to a row of small dressing rooms on wheels parked behind her modest yet private trailer.

"How do they even get dressed in there? They're so teeny."

"They have to go down to the wardrobe room to dress . . . The way you had to go to the makeup trailer. Craig is treating you like the leading lady you are." Then he quickly kissed her on the cheek. "You did good this morning."

Chelsea beamed for a moment, but then her face fell with worry.

"What?"

"We haven't had a chance to talk about the next scene. You know, the bedroom stuff."

"Honey, just relax. You can see the way the director's treating you. I'll have someone bring lunch in your trailer for you and Reis, and you can talk to him so you can feel more comfortable . . . You know, get to know him a little better. I'll speak to Craig and see what he has in mind."

"OK," she started to head to her trailer but then turned back. "There's not even any dialogue, so I . . . OK, Stephen. Just tell Reis to come over."

"That's my girl."

A tray piled with plates and food sat untouched in front of Chelsea who sipped nervously on her Coca-Cola while Reis practically inhaled his lunch. He poked his fork at her baked chicken. "Are you going to eat that?"

"No, you can have it. I'm not really hungry." She watched in amazement as he ingested the food. "Do you always eat like that?"

"Yeah, I guess it's my metabolism, or genes or something. I also work out a lot."

She looked briefly at his shoulders; it was hard to avoid noticing this young man's amazing physique. For an instant her thoughts raced back to Trace and the one time they had made love in the backseat of his car. And with that flashback, she immediately got up and excused herself. She had to clear her mind. No, she wasn't going to think about Trace. It hurt too much.

She disappeared into the small bathroom and pulled out her medication from her purse. Considering its contents for a moment, she decided to take two pills instead of one just to calm her nerves, she told herself. After all, she didn't have to say anything in the scene, so it wouldn't matter if her mouth got cottony and dry. No one would know.

When she returned, Reis had finished both their lunches, and she realized they only had five minutes left of their lunch break.

"Hey, I guess I better go and get my makeup touched up, right? Isn't that what you say? 'Touched up'?"

"Yeah." He laughed. "You sound like a pro already." When he got up and gathered their trays to leave, she thought, *this guy is really nice.* He had chatted with her the entire lunch break, interspersing compliments about her work that morning and assuring her that she was a "natural."

And then, as if by cue, he turned back to her with a kind, warm expression. "Hey, listen, if you're worried about this afternoon, let me tell you, I've worked with Craig, and it's all about editing. No one likes to do these scenes. Believe me, I hate doing them. . . . Nothing personal. Bed scenes are always embarrassing, so don't think it's anybody's favorite time of day. The crew doesn't like them; actors don't like them. It's amazing to me how they make any of these scenes look great on screen, but that's what editing is about."

Chelsea shrugged, trying to look casual. "No, I'm OK. I'm sure it will be fine. I just . . . well . . . I'm sure it will be fine."

Reis gave her a wink and exited the trailer leaving Chelsea feeling like a stupid little girl. She chastised herself for being such a wimp.

Just as Reis disappeared from her view, the AD banged on her door. "Three minutes!" she heard him yell. She turned like a rabbit, rushing into the bathroom again to take one more pill for good measure. She was determined not to let her silly little girl nerves ruin her shot at stardom. Besides, Stephen was there, and he would protect her, she told herself.

Irene headed for the driver's side of her BMW when her father intervened. "I'll drive." She hesitated for a moment but realized it would be a losing battle; if her father wanted to drive, that was the way it was going to be. The only reason Lauren had gotten away with being at the helm when they all went out looking for Chelsea was that Sam admitted he was uncomfortable with the unwieldy size of her truck, which he called "the tank."

As Irene rounded the car, she shouted to her dad. "You don't have to come, you know. If you want to finish watching your show, I'll be fine. I know right where the police station is."

"I'm taping it, don't worry. And your mother will put a second one in if we're gone long."

As they both piled in the car, Sam gave his daughter a thumbs-up. "You don't need to take care of all these things yourself, Irene. I'm here."

"Will wonders never cease?" Irene couldn't believe how different her dad was lately. Maybe he had always been like this and she hadn't noticed. No, she confirmed to herself; no, he hadn't always been like this. "Thanks, Dad. I appreciate it."

As he started the car and drove off, she buckled her seat belt, flipping through the papers in the manila file before her.

"I don't want you to get disappointed, Irene, if they can't do anything to help you find this Stephen character, or Chelsea. After all, they haven't done anything wrong and . . ."

Irene cut him off. ". . . Dad, the guy is not answering my calls. If there was nothing wrong, he'd answer my calls. I have a really bad feeling about what's going on with Chelsea. I can't explain it. Maybe it's a mother's instinct."

Sam stopped the car at the red light at the entrance to the cul-de-sac. "I'm not that sure that a gut feeling is going to fly with the Nashville police."

Irene had always been concerned about the blind curve on the four-lane highway beyond the traffic light where Lauren lived. Actually *concern* was not the right word; she was just grateful for it since she was a rather timid driver having lived in Manhattan all her life. Yes, she was used to flying through the streets like a "mad hatter" in the backseat of a taxi or limousine; she had a comfort zone as a passenger even though cars zoomed in and out, missing one another by mere inches. There seemed to be an unspoken etiquette of when to stop and when to go while navigating Manhattan traffic. But when she drove, Irene wanted a clear and wide right of way.

As the light turned green, Irene continued to review the pictures of Chelsea and her written descriptions of her daughter that she was determined to have the police take note of. And then her dad pulled onto the main road.

No, it never occurred to Irene that a tractor trailer would be barreling around that blind corner at a speed that well exceeded the recommended rate. No, she had never imagined hearing the disgusting sound of squealing tires and mashing metal that suddenly invaded her in surround sound as the big rig slammed into the driver's side of her station wagon, pushing it down the road like a tinker toy hit on a train track.

The first impact came out of nowhere and was so intense that, despite her seat belt holding fast, it threw Irene like a rag doll over onto Sam who was pressed against the driver's door. The intrusion was so sudden, Sam didn't have time even to look in its direction. So, as the eighteen-wheeler plowed the station wagon across the highway, Irene was only able to look up from the centrifugal force that pressed her downward to see her father's face masked in terror.

The moment, enveloped in indescribable horror, seemed like a freeze frame until the second impact hit. The truck slammed the station wagon between its immovable force into the immovable object in their path, a wall of chiseled rock along the side of the mountain pass. And with that, everything seemed to collapse. The car and then Sam as he received the full force of the air bag pinning him against the back of his seat. Irene, having been thrown over, escaped her side of the bag's full force, which now held her captive underneath it for what seemed an eternity. And as the tangled metal of both car and truck grinded and twisted into a settled position, the reality of the situation struck Irene like thunder as she heard her father exhale in pain.

As quickly as the air bags exploded, they retracted, finally allowing Irene to pull herself up to a sitting position. "Dad!" she screamed, but her father didn't respond; his head remained at an unnatural angle against the side window. "Dad!" Her eyes searched the parameters of the car, trying to get her bearings as the realization of what had just happened fully registered.

There was low light that afternoon in the car; the side windows overshadowed by the looming front end of the tractor trailer on one side and the rocky mountain terrain on the other. And it was not long before Irene ascertained that immediate escape was not available to either herself or her father.

She couldn't stop herself from screaming at the top of her lungs as the face of the truck driver appeared in front of her, looking through her windshield, his blood dripping on the glass that miraculously had remained intact during the blow. She could barely hear his muffled screams through the encased interior of the car.

"Hang in there!" She actually read his lips more easily than she could hear his words. "I'm calling 911! Don't move!" And then he was gone.

From then on, she seemed to be in a time warp, metered only by her heartbeat that thumped against her own chest and Sam's labored breathing. Everything she had ever seen on TV or read about or heard flashed through her mind in respect to not moving an injured individual. And although she felt like she had been processed through a metal press, she recognized that whatever her injuries were, they were inconsequential compared to her father's who was laboring for every life-sustaining breath.

"Dad!" She heard herself scream again. "Oh my God, Dad!" Suddenly, other faces, people from various angles, peered in on them, waving and screaming their concerns and encouragement for them to "hang tight. The police are coming! The ambulance is on its way. They'll get you out! Don't worry!"

Suddenly nauseous, Irene vomited, unable to control her actions both physically and emotionally. Sam's hand was locked on the steering wheel, Irene noticed, so tightly that his knuckles were white, as white as his ashen face was turning. Like a ghost, he seemed to be vanishing before her very eyes. She reached for his hand which relaxed at her touch, somehow responding to the connection even though he seemed not to be there. She unbuckled her seat belt with difficulty, collapsing forward from the gravity that pulled her.

"Please, Dad, I'm here. Dad, say something. Oh God. Say something! Daddy, I need you to tell me you're alright." Irene's words rung in her ear; she sounded like a child begging. "Please don't go, Daddy. Please, oh God, please don't go Daddy! They're coming. We're going to get help. See? There are people out there. They're coming to get us Daddy."

She squeezed his hand tighter until she realized that she might be hurting him, so she released her grip, touching his face that seemed suddenly cold.

And in response to his daughter's cries, Sam slowly opened his eyes and patted her hand in reassurance. "Dad. Dad! Dad! Wake up!"

He smiled at her. Even though he couldn't move his head, he smiled at her. "I'm alright, Irene."

"Dad, they're coming! They'll be here any minute. Don't move. Come on, Dad. I love you. Daddy, I love you."

He blinked his eyes that shone bright and luminous. "I have to go now."

"No, Dad. Don't go . . ."

"It's alright, Irene. I have to go, but I'm alright. I'm at peace . . . I'm safe. I love you. Tell your mother I love her, and Lauren and Tucker."

"No, Dad. No, I won't. *You* tell them! *I'm* not going to tell them. *You come back!*"

He smiled at her one more time. "Your mother has been such a gift to me. What a lady. . . . Irene, you're a good girl.

I'm proud of you and your sister. . . . Please take care of your mother for me. . . ."

"Dad don't!"

But his eyes were suddenly different—vacant, staring past her. "Dad?" she squeezed his hand as if she could squeeze life back into him. "Dad don't go! Please, Daddy, please! . . ."

It took almost an hour for the "jaws of life" machine to release the encased car so the paramedics could remove Sam and Irene from the wreckage.

And while she waited, Irene was beyond words and emotion as she had laid her head on her father's chest during all the commotion. She kept hoping, waiting for Sam to take a breath, for his heart to beat once more, but it never happened. He never moved again or responded to her pleas. And as she lay on him, she knew that her father was gone. He was not there anymore. Yes, his body was, but his life force, his spirit had left him.

She had never thought about death much other than when Ford died, and she was glad for his demise. No, she never considered losing her father, especially since she was just beginning to really find him.

Chapter 21

Final Cut

They call it a "closed set." Chelsea was to learn that that term meant nobody extra, including the still photographer, was allowed on the set during the shooting of the bedroom scene between Reis and Chelsea. She kept reminding herself that the lovemaking wasn't between Reis and Chelsea, it was between *Cathleen and Alan,* the starring roles' names in the movie.

Stephen had pounded into Chelsea's head from the time that they had the offer to fly out to LA and read for the part in the movie, "You're an actress. You're not the 'part.' This is different from what we're doing with you musically. So enjoy it. Enjoy the fairy-tale life of playing other roles. As soon as you figure out that it's not you on the screen but the character you're playing, the faster you'll fine-tune your craft."

But despite all of the promptings the director had given her since she'd come on that set after lunch break, and all of Stephen's words of wisdom, and Reis's encouragements, she still felt like Chelsea sitting in the bed on that Hollywood set, not her character. Nope, it was *Chelsea* in bed next to a half-naked actor, and no matter how sweet he was, she was not comfortable with only her panties on and her bra with the straps down to make her look bare shouldered.

She told Stephen she understood the director's "vision" for the scene—How the audience would be swept away by the beauty and romance of these characters' lovemaking. Yes, in fact, they were shooting the end of the movie on the first day. And yes, Chelsea was told how often that happened and how difficult it was, especially as a novice actress to imagine all the scenes between the opening sequence to the end titles.

And as Craig paced around the bed like an army circling the wagons, his tone had gone from commanding to soothing once he insisted that even Stephen leave the set for the privacy of the actors.

"OK, Chelsea," Craig Brandon continued, "everybody's gone, except the makeup girl who is staying to make sure you look gorgeous, and the script girl. And there's the DP, that's Stanley over there. He's made over a hundred films. He's the director of photography, so he has to be here in case the lighting changes. The camera operators and I even put the sound men out in the hall. I have spent forty-five minutes with you, happily so," he offered her a snarl of a grin, "So we can get this shot before we have to call a wrap. We've talked through the character's past history, and you're just going to be lovely in the role. You seem to know where Catherine's coming from, where she wants to go. And now is the moment, the crescendo. . . . It's the sealing of the kiss. Now we let the audience know, without words, that these two young lovers will be together forever and that Cathleen's sacrifice for the man she loves will make her a heroine to the audience. She wins her man in these moments of lovemaking as she turns from a girl into a woman."

Then the director's eyes shifted to Reis. "And during this scene, Alan realizes that he will never find anyone better for him than Cathleen. They share animal magnetism. . . . They're passionate, compelling." Craig took a step back. "Now I will have three cameras running so you two only have to do this one time. . . . One time, right? We've rehearsed the basic moves, and you know the parameters of the scene. So all we need to do is shoot it."

Chelsea nodded obediently having embraced a certain level of comfort over the last hour in the bed with her fellow actor. Yes, they had talked through the whole scene, motivation and all, and now it was about to be filmed. Recorded for all time. She was thankful her pills had kicked in for her celluloid launch into the annals of great performances, she told herself. And she was ready, comforted by the bedsheets and blanket that covered her, leaving, she reminded herself, everything to the imagination.

It would be just like play-acting, like she had done all her life, it seemed. She had gotten really good at selling herself whatever tale she wanted to tell so that she could deal with whatever was going on in her life. She was in control. This was her choice. It wasn't like when Ford messed around with her after she realized he shouldn't be doing what he was doing; that she wasn't "special." No, this was *her* choice. She was stepping into the shoes of greatness.

But then she heard the director say, "Alright now, take off your clothes, and as soon as you're ready, let me know, and we'll start rolling." She froze.

Stunned, she looked at Reis for some understanding, but he was already complying with Craig's request under the covers, pulling off his briefs. She sat there immobile, not even able to find her voice to call Stephen who promised that he'd be right by the closed-set door if she needed him.

Reis realized that his costar's hesitation wasn't born of a momentary sense of insecurity or propriety, so he offered a helping hand lightly on her shoulder to reassure her. "Chelsea, this is Alan who is going to make love to Cathleen. And he's waited so long for this affirmation that she truly loves him."

The director slowly stepped back into the shadows, knowing that the actor's words were probably the only convincing Chelsea would need. She removed his hand as she pulled her shoulder back, confused. Who was talking, the character? Him?

Then he winked at her, like he did at the end of their lunch. "Chelsea, listen, I hate this, and I promise, I won't look. I won't do anything to you. This is not the real deal. It's a movie, and I've worked with Craig before. It's all about the editing—I told you that. That's why they have three cameras going. You need to relax, and let's just get this done because hey, you know me, I'm starving, and I've got a six o'clock with my trainer at the gym."

She stared at him long and hard and then looked around the room that started to swirl, suddenly realizing she was perspiring when the makeup girl patted down her forehead. "You'll be alright," she said softly as she now powdered Chelsea's nose. "That's why I'm here. You look beautiful. Don't worry about anything." Then she ran a brush through Chelsea's long blonde hair as if she were a child. For a moment Chelsea almost relaxed until she heard herself scream, "Stephen!"

Her plea audibly fell off in intensity at the end syllable of his name, realizing how furious he was going to be with her.

DOA was a term Lauren had only heard on television in her favorite detective series; but when she received the frantic call from Margaret that Irene and Sam had been in an accident, she called the hospital as she rushed over to pick up her mother. The information she received from the admitting desk was that her father was dead on arrival, but that Irene would be alright. The woman's voice at the other end of the phone was not cold or callused; she had remembered Lauren from her time in the hospital with Chelsea. Centennial was a small town, after all.

As intent as Lauren was on getting to the hospital to be with Irene, she decided to tell Margaret about Sam at home, not sure how her mother would react to the news that the love of her life was gone. Amazingly, Lauren's concern for her mother superceded her own shock at the sudden loss of her father. Or maybe she was just numb.

Driven into her caregiver mode, Lauren efficiently covered the immediate details of the emergency: Tucker would be with Brian, assuring him that it would be best to keep their son from all the sorrow. "No, Bri. Please don't just show up. Don't bring Tuck to the hospital. And don't come to the house. I don't know when we're going to be there. Just please let me know that Tucker's with you and I don't have to worry about him."

Brian's voice remained calm, "Are you sure? I can take Tucker over to a friend's house. You know that boy that he plays with all the time. Then I can be with you."

Lauren lost it, "Bobbie is in New York!"

"Take it easy, Lauren. I'm not talking about Bobbie. I'm talking about that little blond boy down the street."

"Oh, yes. I'm sorry, I'm sorry. Look I have to go and get Mom. Please, keep Tucker with you. Keep him safe and keep him with you. And don't let him go anywhere. Just keep him safe!"

"OK." Brian lowered his voice so others in his office wouldn't overhear. "I've got it covered, don't worry. I'll be by the phone. Just call me when you need me. . . . If you need anything."

"I will . . ."

❧

It was only four hours and thirty-seven minutes after the initial impact that Irene found herself back at home, miraculously only bruised and battered physically but devastated emotionally. There was so much pain and sadness, one almost had to take one's turn at the altar of grief. Despite Irene's devastating afternoon and personal witness of her father dying, Margaret's profound loss was even more monumental.

Lauren was on overdrive trying to care for her family as she escorted Irene to the powder room; her sister was numbed up on pain pills and clearly shaken. Still, her concern for her mother overrode her personal pain.

"I think Mom's in shock." Irene moved slowly into the bathroom.

"She must be in shock. She hasn't said much. She only cried for a couple of minutes when I told her that Dad was already gone." Lauren had held fast to Irene's arm for support down the hall, but now she carefully released her to back out of the bathroom. "I'll be right outside. Do you need me to help you at all? You're not dizzy are you?"

"I'm alright," Irene nodded, leaning on the sink for more than physical support. "I think we're all in shock, Lauren." And with that she broke down in tears, sobbing over the sink.

Lauren immediately covered her sister with a hug. "It's OK, Rene."

Suddenly, Irene whirled around, pushing Lauren against the wall. "No, it's not OK! Everything is not going to be alright! Dad's gone. Chelsea's gone! Don't you dare say 'chin up' to me or I'll deck you one!"

Imagining the delivery of her threat, Irene totally broke down; all the tension released from her mind and body in a display of gales of laughter. Lauren decided to think her sister's onslaught of hysterics as a good thing, knowing full well how abusive pent-up emotions can be.

Lauren locked Bingo and William up in her bedroom so they wouldn't be underfoot, then assisted Irene back toward their parents' apartment when they noticed the door was wide open with light shining down the hall. "Mom!" Lauren called. "Are you OK?"

"Yes, I'm in here. I just opened the door for you." Margaret's voice was unwavering. The sisters looked at each other briefly, surprised by Margaret's almost upbeat attitude. And when they had made it into the apartment, Margaret was by the TV set, pulling out a tape from the VCR machine. She waved it about almost triumphantly. "I got both of your father's games on one tape! Can you imagine?"

Lauren helped Irene into a chair and then just stood there; neither sister knew quite how to respond as their mother neatly placed the video on the shelf. Then Margaret turned to address her daughters. "Your father looked surprisingly well, don't you think? Almost like he was smiling. Then again, you know Sam. He had pretty healthy jowls, so I'm sure they just delicately pulled his face into a serene expression."

"Mom," Irene started slowly, "He *was* serene, in the end." And then she suddenly couldn't talk anymore.

"Really?" Margaret looked imploringly at her daughter.

"Yes. Dad said that he loved you, and that he was alright."

Margaret digested her daughter's words for a moment as Irene then turned her gaze on to Lauren, "You, too. He said he loved you, and me, and Tucker."

Margaret threw her head back, realizing the finality of Irene's words. "Was he in pain? Your father couldn't even handle a cold without complaining. Was he in pain?!"

"I don't think so, Mom." And then with a lurch, Margaret seemed to fly across the room to the shelf she had just placed the video on, and with a warrior's yell she pulled all of the neatly piled videos off the shelf in a frantic expression of grief.

And with that, the floodgates opened as she screamed. "He won't need these anymore! All his football and tennis tapes . . . ! I want him back! I want to see the back of his head watching the stupid television screen! I want to talk to him! I want to do the crossword puzzle with him! I want to dance, and I want to go out to dinner! I want to hear him snore! I want my lover. . . . I want my husband! I'm not ready to be alone . . . Not without Sam!"

She collapsed to the floor; Lauren and Irene followed suit, holding Margaret in a circle of hugs.

Margaret sobbed, "I want my husband back. He was a good man. A good man, do you both hear me? You always seemed to complain about him. He was never 'there for you,' 'never enough' for you two. But he loved you. He took care of us. He was a good man! He was an honorable man. And he was a better man every day of his life."

The coming together of these three women was beautiful. Old hurts and unforgiveness melted away and were replaced with unconditional love. And somehow it seemed that Sam was there, watching over his girls, his impact and influence intact. Sure, he was a short-tempered, stiff-necked, yet charming mish-mash of identities that summed themselves up in the personality of an unforgettable individual.

Why is it so often that one has to lose someone to appreciate them fully? But that was not true of Margaret. No, she always appreciated Sam, and she had always kept all her criticisms about her husband between themselves. Oh, of course she would let him know when he was out of line privately and without equivocation, but never publicly. And that was an admirable habit of Margaret's.

As the three women rocked back and forth on the floor encased in their unified emotions, Lauren spoke first. "Mom, it wasn't that we didn't know who Dad was, or what a good man he was. I think Rene and I just wanted to have a little more of him . . . Like he had been lately."

All of Margaret's makeup had been smeared down her face as she looked up, first at Lauren and then at Irene. "I didn't mean to keep him from you." Her words were slow in coming and carefully thought out. "It was the way I was raised."

Lauren looked at Irene, confused by her mother's meaning; the softness in her tone vanished for an instant. "But Mom, you were really close to your mother. . . ."

Margaret interrupted. ". . . But not to my father! My mother was all about her children. She had no relationship with her husband to speak of. . . . She had no relationship with my father. And so I swore when I married Sam that it would be different with us, that he would come first. He felt the same way about me. And I'm sorry if that didn't work for you girls, but we took good care of you, or at least the best care we could."

And with that, Irene melted; the tough veneer she had carried for so many years was finally chipping away by the events of the day and her mother's words. "It's OK, Mom. We're fine, and we're together. We're all together now."

Lauren continued. "We love you, Mom. And we're here for you. You're not alone. I know we're not Dad, but we're here, . . . OK?"

The tenderness was invaded by the sudden and persistent ringing of the front door bell. Lauren pulled herself off the floor, miffed and muttering under her breath, "Brian, I told you to not come over here!"

⊱✦⊰

Ham and Eleanor stood on the porch as Lauren flung open the door with annoyance. Upon seeing her friends, she relaxed. "It's good you're not Brian because I was about to punch you."

Eleanor didn't wait for a "please come in"; she simply barged through the doorway, hugging Lauren like a giant panda bear.

Ham looked like he was on red alert, scanning the room to plot his next move. "Sorry about the doorbell, but there was no one letting us in." Ham asserted. "Pam and Tonya send their love and prayers. They'll be flying back tomorrow."

"Flying back?" Lauren's voice was muffled under Eleanor's hug.

"There, there," Eleanor cooed. "Pam went to visit Tonya in New York, but everyone will be comin' in on the first flight to Nashville."

Lauren finally pushed away from Eleanor's embrace, who now stood back in respect. "What are you doing here?"

Stunned, Eleanor regarded Lauren. "Brian called us. He thought we should check on you . . . on your family while he watched Tucker."

Lauren didn't know whether she was angry or relieved that Brian had called in the "fortress."

"I don't mean to be nosy now, Miss Lauren." Eleanor leaned in as she adopted a whisper, "But you got to let that man into your life . . . the good along with the bad. Nobody likes to be put on hold when they have a vested interest in lovin' others."

Not prepared for a lecture, Lauren restrained herself long enough to accept Eleanor's words as advice, not criticism. "OK . . ."

Ham stood at attention. "Where are Irene and your mother?"

Now it was Lauren's turn to hug Eleanor, looking at Ham over his wife's shoulder. "Thanks for coming guys. . . . But I don't want the girls flying back. Same with Suz. Prayers are just as good long-distance."

"I suspect there won't be any stoppin' them. That's what friends are for according to our Book."

The discomfort clearly felt by Irene and Margaret at the invasion of Ham and Eleanor was fleeting. Yes, it only took the time for Lauren to heat up some coffee before Ham and Eleanor's kind words of consolation dispelled any tensions.

Although Ham held court for only a few minutes, he was magnetic, his influence coming from a source beyond. His words were compelling, compassionate and complete. And his assurance that Sam had found his Maker was revelatory.

"Miss Margaret," he stood before her at a respectful distance, yet close enough to maintain authority. "The other night Lauren, Tucker, Irene and your husband came into the diner after looking for Chelsea. And we all prayed. Please let me assure you that I know, madam, that praying with others was not customary for Sam. Although I would never be so bold as to say where anyone's relationship is in their faith, this was my impression. Within moments of taking hands, a presence superseded any discomfort, nerves, or unfamiliarity, and I believe with all my heart that what I'm about to tell you is the truth. Your husband, Sam, accepted Christ that night. In fact, before he left the diner, I made a date with him to have some coffee and talk further. He did want to know more."

Margaret was speculative. "Sam doesn't go out and have coffee with people. It's not that I don't believe what you're saying, it's just that I've never heard of such from Sam." And then she became suddenly angry, her emotions flaring again from all the stress. "I think I know my husband better than you, so . . ."

But Hamilton, as was his way, stepped in to ease what was quickly becoming a confrontational experience. ". . . Please understand that I am not being rude or assumptive in any sense."

Lauren was quick to observe that Eleanor had stepped back to let her husband take the forefront of the conversation. Her actions were noted by Lauren as a gracious style she would like to adopt, not unlike the respect her lovely friend Suz gave to her husband.

By this time Irene was finally succumbing to the exhaustion of the day's events, her eyes blinking to focus on what seemed to be another unbelievable exchange before her. Lauren slowly moved toward her mother in hopes that she might now succeed where she seemed to have failed in the past. "Mom, maybe this is the wrong time to tell you this, but I was there. I saw Dad's face in the diner when we all prayed. I believe in my heart of hearts that he has eternal life. He'd softened so much over the last period of time. Didn't you notice? You must have noticed. Dad was definitely different. . . . Remember what he said to Irene in the lawyer's office?"

Although Eleanor and Ham had not been present at the incident Lauren was describing, she had told them about the incredible changes in her father that day. And surely Irene and Margaret had to remember the words Sam had spoken so sincerely, words that had never been part of his normal conversation:

"Irene, I was always hard on you because you were the oldest. . . . And, well, . . . your mother used to point out to me that I was expecting to have a boy first, so I treated you like one without realizing it."

Although Sam was having trouble letting his true feelings show, he was determined not to have Irene misinterpret his words. "Hey, of course I was happy to have you. But I still expected you to be tough and strong, to take care of your little sister. And you did that, but along the way I think I forgot that you were a little girl, too."

Sam looked away again, choking back his tears as he cleared his voice. Then he took a big breath and regarded his daughters again who stood before him speechless (as did his wife). And as uncomfortable as he was, it was as if he had waited years for this moment, and he wasn't going to let it slip by out of embarrassment. Then he laughed slightly from being so open in front of the women of his family.

"But you girls spoiled me, didn't you?" Now he looked at Lauren. "You were more the tomboy type, and I got to throw some baseballs with you." He grinned slightly at his younger daughter.

"And a little touch football, huh? Except when I got too rough and your mother would yell out the window, 'Don't forget she's a girl, Sam!'" He adopted a falsetto voice for effect as he quoted Margaret. "But I never really forgot that, even when I broke your arm. . . . You know I didn't mean to do that. That was about the slippery grass, right?"

Lauren nodded, stunned at her father's words. "Right, Dad."

"And I never told you this, Irene, but I wanted to punch that first husband of yours in the face more than once. He never treated you right. But your Mother and I decided to stay out of it because, . . . who knew, you might work it out in the long run with the clown and then he'd hate my guts. And then where would we be? Spending Christmas apart or watching football games on Thanksgiving at opposite ends of the couch. Stupid guy things. But I swear, I regret that I didn't nail him for hurting you so badly; and if I ever see him again, he's going to have to answer me because no one treats my little girl like that." There wasn't a dry eye in the room while Sam paused briefly to gather his thoughts. "And Lauren, same thing goes for you and that pip-squeak of a first husband, as your mother called him. Bottom line, what I'm trying to say is that you probably think I was never there for you because . . ." And now Sam really choked on his words. ". . . Because I wasn't, in a lot of ways. Now, I'm not sorry for the rights and wrongs I taught you both. I think it was a good thing I scared you because your mother was such a softy. But I never told you I loved you or that I was proud of you both. I never took my girls to the movies or the circus or even out for a hamburger alone. And now your mother and I are trying to make up for that with Chelsea and Tucker. . . . So maybe you'll forgive . . ."

Sam was interrupted by a light knock on the door. His demeanor instantly changed as everyone stood at attention. "Just a minute, OK?" He responded gruffly. "We'll be right out." He looked back at his daughters. "I'm just saying that I'd give my right arm to go in that courtroom and make this alright for you, Irene. I'd do anything in my power to make that happen . . . to protect you, you know?"

And with that Sam opened the door without waiting for a response from anyone. "So let's go. We're going to win this thing, whenever it gets to trial, you hear me?"

The man couldn't even let the moment settle, and yet he had said what had been on his heart for a number of years. But instead of making a quick exit, he surprised everyone again by standing back and holding the door open for his wife and two girls. And that felt really good to this man.

As Irene passed her father, she whispered, "Thanks, Dad."

Lauren merely touched his hand in gratitude. And when Margaret passed, she looked up at her husband with renewed respect. And Sam thought, if he didn't live another moment in his life, he had just lived the best one.

As Lauren finished describing her father's past expressions of love, Irene spoke up. "I don't want to steal anyone's thunder in regard to loss and pain. . . . Mom," she lured her mother in with her eyes, "I love you very much, and I'm here for you like Lauren is. I can't imagine what you feel right now because I've never had what you had with Dad. The little I know about Ham and Eleanor, they probably could address that issue with you better, but they still have each other. . . . I guess what I'm trying to say is that we need to let each other in. And what Ham was saying happened to Dad that night, I don't know. . . . But he's right, *something* happened."

Lauren dared not breathe as Irene paused, finally continuing in a lower timber. "I'm like you, Mom. I think when we die, we just go to dust and we're dead, but I don't know. Something did happen to Dad that night. And I saw that something . . . whatever it was, in him today. Just because I can't make sense of it, doesn't mean I shouldn't tell you what he said."

Margaret now moved toward Irene. "What, darling? What? You told us that he said he loved us all."

"I know, but he also said something else." Irene's words didn't come easily because her thoughts were foreign to her. In the car that day, Irene did not know how to interpret her father's meaningful statements so she had quickly decided to dismiss them on the surface. But now it was becoming clear to her that she needed to talk of what her father had said to her with her mother in full disclosure to be heard by those who might embrace his meaning without edit.

"Mom," Irene looked at Lauren, then at Ham and Eleanor. "He said that he was *alright*. . . . He said he was *safe*."

Everybody was waiting for more, especially Margaret who shook her head at her daughter. "He was *safe*?"

"He said it, Mom, in a way as if he was looking forward to where he was going. Not to worry about him. That was in his meaning. That's what I got from his words. He wanted to let us know that he loved us and that he was going someplace good. . . . And then he said he had *peace*. . . ."

With that said, there was a long pause while Irene considered the true meaning of her father's last words. And although she wasn't sure exactly what Sam was telling her, she surely was not going to dismiss his words. And when she looked into her mother's eyes again, it was clear neither was Margaret. It was a sacred, lovely, tender revelation for all.

Not much more was said for the next twenty minutes or so as coffee was served other than freely confessed expressions of love. In fact, everything had taken on such a serene tone, Lauren was actually just considering calling Brian to bring Tucker home for bed. Yes, it seemed that a year had passed, but in fact it was only a little before nine in the evening.

But before Lauren made it to the phone, it startled her with a ring. And of course, her first thought was, "He jumped the gun on me again." But to her surprise, it was Stephanie on the other end, not the woman Lauren knew to be ever reasonable and calm in all situations. Frankly, she had never heard her friend sound so flat-out hysterical.

The whole skyline of Centennial was red and smoky set against the streetlights, the news helicopters, and the searchlights from the fire trucks that surrounded Norros Diner, ablaze amid a late spring frost.

Stephanie was wrapped in a blanket, shivering at the entrance of the open ambulance door. No, she was not sitting complacently; she was up and down off her feet like a pogo stick, searching the area for Trace.

She had been told in no uncertain terms by the police and firefighters, to "step back and let them do their job." Part of that job included safely getting Trace out of the inferno before her. Yes, the boy had hung back inside like a renegade cowboy trying to save the diner single-handedly against a blaze that was now threatening to engulf all of Main Street, downtown Centennial. Oh, how lives change so quickly with the impact of an accident or a fiery blaze.

It had quickly been determined by the fire chief that the destruction of Norros Diner had been sparked by arson. It couldn't have been anything else. Stephanie's cook crew was immaculate, and she was ever vigilant in checking the stoves for built-up grease or leaky gas valves. No, it was all too strange that night; everything was fine until Stephanie had heard from Eleanor and Ham that Sam had died in a car crash, and thankfully, Irene had survived. These were people Stephanie considered family, especially after what she had gone through with Irene concerning Chelsea's pregnancy. There was no hesitation on Stephanie's part to slap the "closed" sign on the diner's front door as she turned the people away who had been waiting in line for their dinner reservations. And just as quickly, she scurried those out who had already been seated and were enjoying their meals. Yes, she was the new restaurant owner, but the disappointment of her customers took a far second place next to being there for one of her *circle of friends.*

⚜

Stephanie had reviewed every move she had made since she'd opened the diner that morning. And up until she had told her crew to go home and had called Trace over to help her close up so they could go over to Lauren's, there were positively zero oversights on her part that could possibly have caused the raging fire before her.

But "fault or cause" was not on her mind now; Stephanie's total focus was on Trace. Yes, her son had pulled her out of the building at the first sign of fire, and then had run back to see if he could grab one of the many fire, extinguishers around the establishment to thwart the flames that were, at that time, small yet threatening.

Oh, she thought as she rubbed her hand across her forehead in disbelief, *Trace is so like his father . . . ever ready to be the hero and ever insistent on protecting me.* Stephanie was living a surreal moment, literally held back by the paramedics who were trying to attend to her burned hand.

Between the backlit haze of the smoke and the massive flames, she watched for her son to walk out of danger. Although the firefighters had assured her that they had the situation under control, their words defied what she saw before her, a raging fire and no Trace.

Stephanie had finally hit her emotional wall as she ripped a cell phone off of one of the attendant's belts. "I'm making a call," she announced, balancing the phone at her ear after pounding Lauren's number out with her thumb. And as she waited for someone to answer, there was no question in her mind or heart that she would trade places with Trace in a nanosecond, wherever he was.

"Oh God," she prayed. "Cover him. Let him walk though the fire unscathed. Don't bring him this far to let him fall before he runs for you, Lord!"

She whispered her prayer as the phone rang and rang. "I know he's yours, Father, but let him be mine just a little longer. I know you must have something amazing in mind for him since he's being so threatened by the enemy. I trust in you Father God. . . . Hello? Lauren!" She simply could not calm herself, "Norros is on fire, and Trace is still inside somewhere!"

And although it seemed beyond comprehension to Lauren that one more life-changing event could possibly happen in a single day, she still knew in her heart that God was in control, even if she didn't understand his plan right then.

A story about the unique bonds of faith and
courage between women and their

CIRCLE
of FRIENDS

A Fall Together
Circle of Friends, Just Off Main, Book One
978-0-8054-4195-6

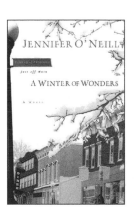

A Winter of Wonders
Circle of Friends, Just Off Main, Book Two
978 0 8054 4196 3

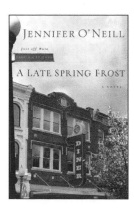

A Late Spring Frost
Circle of Friends, Just Off Main, Book Three
978-0-8054-4197-0

Available at your local bookstore or
by calling B&H Publishing Group at
1-800-251-3225.
www.BHPublishingGroup.com

PUBLISHING GROUP